D1448630

ROYAL HISTORICAL SOCIETY

STUDIES IN HISTORY

New Series

JACOBITISM AND ANTI-JACOBITISM IN THE BRITISH ATLANTIC WORLD 1688–1727

JACOBITISM AND ANTI-JACOBITISM
IN THE BRITISH ATLANTIC WORLD
1688–1727

David Parrish

THE ROYAL HISTORICAL SOCIETY
THE BOYDELL PRESS

First published 2017

A Royal Historical Society publication
Published by The Boydell Press
an imprint of Boydell & Brewer Ltd
PO Box 9, Woodbridge, Suffolk IP12 3DF, UK
and of Boydell & Brewer Inc.
668 Mt Hope Avenue, Rochester, NY 14620–2731, USA
website: www.boydellandbrewer.com

ISBN 978-0-86193-341-9

ISSN 0269-2244

A CIP catalogue record for this book is available
from the British Library

The publisher has no responsibility for the continued existence or accuracy of
URLs for external or third-party internet websites referred to in this book, and
does not guarantee that any content on such websites is, or will remain, accurate
or appropriate

This publication is printed on acid-free paper

Typeset by Fakenham Prepress Solutions, Fakenham, Norfolk NR21 8NN

Printed and bound in Great Britain by
TJ International Ltd, Padstow, Cornwall

TO AMANDA, PIPER AND SYLVIE

Contents

Acknowledgements

As odd as it may sound, this book was born out of an unapologetic love of adventure novels. Had it not been for Bill Horrell's contagious love of literature and his recommendation that I read Raphael Sabatini's *Captain Blood*, I might never have stumbled upon a subject that has since consumed many years' worth of my thoughts. Despite its rather dubious origins, like so many other books, this is a product of years of research and writing. More important, it is the work of many hands.

In working on this project, I have gained numerous friendships and accrued many debts. First and foremost, my wife Amanda, who has through her support and encouragement kept me sane, deserves so much more appreciation than this book and acknowledgement can ever express. My two daughters, Piper and Sylvie, also deserve special praise as they have been both a source of joy and exhaustion, and all the while reminding me that Jacobitism can demand only so much of my attention. To our many friends in Glasgow, you made our time there some of our happiest years to date.

I owe a special thanks to those who have read and critiqued countless drafts of chapters and articles, pointed me towards various sources, and suffered through my presentations. Karin Bowie, Murray Pittock, Daniel Szechi, Simon Newman, Don Spaeth, Lionel Glassey, Colin Kidd, Matthew Dziennik, Kieran German and Darren Layne have been exceedingly generous with their time. They have transformed this book from a sprawling mess of ideas into what I hope will be a book worthy of their time and efforts.

I have also benefitted greatly from the financial support that I received from a Jacobite Studies Trust fellowship offered through the Institute of Historical Research.

I must also thank colleagues, librarians and student workers at the College of the Ozarks, all of whom have been tremendously helpful. Brad Pardue and David Dalton have kindly commented upon draft chapters, and the staff at the library has patiently acquired countless books and articles, no matter how obscure they might seem. Lauren Darnell, Alex Flynn, Stephen Meek, Michaella Ruth, Mollie Rozean, Ariel Smith and Brandi Craig graciously edited and formatted the footnotes and bibliography.

Finally, I must thank those working with the Studies in History series. Guy Rowlands has patiently and selflessly critiqued individual chapters and the entire manuscript. I trust that his assistance has made me a better, more thoughtful writer.

If this seems a bit long-winded, just remember that you have not even made it to the beginning.

David Parrish
June 2016

Abbreviations

BL   British Library
CTP   Council of Trade and Plantations
FP   Fulham papers colonial
LPL   Lambeth Palace Library, London
MHS   Massachusetts Historical Society
NAS   National Archives of Scotland, Edinburgh
RHL   Rhodes House Library, Oxford
SPG   Society for the Propagation of the Gospel in Foreign Parts
TNA   The National Archives, Kew

AOM *Archives of Maryland: proceedings and acts of the general assembly of Maryland, April 26, 1715–August 10, 1716*, xxx, ed. William Hand Brown (Maryland Historical Society, 1910)
AWM *American Weekly Mercury*
BNL   *Boston News-letter*
CSPC *Calendar of state papers colonial, America and West Indies*, ed. W. Noel Sainsbury, J.W. Fortescue and Cecil Headlam, London 1860–1969
JBS   *Journal of British Studies*
JBTP *Journal of the Board of Trade and Plantations (1704–1782)*, ed. K. H. Ledward, London 1920–8
NEC   *New England Courant*
NJA   *Documents relating to the colonial history of the State of New Jersey*, xiv (New Jersey Historical Society, 1880)
ODNB *Oxford dictionary of national biography*
PH   *Parliamentary History*
WMQ *William and Mary Quarterly*

Introduction

Almost from the moment that William of Orange landed on the Devon coast on 5 November 1688, Jacobitism – support for James II&VII and his immediate heirs – captured the imagination of Britons including those located both within and beyond the shores of the British archipelago. Preachers in London and Boston condemned rebels or defended hereditary right while newspapers and pamphlets circulating throughout the English-speaking world kept nervous readers apprised of events. The flight of James II&VII to France and the subsequent coronation of William and Mary created within the various political entities previously ruled by the Stuarts fault lines between Jacobites and their opponents that were to last for well over half a century. From 1688 to 1746 Jacobites sought to restore the Stuart dynasty through various means, including civil wars in Scotland and Ireland, conspiracies and rebellions in 1708, 1715, 1719 and 1745. Yet it is often forgotten that in the early eighteenth century residents in what were then the English (and later British) colonies on the east coast of North America were also primarily Britons. Thus, these events were profoundly important to those living in remote areas across the Atlantic. Nor was it interest alone that was geographically unconstrained. Political and religious divisions were replicated across the British Atlantic world, so much so that one contemporary considered them to be 'an echo to that on the other side'.[1]

The argument of this book is two-fold. First, that Jacobitism and anti-Jacobitism were integral facets of the cultural totality of Britain's Atlantic empire in the early eighteenth century and, as such, were significant elements in transatlantic political culture, religious controversies and the public sphere in the British Atlantic world from 1689 to 1727, that is from the accession of William and Mary to the demise of the first Hanoverian, George I. Second, that Jacobitism and anti-Jacobitism played an important role in the anglicisation of the British Atlantic. In so doing, it illustrates a dynamic transatlantic political culture and sheds light on how Britain's budding empire came to encompass a cohesive and anglicised, yet still heterogeneous, transatlantic political and religious culture. This book is therefore a study of anglicisation writ large. One recent study defines anglicisation as 'the process through which the English colonies of the Americas emerged from their diverse beginnings to become increasingly more alike, expressing a shared Britishness in their political and judicial systems, material culture, economies, religious systems, and engagements with the empire'.[2] Yet, arguably, anglicisation was also occurring within

---

[1]   Robert Hunter to William Popple, 27 July 1717, CSPC, item 674.
[2]   Ignacio Gallup-Diaz, Andrew Shankman and Daniel J. Silverman (eds), *Anglicizing America: empire, revolution, republic*, Philadelphia 2015, 1.

1

the various constituent territories of the British Atlantic world as many Scots, Irish, English and colonials together became British. Care must be taken not to assume that 'Britishness' – and therefore anglicisation – can be defined easily; during the early eighteenth century Britishness was a contested idea. Jacobitism and anti-Jacobitism were important elements of this development within Britain itself,[3] but this was no seamless process. On the contrary, it was fraught with contest and conflict.

This is not the first attempt to make sense of Jacobitism in a transatlantic context. Unintentionally echoing the cynical plea of an eighteenth-century individual accused of Jacobitism that 'any man would be ashamed to make use of such evidences or talk of dethroning a great prince among the pine trees 4,000 miles from her', historians encountering Jacobitism in a colonial context have tended to view it as an 'imagined' threat, an image in the minds of overheated, paranoid imaginations, or a 'rhetorical hysteria'.[4] As such, it is treated as a Catholic bogeyman. Consequently, Jacobitism becomes little more than a foil or means of explaining unique cultural developments in the colonies rather than being a subject worthy of study on its own terms. For example, Thomas Kidd uses accusations of Jacobitism as a means of explaining the construction of 'the Protestant interest's identity', in which Jacobitism operated as the Catholic other.[5] Thus, while having noted its significant influence over local events and debates, it has remained decidedly foreign. These contrasting views raise a fascinating question: is Jacobitism in Britain's Atlantic colonies a faint echo, or is it very much part of the British political sound and fury?

Answers to this question are contingent upon how Jacobites and Jacobitism are understood. If viewed as 'spasmodic' episodes of Scottish resistance to British integration, or as a ragtag army of '9,000 swordsmen', then the Jacobite rebellions could not have been serious enough to create an echo forceful enough to cross the Atlantic.[6] Ned Landsman's comment that 'there were few avowed Jacobites in America' articulates the opinion of many historians who would probably argue the former: that Jacobitism in the Americas was but a weak echo of British politics.[7] This highlights the difficulties inherent

[3] Linda Colley, Britons: forging the nation, 1707–1837, 2nd edn, New Haven 2005.

[4] Thomas Nairne to [Charles Spencer, 3rd earl of Sunderland?], 28 July 1708, CSPC, item 662 (quotation); Thomas S. Kidd, The Protestant interest: New England after Puritanism, New Haven 2004, 116; Jonathan Clark, The language of liberty, 1660–1832: political discourse and social dynamics in the Anglo-American world, Cambridge 1994, 255. See also Thomas Wendal, 'Jacobitism crushed: an episode concerning loyalty and justice in colonial Pennsylvania', Pennsylvania History xl (1973), 58–65.

[5] Kidd, The Protestant interest, 116–17.

[6] Ian K. Steele, 'The annointed, the appointed, and the elected: governance of the British Empire, 1689–1784', in Peter Marshall (ed.), The Oxford history of the British Empire, II: The eighteenth century, Oxford 1998, 105–27; Stephen Saunders Webb, Marlborough's America, New Haven 2013, 32.

[7] Ned Landsman, From colonials to provincials: American thought and culture, 1680–1760,

in a study of Jacobitism, for although his statement is probably accurate, the absence of vocal, avowed Jacobites – however one imagines them – cannot be equated with the absence of Jacobitism.

Lest this seem like little more than an exercise in semantics, it must be remembered that any study of Jacobitism is beset with ambiguities, and the definition of terms becomes crucial. Before making a case for the existence and significance of Jacobitism and anti-Jacobitism in the British Atlantic, it is necessary to define what is meant by Jacobitism. In its broadest sense it entails support for James II&VII and his heirs. But this seemingly simple definition masks a deceptive complexity inherent in the idea of support. What counts as support and how much 'support' must one show in order to be counted a Jacobite? If rebellion is not the measure, what is? According to Paul Monod, Jacobitism is both 'the idea and the expression of support' for the Stuarts. Moreover, these ideas and expressions possess an internal coherence. As such, they are a subcultural element of the larger English political culture.[8] This definition is useful and applicable to the larger British Atlantic world. Expressions of both Jacobitism and opposition to a perceived Jacobite threat in the colonies are thus examples of a complex British political culture in a remote British province. Expressions of Jacobitism in Scotland, Ireland or one of the various colonies are not necessarily examples of a distinct or independent Jacobite subculture; they are representative of a larger transatlantic political culture. This is not to imply a monolithic Jacobite movement or a sophisticated transatlantic Jacobite organisation, but rather to suggest the existence of a transatlantic political culture bound by a series of shared words, images and forms of behaviour.[9]

With this broader definition in mind, it should be clear that the absence of Jacobite-led or inspired rebellions in the Atlantic colonies cannot be used to prove the absence of Jacobitism as an idea, expression or even political culture. Certainly, an active ideological Jacobitism or explicit support for the exiled Stuart dynasty directly comparable in scope or power to that in Scotland, England and Ireland did not exist. Historians of Britain have, however, successfully employed this broader definition as a means of explaining Jacobitism as a part of the transatlantic cultural, social and political *milieu* of Britain. To risk taking the metaphor of echo too far, it was this *milieu* that resonated across the Atlantic. It was replicated even if it was more muted in practice, and yet it also helped to shape the broader political culture of Jacobitism and anti-Jacobitism, even in the absence of widespread rebellion. We must seek to understand how and why this culture existed despite the lack of rebellion, riots or protests. This means that a proper understanding of Jacobitism as a part of a transatlantic political or religious culture, and transatlantic public sphere, is all the more important in an Atlantic context.

New York 1997, 151.

[8]   Paul Monod, *Jacobitism and the English people, 1688–1788*, Cambridge 1989, 7–8.

[9]   Ibid. 7.

If Jacobitism were expressed *via* a series of shared terms and ideas, then it is likely that its opponents would have possessed a heightened awareness of such expressions. Many Congregationalists in New England were quick to use accusations of Jacobitism against those who professed High Church Anglican beliefs. With the benefit of hindsight, it can be presumed that there was no great likelihood of a local Jacobite rebellion seeking to topple a colonial government, but contemporaries could not have known that. Accusations should not be lightly dismissed as paranoia or empty rhetoric. Is it paranoia if it is rooted in reality? As the 1689 collapse of the Dominion of New England and the Leisler episode in New York of the same year illustrates, successful rebellion by influential malcontents was possible. Moreover, the increasingly transatlantic nature of party politics meant that, by the early eighteenth century, influential malcontents might be connected to a transatlantic party interest suspected of embracing Jacobite sympathies. Thus, anti-Jacobitism must also be taken seriously. Like its counterpart, anti-Jacobitism shared its own tropes, images, terms and ideas.[10] Moreover, such rhetoric was often employed in response to specific events or publications. Reactions against local manifestations of a transatlantic Jacobitism or responses to a transatlantic Jacobite threat – however distant from the seats of power – suggest both the diffusion of cultural understandings regarding Jacobitism as well as the importance of Jacobitism as a significant part of the cultural totality of the British Atlantic world.

Rather than assuming that the absence of rebellions leaves little to be studied, or that evidences of Jacobitism in the colonies can be easily explained away as an unwanted political import, a cultural anomaly, or a fanciful fabrication, examples of Jacobitism and anti-Jacobitism indicate cultural diffusion within a dynamic transatlantic political culture. Jacobitism was an enduring part of eighteenth-century British political, religious and print culture and it therefore follows that it was an important element in an eighteenth-century British Atlantic culture. In fact the very existence of both Jacobitism and anti-Jacobitism as a part of the colonial vernacular culture illustrates their contemporary relevance in a wider geographical context than has previously been known.

Recent scholarship has rescued Jacobitism from its exile in the realm of 'reactionary nostalgia'.[11] Having largely moved away from the contested territory of high politics,[12] scholars have much more convincingly identified Jacobitism

---

[10]   Chris Whatley, 'Reformed religion, regime change, Scottish Whigs and the struggle for the "soul" of Scotland, *c.* 1688–*c.* 1788', *Scottish Historical Review* xcii (2013), 66–99; Hannah Smith, *Georgian monarchy: politics and culture, 1714–1760*, Cambridge 2006.

[11]   Paul Monod, 'A restoration? 25 years of Jacobite studies', *Literature Compass* x (2013), 311–30. See also J. C. D. Clark, 'The many restorations of King James: a short history of scholarship on Jacobitism, 1688–2006', in Paul Monod, Murray Pittock and Daniel Szechi (eds), *Loyalty and identity: Jacobites at home and abroad*, Basingstoke, 2010, 9–56.

[12]   Eveline Cruickshanks, *Political untouchables: the Tories and the '45*, New York 1979;

and anti-Jacobitism as pervasive themes and motifs in the language and discourse of the three constituent kingdoms of the eighteenth-century British archipelago.[13] Daniel Szechi, for instance, having amply detailed the existence and manoeuvres of a Jacobite wing of the Tory party in the years leading up to the Hanoverian accession, has shown that frenetic Whig accusations of Tory Jacobitism were not simply imagined.[14] Not surprisingly this ambiguous relationship both created and reflected a political culture in which Jacobites and Tories shared a 'common currency of discourse ...which allowed Jacobite and Tory to shade equivocally into each other'.[15] This political culture rested on religious foundations, and Jacobitism was therefore inextricably intertwined with religious beliefs.[16] Scottish Episcopalians, High Church Anglicans, nonjurors and Roman Catholics each provided ideological pillars of Jacobite resistance.

One of the most important results of this work is that historians have broken Jacobitism out of an 'othered' Celtic fringe and established it as a fixture in mainstream British society. Detailed studies of the Jacobite armies which partic-ipated in the rebellions of 1715 and 1745 have undermined the notion that the Jacobite armies were almost exclusively Highland and Catholic. Szechi's work on the 1715 rising and Murray Pittock's examination of the composition of the army in the rising of 1745 have shown that the armies had substantial numbers of Scottish Episcopalians and Lowlanders thus demonstrating the extent to which Jacobitism was central to various constituencies within British politics.[17]

As part of a larger cultural turn, party politics, nationalism, poetry, painting, medical controversies, theatre and print culture have become fertile ground for scholars examining the influence of Jacobitism in eighteenth-century Britain.[18]

Linda Colley, *In defiance of oligarchy, 1714–1760*, Cambridge 1982; Romney Sedgwick (ed.), *The history of parliament: the House of Commons, 1715–1754*, London 1970; J. C. D. Clark, *English society, 1668–1832: religion, ideology, and politics during the ancien régime*, Cambridge 1985; Andrew Hanham, '"So few facts": Jacobites, Tories and the Pretender', *PH* xix (2000), 233–57.

[13]   Monod, *Jacobitism*; Murray Pittock, *Poetry and Jacobite politics*, Cambridge 1995; Eaomon O'Ciardha, *Ireland and the Jacobite cause, 1685–1766: a fatal attachment*, Dublin 2002; Paul Fritz, *The English ministers and Jacobitism between the rebellions of 1715 and 1745*, Toronto 1975; Smith, *Georgian monarchy*; Whatley, 'Reformed religion', 66–99.

[14]   Daniel Szechi, *Jacobitism and Tory politics, 1710–1714*, Edinburgh 1984.

[15]   Clark, *English society*, 143.

[16]   Bruce Lenman, 'The Scottish Episcopal clergy', and Mark Goldie, 'The nonjurors, episcopacy, and the origins of the Convocation Controversy', in Eveline Cruickshanks (ed.), *Ideology and conspiracy: aspects of Jacobitism, 1689–1759*, Edinburgh 1982, 36–48, 15–35; Clark, *English society*, 83–105; Daniel Szechi, *The Jacobites: Britain and Europe, 1688–1788*, Manchester 1994; Monod, *Jacobitism*, 126–58; Gabriel Glickman, *The English Catholic community, 1688–1745: politics, culture, and ideology*, London 2009

[17]   Daniel Szechi, *1715: the great Jacobite rebellion*, New Haven 2006, 102–98; Murray Pittock, *The myth of the Jacobite clans: the Jacobite army in 1745*, 2nd edn, Edinburgh 2009, 65–109.

[18]   Murray Pittock, *Material culture and sedition, 1688–1760: treacherous objects, secret places*, Basingstoke 2013; Monod, *Jacobitism*, 45–94; 'The Jacobite press and English censorship,

By examining political cultures, Paul Monod has demonstrated the remarkable depth of Jacobite sympathies among High Church Anglicans.[19] Murray Pittock has challenged the 'myth of the Jacobite clans', by exploring the prevalence of cultural Jacobitism outside the Scottish Highlands, and Daniel Szechi has shown the complexity of the Scottish Jacobite *mentalité*.[20] Furthermore, ties in Britain between Jacobitism, party politics and the religious controversies of the period, described by Geoffrey Holmes, Mark Knights and Brian Cowan, among others, have clearly revealed the importance of Jacobitism in the partisan divide and public sphere during the reign of Anne (1702–14).[21] Much the same could be said of Irish Jacobite culture, which too has received a great deal of recent attention.[22]

Building on the numerous works establishing the place of Jacobitism in the British Isles, studies have also begun to examine Jacobitism outside Britain, focusing attention on a great variety of different topics including diasporas, identity, empire and exiles.[23] Many Jacobites left England, Scotland and Ireland in search of a new home or new opportunities and consequently created or joined exile communities throughout Europe. Some of the most important work in this area has focused on the Stuart courts in exile, and has shaped our understanding of the significance of Jacobitism on a European stage.[24]

1689–1695', in Edward Corp (ed.), *The Stuart court in exile, and the Jacobites*, London 1995, 125–42; and 'Pierre's white hat: theatre, Jacobitism and popular protest in London, 1689–1760', in Eveline Cruickshanks (ed.), *By force or default? The Revolution of 1688–89*, Edinburgh 1989, 159–89; David Parrish, 'A party contagion: party politics and the inoculation controversy in the British Atlantic World, *c.*1721–1723', *Journal for Eighteenth-Century Studies* xxxix (2016), 41–58; Neil Guthrie, *The material culture of the Jacobites*, Cambridge 2013; Eirwen Nicholson, '"Revirescit": the exilic origins of the Stuart oak motif', in Edward Corp (ed.), *The Stuart court in Rome: the legacy of exile*, Basingstoke 2003, 25–48; Allan I. Macinnes, Kieran German, and Lesley Graham (eds), *Living with Jacobitism, 1690–1788: the three kingdoms and beyond*, London 2014

[19]   Monod, *Jacobitism*

[20]   Pittock, *The myth of the Jacobite clans*, and *Jacobitism*, Basingstoke 1998; Daniel Szechi, *George Lockhart of Carnwath, 1689–1727: a study in Jacobitism*, East Linton 2002

[21]   Geoffrey Holmes, *British politics in the age of Anne*, 2nd edn, London 1987; G. V. Bennett, *The Tory crisis in Church and State, 1688–1730: the career of Francis Atterbury, bishop of Rochester*, Oxford 1975; Brian Cowan, *The social life of coffee: the emergence of the British coffeehouse*, New Haven 2005, 209–22; Mark Knights, *Representation and misrepresentation in later Stuart Britain: partisanship and political culture*, Oxford 2005; Lenman, 'The Scottish Episcopal clergy', 36–48; Goldie, 'The nonjurors, episcopacy, and the origins of the Convocation Controversy', 15–35; Nicholas Rogers, *Crowds, culture, and politics in Georgian Britain*, Oxford 1998, 21–57

[22]   O'Ciardha, *Ireland and the Jacobite cause*; Breandán Ó Buachalla, 'Irish Jacobite poetry', *Irish Review* xii (1992), 40–9.

[23]   Monod, Pittock and Szechi, *Loyalty and identity*; Geoffrey Plank, *Rebellion and savagery: the Jacobite rising of 1745 and the British Empire*, Philadelphia 2006, 77–100; Margaret Sankey, *Jacobite prisoners of the 1715 rebellion: preventing and punishing insurrection in early Hanoverian Britain*, Burlington, Vt 2005.

[24]   Edward Corp, *A court in exile: the Stuarts in France, 1689–1718*, Cambridge 2004; *The*

Furthermore, through Freemasonry and other social networks, Jacobites maintained extra-institutional connections with like-minded people throughout Europe.[25] This is an increasingly fascinating area of study as it places Jacobitism in a larger European and world context. There have been other excellent works examining diasporic communities of Jacobites including soldiers and merchants.[26] Jacobite exiles of all social classes made new homes in Spain, France, Russia and the British colonies.[27] There is still a great deal of research to be done regarding how Jacobite exiles interacted with their adopted societies.

Moving beyond Britain and Europe, Margaret Sankey has examined the transportation of Jacobite prisoners after the 1715 rebellion and Geoffrey Plank and others have explored the impact of the 1745 rebellion within an imperial context.[28] Furthermore, over the last quarter-century, David Dobson has documented a great number of Jacobites transported to the British colonies in America.[29] These studies hint at the likely import of Jacobitism into the British Atlantic. Although its significance in the history of Britain has been reasserted and the advent of 'Atlantic history' has reminded us of the dynamism of cultural and political exchanges, the subject has not yet received sufficient attention in Atlantic or colonial history,[30] although recent work suggests that Jacobitism may have cultural significance in the British colonies.

Stuarts in Italy, 1719–1766: a royal court in permanent exile, Cambridge 20111; and *The Stuart court in Rome*.

[25] Steve Murdoch, 'Tilting at windmills: the Order del Toboso as a Jacobite social network', in Monod, Pittock and Szechi, *Loyalty and identity*, 243–64; Robert Collis, 'To a fair meeting on the green: the Order of Toboso and Jacobite fraternalism, 1726–c. 1729', in Macinnes, German and Graham, *Living with Jacobitism*, 125–38.

[26] Nathalie Genet-Rouffiac, *Le Grand Exil: les Jacobites en France, 1688–1715*, Paris 2007; Siobhan Talbott, 'Commerce and the Jacobite court: Scottish migrants in France, 1688–1718', in Macinnes, German and Graham, *Living with Jacobitism*, 99–110.

[27] Steve Murdoch, *Network North: Scottish kin, commercial and covert associations in Northern Europe, 1603–1746*, Leiden 2006, 313–48; Rebecca Wills, *The Jacobites and Russia, 1715–1750*, East Linton 2002; Thomas O'Connor (ed.), *The Irish in Europe, 1580–1815*, Dublin 2001.

[28] Sankey, *Jacobite prisoners*, 59–75; Plank, *Rebellion and savagery*, 77–100; Jonathan Hawkins, 'Imperial '45: the Jacobite rebellion in transatlantic context', *Journal of Imperial and Commonwealth History* xxiv (1996), 24–47.

[29] David Dobson, *Scots on the Chesapeake, 1607–1830*, Baltimore 1992; *Directory of Scots banished to the American plantations, 1650–1775*, 2nd edn, Baltimore 2010; and *Scottish emigration to colonial America*, Athens, GA 1994.

[30] For an overview of the development of Atlantic History see Bernard Bailyn, *Atlantic history: concepts and contours*, Cambridge, MA 2005. For histories of the British Atlantic see David Armitage and Michael Braddick (eds), *The British Atlantic World, 1500–1800*, Basingstoke 2002; Joyce Chaplin, 'The British Atlantic', in Nicolas Canny and Phillip Morgan (eds), *The Oxford handbook of the Atlantic world, c. 1450–1850*, Oxford 2011, 219–34; and Carla Pestana, *Protestant empire: religion and the making of the British Atlantic world*, Philadelphia 2009. For exceptions see David Lovejoy, *The Glorious Revolution in America*, New York 1972, and Owen Stanwood, *The empire reformed: English America in the age of the Glorious Revolution*, Philadelphia 2011.

Without question, the various Atlantic colonies under the control of the late Stuart and early Georgian monarchies were an important part of the British world, and the language and rhetoric of Jacobitism and anti-Jacobitism, which were so prevalent in the British Isles, were pervasive themes in the larger British Atlantic. Scholars have increasingly recognised that the colonies were cultural provinces of Britain whose 'legal and social systems, perceptual frameworks, and social and cultural imperatives were inevitably in large measure British in origin'.[31] These Atlantic and colonial American historians, while examining themes and events closely related to Jacobitism such as a monarchical political culture and anti-Catholicism, have not yet sufficiently integrated many of the advances made by Jacobite studies into their respective historiographies.[32]

While demonstrating important transatlantic cultural links, these works have displayed 'homogenizing tendencies in their relentless search for connections' and have tended to portray a homogenous transatlantic British Whig political culture, often with little reference to Tories or Tory political culture.[33] Thus, many aspects of history which have created such a rancorous debate in the historiography of Britain over the previous four decades, such as the heterogeneous and contested political culture evident during the first half of the eighteenth century, have not yet been incorporated into colonial American history. Studies of the 'anglicisation' of the Atlantic colonies have been viewed primarily through a largely Whiggish lens. In so doing, they have minimised the contested nature of this fraught process.[34]

One purpose of this book is both to build upon and complement these works. Britain's political culture encompassed a bewildering variety of opinions. Some of this complexity should be injected into the narrative of anglicisation. As the colonies became more British, they increasingly participated in a British political culture that was informed not just by English norms, but by Scotland and Ireland as well. Therefore, approaching this within the confines of Atlantic history provides an expansive comparative framework which can better account for the interactions between various kingdoms and colonies.

The book will set a strong contextual background by examining manifestations of Jacobitism and anti-Jacobitism in various aspects of the culture and society of the British Atlantic world. Part I of the book will pursue a thematic

---

[31] Jack P. Greene and J. R. Pole, 'Reconstructing British-American colonial history', in Jack P. Greene and J. R. Pole (eds), *Colonial British America: essays in the new history of the early modern era*, Baltimore 1984, 1–17 at p. 14.

[32] Kidd, *The Protestant interest*; Stanwood, *The empire reformed*; Brendan McConville, *The king's three faces: the rise and fall of royal America, 1688–1776*, Chapel Hill 2006.

[33] Trevor Burnard, 'The British Atlantic', in Jack P. Greene and Phillip D. Morgan (eds), *Atlantic history: a critical appraisal*, Oxford, 2009, 111–36 at p. 128.

[34] John M. Murrin, 'Anglicizing an American colony: the transformation of provincial Massachusetts', unpubl. PhD diss. Yale 1966; T. H. Breen, 'An empire of goods: the Anglicisation of colonial America', *JBS* xxv (1986), 467–99; McConville, *The king's three faces*.

approach, encompassing the entirety of the British Atlantic. The first chapter will examine the relationship between Jacobitism, party politics and imperial governance following the revolution of 1688. Issues around the legitimacy of William's invasion and accession were not solely debated in the British Isles. Whig and Tory party divisions in Britain influenced political developments throughout the British Atlantic, including imperial appointments, the development of colonial interest groups and the appropriation of party-infused rhetoric. Thus, colonists were not only exposed to the consequences of British party political divisions, they were also willing participants in the 'rage of party'. This connected them directly to elements of a transatlantic political culture in which Jacobitism was increasingly linked with elements of Toryism and thus influenced Whig perception of a Tory/Jacobite threat.

Chapter 2 will address the relationship between Jacobitism and religious beliefs. Jacobitism was rooted in the ideologies of divine hereditary right, passive obedience and non-resistance prevalent both in the Church of England and among Scottish Episcopalians. These confessional groups provided an ideological foundation for Jacobitism and it is therefore necessary to examine the role of the Churches in an Atlantic context to fully appreciate colonial understandings and expressions of Jacobitism and disaffection. Moreover, the Whig and Tory divisions discussed in the first chapter were inherently connected to religious differences. Divisions between High Church and Low Church Anglicans, and Anglican and Episcopalian attitudes towards dissenters, were flashpoints in the British party political system and political culture, a problem exacerbated by the conspicuous High Church Tory relationship with Jacobitism. Much of the resistance to the establishment of an episcopate in the colonies was a consequence of the thorny relationship between the Church of England and Jacobitism. The rapid expansion of the Church of England in the British Atlantic world, therefore, was fraught with political baggage inseparable from Jacobitism. Predictably, colonial fears of Catholicism, too, were inherently tied to Jacobitism due to the religious affiliation of the exiled Stuarts.

Chapter 3 posits the existence, and discusses the importance, of transatlantic Jacobitism and anti-Jacobitism within an Atlantic public sphere. As recent scholarship has shown, Grub Street, coffee houses, inns, taverns and the popular press were instrumental in shaping political and religious debates in London outside parliament and the Anglican Convention and similar patterns were emerging in the colonies. Slanderous polemics, religious and political pamphlets, newspapers and broadsides were part and parcel of a transatlantic print culture and, where printing was not widely available, in private correspondence which often included coded language. Such informal and non-institutional networks of information exchange facilitated the communication of elements of a Jacobite subculture as well as anti-Jacobite rhetoric.

Part II of the book provides separate case studies, each illustrating aspects of the broader context but within a specific colonial context. These have been chosen for two reasons. Firstly, the colonies selected possessed religious establishments or political contexts that made expressions or accusations of

Jacobitism more likely. There is therefore a greater body of evidence upon which to draw. Second, when viewed together the events and chronology associated with each chapter help to demonstrate changing perceptions or manifestations of Jacobitism over time. Chapter 4 examines the debate surrounding the passage of Establishment and Test Acts in South Carolina in 1704 and its relationship to debates about occasional conformity in England. The passage of these acts was tied to party political developments in London and clearly demonstrates elements of a transatlantic political culture. The controversies surrounding the acts resulted in numerous accusations of Jacobitism aimed at High Church Tories. Furthermore, the acts were an essential component in the subsequent development of a transatlantic High Church culture in the colony, a culture which encouraged and inculcated Jacobitism for years to come. Chapter 5 explores the relationship between a nascent High Church culture, a Whig governor and Jacobitism in the mid-Atlantic colonies of New York, New Jersey and Pennsylvania in the period leading up to and surrounding the Jacobite rebellion of 1715. This chapter provides a colourful example of the heady mix created by imperial politics, religious developments and an emerging print culture. Chapter 6 demonstrates the relevance of Jacobitism and the significance of debates about Jacobitism in New England's increasingly vibrant print culture, focusing especially on the years surrounding the 1722 Atterbury plot. Though predominantly supportive of the Hanoverian succession, New England was not isolated from British Atlantic developments. Its maturing print culture fostered a series of religious controversies reflecting expressions of the transatlantic Jacobite political culture and, consequently, elements of an informed, political and religiously-minded anti-Jacobitism.

The aim of this book is to encourage conversation between the often disparate fields of eighteenth-century British history, Atlantic history, Jacobite studies and colonial America. For the broad fields of eighteenth-century British and Atlantic history, it provides a wider Atlantic context to recent work on the Glorious Revolution and post-Revolutionary politics, religious culture and the public sphere. For Jacobite historians the book will add an Atlantic dimension to the four separate but interconnected branches of Jacobitism: those of England, Scotland, Ireland and the Continental European diaspora. For historians of colonial America, it contributes complexity to, and further reinforces, arguments detailing the monarchical, increasingly anglicised character of the British colonies in the early eighteenth century.

PART I

CONTEXT

1

Jacobitism, Party Politics and the British Atlantic World

In the late seventeenth century the British Empire in the Atlantic was a variegated, institutionally disjointed entity, in many respects little more than a patchwork of diverse religious, political, ethnic and economic cultures. Though the population was primarily English, settlers also migrated from Scotland, Ireland and Continental Europe under the aegis of a composite British monarchy. Government structures and church establishments varied from colony to colony, adding a layer of institutional confusion. Pennsylvania, Maryland and South Carolina, among others, were governed by proprietors, not by the crown. Virginia and a number of the Caribbean colonies were royal colonies whose governors were royal appointees answerable to the king. By the late seventeenth century England and Scotland possessed, through plantation or conquest, nearly twenty Atlantic colonies, each with a separate and unique government or charter, creating a lively variety of local institutions and political cultures. These diverse settlements, looking to London as the metropolitan centre of an expanding empire were united by a shared history, heritage, economy, a public sphere and, increasingly throughout the early eighteenth century, the rage of party.

Prodigious amounts of scholarship have debated the origins, structures and ideological features of British party politics in the early eighteenth century.[1] Parties were divided by issues of religion, finance and theories of empire. Although such conflict is well established within the context of England, Scotland and Ireland, there is much more to be said about its trans-atlantic impact. Party conflict affected political appointments, among other things, directly connecting colonial political cultures to British party divisions. Moreover, issues undergirding the rage of party were also undoubtedly linked to questions concerning the Protestant succession, an event with dramatic imperial consequences. The overlap evident in Jacobitism and Tory political culture during the rage of party in Britain, especially the years 1710 to 1714,

[1]   Holmes, *British politics*; W. A. Speck, *Tory and Whig: the struggle in the constituencies, 1701–15*, London 1970, and *The birth of Britain: a new nation, 1700–1710*, Oxford 1994; Tim Harris, *Politics under the later Stuarts: party conflict in a divided society, 1660–1715*, London 1993; Aaron Graham, *Corruption, party, and government in Britain, 1702–1713*, Oxford 2015; David Stasavage, *Public debt and the birth of the democratic state: France and Great Britain, 1688–1789*, Cambridge 2003, esp. pp. 1–25, 99–129.

did not go unnoticed in the colonies.[2] As the appointments illustrate, a hazy distinction between Toryism and Jacobitism was instrumental in shaping colonists' views of Jacobitism. The existence of Jacobitism and Toryism in the British Atlantic, whether the result of local politics or imperial appointments, suggests the likelihood and significance of both in larger transatlantic interactions. Jacobitism was a central aspect of Tory and Whig political divisions, and therefore a significant element in an increasingly cohesive, though multifaceted, transatlantic political culture.

This chapter seeks to outline the significance of Jacobitism and the rage of party in the British Atlantic and suggests that both Jacobitism and anti-Jacobitism, part of the cultural totality of the British Atlantic and an integral facet of Whig and Tory divisions, acted as linking elements joining disparate political cultures in the British Atlantic world to a divided British body politic. Moreover, Jacobitism and anti-Jacobitism, key shapers of British party divisions, were inherently tied to other integrative features linking Britain's Atlantic world such as anti-Catholicism and the Protestant succession, thus forging stronger ties between transatlantic party interests. The chapter first examines overt expressions of Jacobitism in the British Atlantic and demonstrates the existence of elements of a Jacobite subculture within the British Atlantic colonies, especially in the years between 1689 and 1727. The very existence of elements of a Jacobite subculture elucidates the prevalence of a virulent anti-Jacobitism. Seemingly paranoid responses to both perceived and real Jacobitism were, in fact, local expressions that were deeply rooted in a transatlantic cultural and political context. Building on the evidence of a transatlantic Jacobite subculture, the chapter then explores the impact and importance of British party politics in the management of Britain's Atlantic empire as a means of explaining manifestations or accusations of Jacobite sympathies among people in the colonies. Moreover, the changing character of accusations of Jacobitism from being anti-French, anti-Irish and anti-Catholic to anti-Tory or anti-High Church suggests the changing nature of the Jacobite threat. This, in turn, helps to explain the lasting currency of accusations of Jacobitism. It contributes to the larger discussion of the remarkable transatlantic impact of Britain's politically divided society and thus demonstrates the significance of Jacobitism and anti-Jacobitism in the political culture of the British Atlantic world.

After the restoration of the monarchy in 1660 the British presence in the Atlantic expanded rapidly. Charles II and James II&VII actively pursued imperial projects. They oversaw the acquisition of new territories through conquest and also used land grants to reward supporters which resulted in the proprietary colonies of New York (1664), Pennsylvania (1682), the Jerseys (1664)

---

[2]   For the most comprehensive examination of the complex relationship between Jacobitism and Toryism during the rage of party see Szechi, *Jacobitism and Tory politics*.

and Carolina (1663). Each colony had a unique governmental structure and ethnic make-up creating a vast diversity of experience. Institutional diversity caused numerous problems of government and administration, not least the constant tension between the English government and the colonial peripheries concerning constitutional issues.[3] Unable to maintain imperial control during periods of uncertainty, the few imperial officials on hand in the colonies were ineffectual during times of institutional chaos, especially in 1689. The proprietors in the Jerseys and elsewhere were constantly in conflict with settlers, and colonists throughout the British Atlantic pursued illicit trading and smuggling in order to avoid the restrictions on trade imposed by the Navigation Acts. In order to curtail colonial resistance to the acts and create a more centralised empire, Charles II and James II&VII had begun by 1685 the process of revoking proprietary colonial charters and reorganising the empire in a manner similar to the Spanish empire in the Americas as a means of centralising authority in the crown.

Their schemes ended abruptly in 1689. The effects of the revolution of 1688 reverberated across the Atlantic and resulted in a number of local revolts. Those in Boston, New York and Maryland capitalised on William's invasion and ousted the appointees of James II&VII or, in the case of Maryland, of the proprietor.[4] Rooted in a profound fear of Catholicism and the possible tyranny of central authority, the revolts reflect a shared political culture antithetical to popery while also demonstrating the colonial elites' dissatisfaction with the local impact of James II&VII's imperial designs. As a result, though in ways profoundly local, the revolts acted as a catalyst for the anglicisation of the empire and fostered elements of a predominantly Whig transatlantic political culture, a key component of which was the Protestant succession and Protestant monarchy.[5] Yet the Protestant succession was not without its critics in Britain, and after 1688 there was a brief civil war in Scotland, a three-year long war in Ireland and almost constant political unrest in England.

Similarly, William of Orange's accession did not go uncontested in the colonies. While few in the mainland colonies proved to be overly sympathetic to the plight of the Catholic James II&VII, numerous colonial officials in the Caribbean were less reluctant openly to support James for a variety of reasons echoing responses from the British Isles. For example, in April 1689 Nathaniel Johnson, governor of the Leeward Islands, wrote to an unknown correspondent

---

[3]   Jack P. Greene, *Peripheries and center: constitutional development in the extended polities of the British Empire and the United States*, Athens, GA 1986.

[4]   Stanwood, *Empire reformed*; Lovejoy, *The Glorious Revolution in America*; Richard Dunn, 'The Glorious Revolution and America', in Nicholas Canny (ed.), *The Oxford history of the British Empire*, I: *The origins of empire: British overseas enterprise to the close of the seventeenth century*, Oxford 1998, 445–66.

[5]   Stanwood, *Empire reformed*; McConville, *The king's three faces*; Jack P. Green, '"Empire and identity" from the Glorious Revolution to the American revolution', in Marshall, *Oxford history of the British Empire*, ii. 208–30; Kidd, *The Protestant interest*.

in England that he would remain loyal to James despite knowing that he had fled to France. Rooting his support for the king in High Church Tory understandings of passive obedience and non-resistance, Johnson claimed that 'I think the Church of England teaches me the doctrine of non-resistance.'[6] Johnson's eventual resignation from his post illustrates the transatlantic reverberations of the Glorious Revolution by demonstrating that colonial governors were active participants in events roiling Britain, and that at an early stage the colonies witnessed political divisions following the Revolution of 1688.

Nor was Johnson an isolated case. In 1689 the chaplain of a ship commanded by Admiral Hewetson reported that during the period of uncertainty following William's invasion the admiral forced him to continue to pray for King James and continued to do so even after he had received news of William's accession.[7] Sir Thomas Montgomerie, a recent convert to Catholicism in Barbados, carried on an extensive correspondence with French Jesuits in the Caribbean and acquaintances in England. He received updates from his correspondents regarding William's invasion of England and James's intended invasion of Ireland.[8] Montgomerie's pursuit of patronage and power during the reign of James II&VII, including his conversion, had proved somewhat untimely. The governor of the island, James Kendall, acquired Montgomerie's incriminating correspondence and had him arrested for conspiring with the French. A year later, Montgomerie was still in prison and Kendall wrote to England that he believed Montgomerie's crimes were of a treasonable nature and, consequently, he was disinclined to release him. He believed that the prisoner was still inclined to King James and would 'escape to him if released'. He contrasted this with one of Montgomerie's allies, also in prison, who in Kendall's opinion was a 'fat fool' who had changed his religion in hopes of gaining advantage.[9]

Some of those hostile to the Revolution resorted to violence. Following the proclamation of William and Mary's accession and the onset of the Nine Years War between England and France 'malicious people of the Irish nation' in the Leeward Island revolted in support of James. One deposition attested to the fact that the rebellious Irish were flying colours which observers noted they called 'King James's colours'.[10] Another witness remarked that the Irish had 'set up a red flag with four white balls and J.R. thereon', likely referencing Jacobus Rex, and were threatening to kill any who would not declare for King James.[11] Moreover, the Irish were supported by the French, who not only provided a safe

---

[6] Nathaniel Johnson to [?], 25 Apr. 1689, CSPC, item 88.

[7] 'Statement of the passage between Admiral Hewetson and the Rev. Mr Bowerman', 11 July 1689, CSPC, item 247.

[8] Garrat Trant to Sir Thomas Montgomerie, 30 May 1689, CSPC, item 157i.

[9] Governor James Kendall to Charles Talbot, 12th earl of Shrewsbury, 26 June 1690, CSPC, item 968.

[10] John Netheway to William III and Queen Mary, 9 July 1689, CSPC, item 237

[11] 'Remonstrance of the sufferings of the poor people of St Christophers', 11 July 1689, CSPC, item 253ii.

haven for the rebels but attacked the English island of Anguilla, 'administered an oath of allegiance to King James' and installed an Irishman as governor.[12] As late as 1694 the governor of Jamaica wrote that the Irish were providing intelligence to the French and that Roman Catholics and Irish went to serve the French as privateers because they 'thought it their duty to serve King James'.[13]

There were other more subtle acts of resistance to the accession of William and Mary. Officials throughout the colonies refused to take the required oaths of allegiance. In 1691 James Bray, a member of Virginia's House of Burgesses, refused to take the oaths and was disabled as a member. Two months later the lieutenant-governor of Virginia explained that three of Virginia's councillors had refused to take the required oaths from a 'scruple of conscience'.[14] Isaac Richier, governor of Bermuda, noted that the master of a ship and three mariners thought it 'no harm to perjure themselves when it is against the King', suggesting that the men harboured a sense of the illegitimacy of William III&II's accession.[15]

These subtle acts of resistance were not always voluntary. Officials in the colonies often knew of men who might not be reconciled to the accession of William and Mary and used oaths as a weapon to flush them out. In 1698 the council of Maryland was advised that 'Mr. Joseph's seems to be a person disaffected' to the government and the council suggested that Josephs take the oaths appointed by parliament. Josephs refused to take the oaths 'saying that it was his opinion that if he took those oaths he renounced his God'.[16] This is clearly an echo of events in Britain where a number of men, including ten English peers, sixty members of parliament and around a hundred gentry families accepted lives of political exile rather than swear the oaths.[17] Thus, those in the colonies who refused the oaths were not isolated anomalies, but rather were part of a larger, transatlantic disaffected minority. Refusal to swear the oaths was at the very least a tacit acknowledgement that William III&II had usurped the crown, indicating that at least some colonists felt discomfort, if not disaffection, with the Revolution settlement and probably sympathy for the exiled Stuarts.

Seditious words, the cause of regular complaints in the colonies, further demonstrate the existence of a disaffected minority. Although in many cases both the background of the accused and the intentions of the accuser remain

---

[12] Lieutenant-General Christopher Codington to the Lords of Trade and Plantations, 19 Sept. 1689, *CSPC*, item 444.

[13] Lieutenant-Governor Sir William Beeston to Shrewsbury, 18 Aug. 1694, *CSPC*, items 1236, 1236i.

[14] Journal of the House of Burgesses; Francis Nicholson, Lieutenant-Governor of Virginia to the Lords of Trade and Plantations, 18 May, 10 June 1691, *CSPC*, items 1510, 1583.

[15] Governor Isaac Richier to the Lords of Trade and Plantations, 16 Oct. 1691, *CSPC*, item 1843.

[16] AOM xxiii. 513.

[17] Monod, *Jacobitism*, 142.

obscure, the nature of the words reported and the punishment inflicted indicate the seriousness with which authorities viewed the charge. Moreover, seditious words spoken in the colonies reveal a striking similarity to examples from England. Paul Monod has argued that evidence of spoken seditious words might not reveal a deeply committed Jacobite, but it does indicate a level of disaffection, thereby suggesting the persistence of Jacobitism as a meaningful element in British political culture; a claim equally applicable to examples from the colonies.[18] Thus, evidence of seditious words being uttered in the colonies provides a reminder of the cultural connections and discourses spanning the Atlantic. There are other notable parallels. As in England, seditious words document the changing nature of Jacobitism and Jacobite political culture. For example, just as in England, colonial complaints and prosecutions of seditious words appear to have declined during the reign of Anne, a monarch much more acceptable to the disaffected minority than either William of Orange or George I.

Examples of seditious expressions appear as early as 1689, echoing the sentiments of contemporaries in the British Isles. In July of that year the governor of Barbados noted that many people were 'taking the oaths cheerfully' but that a handful of men were in custody and would soon stand trial for using 'dangerous words'.[19] A number of colonists faced stiff penalties. In Maryland in 1697 Richard Smith, a Catholic and a person 'reputed to be a factious person much disaffected to his Majesty', was forced to put up £2,000 of security for countenancing Jacobitism at his house by 'laughing and grinning' when Thomas Johnson said he would 'never take an oath to any but King James'.[20] The Council of Jamaica required James Hands to 'answer for scandalous words spoken against their Majesties' and reported the next week that Hands had been dismissed upon giving security for good behaviour.[21] Another complaint from Jamaica noted a Catholic exclaiming that 'the Prince of Orange was a Dutch bastard' and that 'the people of the West were always rebelling and that he hoped one stone would not be left upon another in Exeter'.[22] Similarly, in 1700, the governor of Barbados reported on the arrest of 'one George Duncan, a Scotchman' who had spoken 'several seditious words against his Majesty'. Resulting from passions aroused by the heady combination of the failure of the Darien colony and strong drink, Duncan had declared that 'the Scotch were as good as the English, no subjects of King William, and that there would soon be a change'.[23] Duncan's outspokenness can no doubt be attributed in part to his fondness for drink, but this does not discount the apparent disaffection

[18] Ibid. 234–44

[19] Lieutenant-Governor Edwin Stede to Shrewsbury, 2 Sept. 1689, CSPC, item 397.

[20] AOM xxiii. 468.

[21] Minutes of the Council of Jamaica, 3, 10 Feb. 1690, CSPC, items 753, 758.

[22] Ibid. 29 Jan. 1690, CSPC, item 874v.

[23] Governor Ralph Grey to the CTP, 23 Mar. 1700, CSPC, items 245, 245ii.

underlying his statements or the importance of the transatlantic context of the words that he chose to use.

Other cases of seditious words indicate that imperial officials were complicit or lenient towards the speaker. In the Leeward Islands in 1697 Captain Robert Arthur, 'formerly commander of H.M.S. Mary', was 'committed for scandalous and treasonable words against the King and Government'. His comments included statements damning the king and suggesting that 'King William had never done good to the Kingdom' because he was cursed by God for 'taking it from his father to whom it justly belonged'. Though brought to trial, Arthur was released because the witnesses necessary for his conviction were sailors whose ship had been sent on patrol by the governor.[24]

Although the numbers were in any case much fewer than in Britain, it is possible to discern a decline in accusations and prosecutions of seditious words in the colonies during the reign of Anne, as happened in England. In the years between 1702 and 1714, either those guilty were less likely to be prosecuted or there was less reason for many to be disaffected, as Anne was much more palatable to the Jacobites than had been William III&II or than George I would be. However, just as in Britain, after the accession of George I in 1714 there were notable examples of outspoken disaffection. Two men in Philadelphia were tried and punished for speaking against George I's right to the throne.[25] In New Hampshire a customs official and 'noted Irish Jacobite' named Robert Armstrong was reported to have said, 'Is it not a shame that we should be governed by Germans and Dutch, and have such a fine English prince of our own, but I hope I shall yet live to see the right heir upon the throne.'[26] The charges against Armstrong were considered so serious that the Board of Trade seems to have removed him from his post.[27]

There was also a remarkable use of Jacobite cant and seditious words by pirates for at least a decade after 1715 which suggests that the language of party politics and seditious words were an essential aspect of British Atlantic culture even as far down the social scale as plebeian criminals: a parallel to the relationship between Jacobitism and crime in England.[28] E. T. Fox has shown that pirates, like smugglers in England, routinely uttered seditious words and some even corresponded with Jacobites in England.[29] For example, the famous pirate Bartholomew Roberts reputedly called King George a Turnip man.[30]

---

[24] Edward Walrond to John Egerton, 3rd earl of Bridgewater, 6 Nov. 1697, CSPC, items 31ii, 31i.

[25] AMW, 23 Mar. 1721, no. 66.

[26] Richard Sharpe to the CTP, 16 Nov. 1722, CSPC, item 345; 'Journals', Nov. 1722, JBTP iv.

[27] Lieutenant-Governor John Wentworth to the CTP, 20 Aug. 1723, CSPC, item 685.

[28] Monod, Jacobitism, 111–19.

[29] E. T. Fox, 'Jacobitism and the "golden age" of piracy', International Journal of Maritime History xxii (2010), 277–303 at p. 286.

[30] Ibid. 288.

Similarly, after the Jacobite Rebellion of 1715 pirates named their ships after prominent Tory leaders involved in the rebellion – the *King James, Ormonde* and *Windham Galley* – suggesting a sharp political and historical awareness.[31] Fox has further argued that the use of these seditious words represented the political beliefs of the pirates involved and that a shared disaffection to the Hanoverian succession was a feature of recruitment.[32] Monod's claim that Jacobitism provided criminals with 'a means to legitimise their defiance of the law' probably applied to pirates too.[33]

Seditious words are suggestive of one of the most striking patterns that emerged in the British Atlantic during the age of Anne: the intensification of a pan-Atlantic integration of political cultures following the Revolution of 1688. If understood as common to a larger British Atlantic political culture, rather than representing colonial abnormalities or local, isolated examples, they reveal cultural and political cohesion in Britain's Atlantic empire. Certain examples, such as those of Duncan, Sharpe or the Irish rebels, illustrate the importance of ethnicity and the migration of people of a variety of ethnic backgrounds, and the consequent integration of Scottish and Irish political cultures into a comprehensive British Atlantic political culture. While these examples reflect larger themes such as a shared antipathy to William III&II and George I, they also demonstrate the expression of uniquely Scottish, Irish or provincial complaints within an Atlantic framework. However, after 1714 seditious words increasingly demonstrated overlap between Jacobite disaffection and Tory political culture, thus offering tantalising glimpses of an evolving, multi-faceted political culture that bridged the Atlantic. Furthermore, evidence of disaffection helps to make sense of changing fears of Jacobitism, suggesting that virulent anti-Jacobitism was rooted in both local and transatlantic political realities.

While seditious words and overt expressions of Jacobitism mark are an important element of cohesion, they represent only a single manifestation of the integration of British and colonial political cultures in the early eighteenth century. The overarching and primary means by which the colonies were integrated into an Atlantic political culture was through participation in the rage of party.

The rancorous division between the Whig and Tory parties was one of the most notable features of the post-1688 British political world.[34] British society was divided by an increasingly polarised political sphere. This increasingly led to the assumption that the opposing political party was antithetical to the economic prosperity or future wellbeing of Britain. Debates about

---

[31] Ibid. 287–8.

[32] Ibid. 296.

[33] Monod, *Jacobitism*, 113.

[34] Holmes, *British politics*; Speck, *Tory and Whig*, and *The birth of Britain*; Colley, *In defiance of oligarchy*; Harris, *Politics under the later Stuarts*.

the Church, political economy and the succession tore constituencies apart and divided England, Scotland and Ireland and, consequently, the British Atlantic. In England relatively sophisticated party systems comprised of various political, religious or economic interests mobilised and facilitated widespread political participation.[35] These party divisions affected, to a large degree, the management of the colonies, including appointments and imperial policies. Consequently, party politics reverberated across the Atlantic.

From 1688 to 1715 Tories and Whigs battled for parliamentary supremacy. Although party interests were certainly diverse, the primary Tory means of garnering political support was by proclaiming that the Church of England was threatened by the growth of dissent and heresy, problems that they attributed to the Toleration Act of 1689. Tory champions such as the High Church cleric Henry Sacheverell used fiery religious rhetoric to ridicule the revolution settlement, and leading Tory politicians responsible for the creation of a 'church party', such as Henry St John, 1st Viscount Bolingbroke, were in contact with the exiled Stuart court, suggesting to antagonistic contemporaries that the Tory party was, at least in part, a Jacobite party. Thus, although the Whigs possessed no symbol of electoral importance comparable to 'the Church in danger', they were able to rally around the Protestant succession to begin fashioning a pro-Hanoverian political culture. One fundamental aspect of this was the identification of Tories as subversive enemies of the Revolution and the succession, especially in the latter years of Anne's reign.[36] As a consequence, Jacobitism and anti-Jacobitism became a vital aspect of party politics in early eighteenth-century Britain. Such party struggles, propaganda and language extended well beyond those Britons immediately involved in elections or governing, and political cultures extended well beyond the confines of the British archipelago.

In fact, there was a symbiotic process by which party politics facilitated political – and therefore imperial – centralisation, and centralisation accelerated the export of party politics throughout the Atlantic. In the aftermath of the revolution of 1688, the English, and after 1707 the British empire experienced a long process of institutional reorganisation, leading to the formation of a new Atlantic political culture.[37] Owen Stanwood and Brendan McConville have convincingly argued that this occurred in the wake of 1688-9 and was due largely to a shared anti-popery, the concerted use of anti-Catholic rhetoric by imperial officials and a 'cult of Protestant monarchy' respectively.[38] Anti-popery

---

[35] Speck, Tory and Whig, 18; Stasavage, Public debt, 99–129.

[36] Szechi, Jacobitism and Tory politics. For the development of a pro-Hanoverian political culture see Smith, Georgian monarchy.

[37] Stanwood, Empire reformed; McConville, The king's three faces; Kidd, The Protestant interest; Alison Gilbert Olson, Making the empire work: London and American interest groups, 1690–1790, Cambridge, MA 1992, and Anglo-American politics, 1660–1775: the relationship between parties in England and colonial America, Oxford 1973; Webb, Marlborough's America.

[38] Stanwood, Empire reformed, 3, 20; McConville, The king's three faces, 15.

and the celebration of Protestant monarchy, however, were, in part, elements of a Whiggish political rhetoric disparaged by many Tories as little more than a means of engendering fear and hysteria.[39] Thus, as the eighteenth century progressed, colonial expressions of anti-Catholicism and support for the Protestant succession demonstrate secondary elements of integration. In fact, in Britain these were rhetorical flourishes employed as key features of British party conflicts, and thus indicate that the rage of party was (along with trade) the primary engine of integration.

Possessing a shared history, heritage and language, provincial Britons were well placed to participate actively in the English – and later British – party system contested by the Whig and Tory parties. This is not to say that colonials created organisations as complex as those in Britain. Local political issues such as taxes and trade, and the practice of politics including elections, appoint-ments and the differences in representation caused by smaller assemblies often differed markedly from those in Britain. Yet these decidedly local issues were increasingly debated within a cultural context defined in large part by British party politics. Consequently, colonists participated in the culture of British party politics and actively identified themselves and their opponents in party terms. The adoption of Whig and Tory party language thus facilitated the creation of Whig and Tory interests in the colonies, a process inevitably linked to attitudes towards Jacobitism and the succession.

This process has remarkable similarities to the integration of Scottish and Irish politics in the early eighteenth century. The introduction of party politics in Ireland was not simply produced by provincials following an English example, but was rather a 'complex interaction between two political worlds'.[40] Although local issues may have predominated, these issues were increasingly recast within the cultural context of English party politics. For instance, the Tory government under Anne restructured the Irish executive along party lines, in effect introducing Whig and Tory politics. As influential individuals associated with an English party rose to prominence, such as the James Butler, 2nd duke of Ormonde, in Ireland, locals appropriated party language and intentionally participated in party disputes, effectively creating a British party dynamic.[41] Party politics were not transplanted wholesale to the colonies nor was the actual practice of politics identically reproduced among local political

---

[39]   Mark Knights, 'The Tory interpretation of history in the rage of parties', *Huntington Library Quarterly* lxviii (2005), 353-73; Scott Sowerby, 'Opposition to anti-popery in resto-ration England', *JBS* li (2012), 26-49, and *Making toleration: the repealers and the Glorious Revolution*, Cambridge, MA 2013, 82-92.

[40]   David Hayton, *Ruling Ireland, 1685-1742: politics, politicians, and parties*, London 2004, 94; 'Traces of party politics in early eighteenth-century Scottish elections', *PH* lvi (1996), 74-99; and 'Irish Tories and victims of Whig persecution: Sacheverell fever by proxy', *PH* xxxi (2012), 80-98.

[41]   Idem, *Ruling Ireland*, 35-95, and 'Traces of party politics', 74-99; S. J. Connolly, *Religion, law, and power: the making of Protestant Ireland, 1660-1760*, Oxford 1992, 74-86.

cultures. What is evident, however, is the increasingly partisan nature of political language, rhetoric, accusations and identifications among colonial officials and colonists. Language was certainly a vital element. As local political leaders were drawn into a British party dynamic and employed loaded party language, their opponents were forced to participate as well. Although the colonies do not exhibit a mirror image of British party organisation, practice or electioneering, some colonists and colonial officials appropriated party language, thus signifying a tacit acceptance of British party politics. Imperial officers such as governors were conscious of their party connections and utilised them to great effect, further reinforcing the import of party politics. As is evident in Scotland and Ireland, political assimilation was made possible by and was inseparable from the Atlantic integration of a more efficient and timely communications network.[42] Newspapers, broadsides, almanacs and pamphlets all contributed to the development in the British colonies of party consciousness and participation in party disputes.

Party politics in Britain affected both the ideological foundations of empire and the day-to-day functioning of imperial business. Ideological divisions, ranging from debates about the Established Church's relation to dissent to foreign policy, separated the Whigs and Tories. Nor was the rage of party 'simply about religious and constitutional issues'. Party divisions affected every area of imperial business including ideas of political economy.[43] Such divisions would undoubtedly have had practical consequences, especially regarding appointments: explorations of Anglo-American politics by Alison Olson and Ian Steele illustrate the assimilation of colonial issues, such as the future of proprietary charters, into the larger orbit of British party conflicts.[44] Thus, ideological contests in Britain had practical consequences and shaped both the conceptions of and day-to-day functioning of the Atlantic empire.

The Nine Years War that erupted between Britain and France in the aftermath of the accession of William and Mary forced British policymakers to reorganise imperial government. The wars also increased the government's need for reliable information about the colonies. In 1696 William created the Board of Trade and Plantations, a small group of seven men who reported to the Secretary of State for the Southern Department, as a means of organising and facilitating imperial correspondence. As the body responsible for gathering information on the colonies, and advising the government on colonial issues,

---

[42] Ian K. Steele, *The English Atlantic, 1675–1740: an exploration of communication and community*, Oxford 1986. The emergent public sphere is discussed in greater detail in chapter 3 below.

[43] Steve Pincus, 'Addison's empire: Whig conceptions of empire in the early 18th century', *PH* xxxi (2012), 99–117, and 'Rethinking mercantilism: political economy, the British Empire, and the Atlantic world in the seventeenth and eighteenth centuries', *WMQ* lxix (2012), 3–34.

[44] Olson, *Anglo-American politics*, 104–5; Steele, 'The anointed, the appointed, and the elected, 105–27.

it acted as a clearing house for a large amount of the correspondence and complaints arriving from the colonies, including information from proprietary colonies. As such it was partly responsible for deciding what needed to be forwarded to the privy council, and primarily responsible for advising the government on colonial issues, and for suggesting candidates for colonial governorships. Appointments to the board were made by the Secretary of State for the Southern Department, a crown appointee and member of the cabinet. Consequently, appointments were both subject to and reflected party divisions, thus confirming the current direction of imperial policy.[45]

When the board was created in 1696, in the aftermath of a plot to assassinate William, it leaned heavily to the Whigs and included figures such as John Locke and John Pollexfen. Of the seven men appointed to the board, only one was a Tory, William Blathwayt. The make-up of the board affected communications with the colonial administrators: for example, two Tory governors received harsh letters from the board which were drafted during periods when Blathwayt was absent from the board's meetings.[46]

British politicians recognised the board's value as a means of shaping colonial policy and, as a result, party politics wrought havoc with its membership, which was hotly contested from 1702 to 1714. In 1702, when the Tories rose to power under Nottingham and Harley, Nottingham replaced two of the Whig members with the Thomas Thynne, 1st Viscount Weymouth, and William Legge, 1st earl of Dartmouth, loyal Tory appointees. The Tories suffered a reversal in 1706 when the Whig Junto rose to prominence and Charles Spencer, 3rd earl of Sunderland, was appointed as Secretary of State for the Southern Department.

Sunderland replaced all the Tory members with staunch Whigs. Following Sunderland's dismissal after the Tory ascendancy in 1710, the new Tory administration once again filled the board with Tories, and by 1713 Bolingbroke was the Secretary responsible for board appointments and colonial policy.[47] British historians have long accepted that Bolingbroke's political aim was 'to fill the employments of the kingdom, down to the meanest, with Tories'; and his role as Secretary of State meant that he could do the same for colonial appointments.[48]

Political battles over membership of the board mirrored the party orientation of the current ministry and thus had implications for officials throughout the empire. In the quickly shifting political waters, governors, who might have been appointed during the administration of one party, might find their allies out of power before they had even arrived at their post. In such cases appointees were forced to correspond with a potentially hostile board. Robert Hunter, for example, recognised the value of a friendly ministry. Governor of New York

---

[45] Ian K. Steele, *Politics of colonial policy: the Board of Trade in colonial administration, 1696–1720*, Oxford 1968.

[46] Ibid. 19–24.

[47] Ibid. 78–149.

[48] H. T. Dickinson, *Bolingbroke*, London 1970, 76.

and New Jersey from 1710 to 1719 and a Whig appointee, Hunter wrote to James Graham, 1st earl of Montrose, in 1714 following four years of Tory rule, that he had been 'hollowing complaints into deaf ears for four successive years'. Moreover, he noted the benefits of the political change after seeing a list of peers responsible for overseeing the successful accession of George I, stating that 'I hope that [hollowing complaints] is at an end' and that 'nothing confirmed me more that it was so then the reading your Grace's name in the list of the Lords of the Regency'. He added that he did not 'doubt your Grace's patronage'.[49] Hunter also wrote to his friend, the Whig essayist Joseph Addison, congratulating him on his being 'imployed' in the new ministry. Knowing he had a sympathetic ear, he noted having suffered due to not having received a reply to his 'enumerable complaints' during the 'late administration'.[50] Similarly, the Tory governor of Antigua, Daniel Parke, was elated when his antagonist, the Whig Charles Spencer was replaced in 1710.[51] Likewise, the Whig governor of Nova Scotia Samuel Vetch (1710–13) had good reason to complain in 1714 in a petition to the king that he had been 'intirely neglected or rather abandoned by the ministry at home' and despairingly related to another correspondent that he had sent repeated entreaties to the late ministry only to be ignored.[52] The Whig Richard Coote, 1st earl of Bellomont, governor of New York, lamented to the Board of Trade that it was 'a misfortune to me and great prejudice to the King's affairs here that your Lordships send me no orders' and that his opponents were exulting in the fact that he was not receiving letters because they said it was a mark of disgrace.[53]

If governors felt secure when they had the support of a friendly board, so too did the colonists whom they governed. In 1719 the critics of Robert Lowther, the Whig governor of Barbados, noted that Lowther thought his opponents' political tranquillity cowardice, saying that it proceeded only from 'their knowing that he stood so well with the ministry'.[54] As a consequence, prominent colonists were also keen on knowing the make-up of the current ministries, especially if they were likely to be friendly to their interests. Perhaps the most telling evidence of this is the New York merchant Robert Livingston's possession of handwritten ministerial lists from 1715.[55]

The contested membership of the board, and its vital role as a clearing-house for much of the correspondence and complaints arriving from the colonies,

---

[49]   Hunter to James Graham, 1st duke of Montrose, 20 Dec. 1714, NAS, Edinburgh, GD220/5/1895.

[50]   Hunter to Joseph Addison, 8 Nov. 1714, BL, MS Egerton 1971, fo. 15.

[51]   Webb, *Marlborough's America*, 278.

[52]   Petition of Colonel Samuel Vetch, late governor of Annapolis Royal, to the king, Dec. 1714, CSPC, item 122i.

[53]   Governor Richard Coote, 1st earl of Bellomont to the CTP, 1699, CSPC, item 116.

[54]   [William Gordon], A *representation of the miserable state of Barbadoes*, London 1719, 21.

[55]   'A list of the names of the new ministry', 27 Jan. 1715, Livingston family papers, Franklin D. Roosevelt Presidential Library, New York, microfilm, reel 3.

directly connected imperial officials and correspondents in the colonies to party divisions in Britain. The board became an important point of contact for complaints and updates as it looked to colonial interest groups, governors and individual colonists for information. As a consequence, it encouraged colonists, colonial officials and the agents whom they sent to represent their interests in Britain to appropriate party language as a means of securing support from British politicians. Colonists and colonial appointees were quick to capitalise on both institutional and extra-institutional means of combating and influencing officials, a process which disrupted local colonial politics and reshaped colonial political cultures even as it drew colonists and colonial officials into the larger arena of transatlantic party politics.

The Board of Trade was not the only institutional contact available to colonists. The different factions in the various colonies tended to prefer employing differing channels of authority. British Whigs encouraged their friends and devotees in the colonies to attempt to exercise influence by addressing parliament, while Tories tended to favour working through the privy council or informal means such as the SPG.[56] Colonials engaged with the Westminster parliament when necessary, appealing to parliament as a means of contending with governors, the Church or other colonial parties, but in doing so they were forced to involve themselves in British party conflicts.[57] As a temporary colonial agent sent to England to pursue the interests of the colony of Massachusetts, Increase Mather sought the restoration of the Massachusetts Charter as early as 1689 by addressing King William and parliament through petitions and meetings, a process facilitated by Mather's extensive network of dissenting correspondents.[58] Similarly, opponents of South Carolina's Test Act of 1704 appealed not to the Tory-leaning House of Commons but to the stronger Whig presence in the House of Lords, a tactic which allowed the Whig lords to bring the bill to the attention of the queen, securing a royal veto.[59]

There were also a number of extra-institutional avenues for building political connections. Contacts in the Anglican Church, including the current bishop of London or the SPG, provided a means for colonists to cultivate networks directly linking them to the rage of party.[60] For example, High Church clergy and congregations in the colonies were quick to employ the Tory rhetoric of 'the Church in danger' as a means of garnering sympathy among British High Churchmen. In 1712 William Vesey and Jacob Henderson, clergymen in New York and Pennsylvania, worked together to send to the SPG representations against the governor of New York who, after noting the increasing success of

[56]   Olson, *Anglo-American politics*, 104. For the SPG see chapter 2 below.

[57]   Steele, 'The annointed, the appointed, and the elected', 105–27.

[58]   Olson, *Anglo-American politics*, 99; Richard Johnson, *Adjustment to empire: the New England colonies, 1675–1715*, New Brunswick, NJ 1981, 136–82.

[59]   Olson, *Anglo-American politics*, 99.

[60]   In the period covered by this book the bishops of London were, successively, Henry Compton (1675–1713), John Robinson (1713–23) and Edmund Gibson (1723–48).

High Church Tory connections, was forced to respond by employing his father-in-law Thomas Orby to act as his personal agent and defend his interests before the SPG.[61] Similarly, in 1716 a number of prominent Massachusetts clergymen wrote to an unknown correspondent:

> very lately [during the Tory ministry] the charter of our province was threatened by a bill in Parliament, and in great danger of being taken away. This attempt has made us sensible that we need some standing friends in and about London who will naturally care for us on like emergencies, and generally use their interest on our behalf.[62]

Whether working through parliament, the privy council, or through extra-institutional means, colonists began to frame local conflicts in British party terms and rely on party connections as a means of securing support from party interests in Britain.

A brief examination of imperial appointments offers suggestive glimpses of both the institutional impact of the rage of party on Britain's Atlantic colonies and also the subsequent adoption of party-political language. The appointment of officials, especially governors, was subject to the shifting winds of party dominance in Britain. As in Ireland, the importance of a system of patronage inherently tied to party affiliations impressed on colonists and colonial officials the significance of Whig and Tory party divisions, and therefore the need to cultivate party associations. Indeed, the violent swings of the pendulum between the Tory and Whig parties in Britain directly affected the future prospects of colonial officials and therefore their colonial allies, thus shaping the management of the colonies and also influencing the practice and outcomes of local politics. When patrons lost positions of power, the governors whom they had appointed were forced to defend their actions to a hostile ministry. Their colonial opponents were quick to capitalise on this by nurturing their own party connections. Dependency on parties at home for appointment, support or guidance encouraged governors to serve party interests and cultivate party connections for their allies in the colonies. Undoubtedly, this meant that governors also acted as vital links between the two great parties in Britain and emerging party consciousness in the colonies.

The relationships between colonial officials and British party politics moulded perceptions in the colonies. Governors and other imperial appointees consequently remained an immediate, present reminder of the rancorous party divisions of Britain. Officials sent to the colonies utilised party language and rhetoric which was appropriated by colonists, tying the colonies to Britain's political culture. This was especially evident as fears of Jacobitism increased. The growing disaffection of the Tory party and the problematic relationship between Tory political culture and Jacobitism was exploited by Whig officials in

---

61 SPG papers, Rhodes House, Oxford, ser. C, box 1, items 25, 57.
62 Hunter to Thomas Orby, NAS, CH8/196/2, 25 May 1716.

the colonies who were keen to discredit their opponents. This led to a number of interesting accusations of Jacobitism in the British Atlantic inherently tied to party language. Yet allegations of Jacobitism were not merely instances of a transatlantic party rhetoric. They tended to be rooted in the realities of both party ideology and party appointments. Lending credence to colonists' fears that the Tory party was intending to facilitate the return of the exiled Stuarts, there were a number of Tory appointees in the period from 1710 to 1714 who had a Jacobite past. An example is William Keith who had been arrested for suspicion of treason for Jacobite plotting in 1703, but was appointed as Surveyor-General of the Customs of the South District of North America by Bolingbroke's ministry in 1714. That Keith's Jacobitism was well known is verified by requests sent to the Whig Montrose asking for Keith to be replaced after the fall of the Tories in 1715. The letter noted that Keith had not had 'any imployment under the Government since the Revolution, until admitted to this by the late ministry, by the interest of the Lord Bolingbroke' because he was 'far from being lookt upon as a person duly affected'.[63] Moreover, the Jacobite Christopher Fleming, Lord Slane, was reportedly offered the governorship of New York in 1714 during the Tory heyday, but instead opted for an Irish peerage.[64]

The proscription of the Tory party in 1715, a seismic political shift in Britain, was replicated throughout the British Atlantic as the Whigs replaced Tory appointees with those whom they deemed loyal to the Whig party and the Protestant succession. Three examples, Richard Coote, Robert Lowther and Samuel Vetch, emphasise the importance of colonial appointees in the developing party divisions and party consciousness in the colonies. The ethnicity of these three men is emblematic of the integration of Britain's Atlantic, while their careers illustrate how changing political cultures in Britain shaped accusations in the colonies. This places accusations of Jacobitism in a larger context, demonstrating the ideological party realities that accusations underscored in Britain's colonies.

Richard Coote, Lord Bellomont, was appointed governor of New York and Massachusetts in 1696 by the new Whig ministry, replacing the Tory appointee Benjamin Fletcher. Bellomont was a Protestant Irish peer and, like most Irish Protestants in the decade following the Jacobite wars of 1689-91, a staunch supporter of William and Mary.[65] Bellomont's tenure as governor is notable for a number of reasons and coincided with the creation of new imperial structures such as the Board of Trade. One of the most intriguing aspects of his tenure is that he was one of the first governors to employ divisive English party

[63] W. A. Speck, 'Keith, Sir William, fourth baronet (c. 1669-1749)', ODNB; Memorial of Archibald Forbes, [c. 1715], NAS, GD220/6/1754.

[64] Webb, Marlborough's America, 312.

[65] John Gibney, 'Ireland's restoration crisis', and Toby Barnard, 'Ireland, 1689-91', in Tim Harris and Stephen Taylor (eds), The final crisis of the Stuart monarchy: the revolutions of 1688-91 in their British, Atlantic, and European contexts, Woodbridge 2013, 133-56, 157-88.

language in colonial disputes. Bellomont viewed anyone who disagreed with him or contested his authority as a Jacobite or papist, terms which according to many were virtually synonymous in the late seventeenth century.[66] He regularly used anti-Catholic and anti-Tory rhetoric to galvanise support and discredit his opponents. By contextualising colonists in these terms, Bellomont was, in some respects, superimposing metropolitan party conflicts onto provincial politics, a development which encouraged colonists to actively participate in imperial politics.

On Bellomont's arrival in 1698, New York was riven by factional strife, divided between Leislerians and anti-Leislerians, who had vied for advantage ever since Jacob Leisler, the virulently Protestant Dutch militia captain, had wrested power from the royal governor during the revolution of 1688–9 only to be executed two years later. Bellomont quickly sided with the Leislerians who had been supportive of William's bid for the throne in 1689 and had led a rebellion against James II&VII's appointees. The Leislerians viewed themselves as supporters of William and Mary and so it was likely that Bellomont's strong ties with William and the Whig party would endear him to them while also encouraging his opponents in New York to seek out alliances with Tories in England, creating 'durable affiliations' between factions in New York and parties in Britain.[67] Colonists understood the vagaries of Britain's emerging party political system. After the king's death in 1701, the attorney-general of New York noted that this event did not bode well for the Whigs or Bellomont and that the accession of Anne, who was sympathetic to the Tories, would discourage Bellomont's allies in the colony and encourage his enemies.[68] Bellomont's tenure in government, then, is an early example of provincial politics being drawn into ambit of British party conflict.

The two local factions, Bellomont's and that of his opponents, realised the importance of British party politics and used transatlantic connections to effect local changes. Bellomont complained to the largely Whig Board of Trade that the 'Jacobite party' in New York was anxious to see him gone, and noted that his Tory predecessor, Benjamin Fletcher, was writing encouraging letters to his friends in the colony, suggesting that Bellomont's dismissal was imminent, and thereby increasing local opposition by spreading rumours that Bellomont had lost influence at home. The governor lamented his plight to the Board of Trade in 1698, chastising them for their lack of communication as the 'Jacobite party here take great notice of it, and give it out all the county over that I am therefore in disgrace with the King, for that the ministers neglect me'.[69] By 1699 reports stated that the 'Leislerites' referred to their opponents as

---

[66]   Stanwood, *Empire reformed*, 189.

[67]   John D. Runcie, 'The problem of Anglo American politics in Bellomont's New York', *WMQ* xxvi (1969), 191–217 at p. 217.

[68]   Olson, *Anglo-American politics*, 101–2.

[69]   Coote to the CTP, 21 Sept. 1698, *CSPC*, item 835; 21 Oct. 1698, item 914; Dec. 1698, item 116.

the 'Jacobite party', indicating the diffusion of mainland party language among colonial factions.[70]

Nor were the complaints of Bellomont and the Leslerians about a Jacobite party without foundation. In 1699 he noted 'a club of dissatisfied marchands to the number of 28 or 30, where one constant health was, to him that durst be honest in the worst of times', clearly a reference in Bellomont's mind to the exiled Stuarts.[71] The reputed drinking of toasts mirrors a prominent element of mainland Jacobite culture, a reflection of British political culture. He also reported that a member of the House of Representatives in New York moved in relation to a bill referring to the Revolution of 1688–9 as the 'late happy Revolution' that '"happy" might be left out, for he did not conceive the Revolution to be happy'.[72] Whether this was meant to be an insult directed towards the Leislerians who were responsible for the revolution in New York matters little. According to Bellomont, it was a clear sign of disaffection and placed the opposition firmly in the Jacobite camp. The man who reportedly disapproved of the word happy owned a public house, suggesting a means of further ideological diffusion as his opinions would likely have been discussed and spread. Furthermore, Bellomont was certain that in order to avoid taking the oaths to the king, 'a great many men pretended themselves Quakers' but soon after 'pulled off the mask of Quakerism'. The leaders of this party had 'uttered scurrilous and opprobrious language against His Majesty and declared themselves much in favour of the late King James'.[73] Furious factional disputes relating to land grants, taxes and religious differences in New York became enmeshed in British party politics and so came to reflect worries not only about Catholicism, but increasingly concerns about the relationship between Tory politics and Jacobitism. Tory election victories in in England in 1701 at the end of William's reign did not bode well for Bellomont, especially in light of his litany of anti-Tory and anti-Jacobite complaints, and would probably have led to his recall had he not died in 1701, before such a recall could take place.

Bellomont was not the only governor to encounter such difficulties. Robert Lowther, governor of Barbados from 1711 to 1714, and then from 1715 to 1720, also took aim at opponents whom he considered Tory Jacobite sympathisers. Lowther's tenure as governor provides a compelling example of the problems and possibilities presented by the rage of party. It also demonstrates the shifting nature of the Jacobite threat, from papist and nonjuring to Tory and High Church. Lowther was appointed governor of Barbados by Lord Treasurer Godolphin in 1710, just before Goldophin was ousted in the wake of the Tory parliamentary victory. Prior to this Lowther served as a member of parliament

---

[70] *CSPC*, Apr. 1699, item 317.

[71] Ibid.

[72] Ibid.

[73] Ibid. The Quaker relationship with Jacobitism is discussed in more detail in chapter 2 below. For the wider context of this relationship see Sowerby, *Making toleration*.

for Westmoreland from 1705 to 1708. Classed as a Whig during his parliamentary career, he was also noted as being a churchman though 'indifferent to all religions', a latitudinarian low churchman, and thus epitomising the Tory caricature of a Whig.[74] His time in parliament also meant that he was well versed in the practice and language of Britain's party politics.

Upon his arrival in Barbados, Lowther almost immediately fell out with a local party that possessed strong connections to Tory interests. His primary opponents were William Sharpe and William Cleland, two large landowners, and William Gordon, an Anglican minister. All three of these men were members or were soon to become members of the SPG, and they supported a much stronger Anglican ecclesiastical establishment in the colony, including the appointment of a bishop.[75] They actively canvassed the bishop of London, the SPG and the Board of Trade in pursuit of a stronger church establishment, a goal that Lowther vehemently opposed. They were able to capitalise on the Tory victory of 1710 and received sympathetic hearings from the SPG and the bishop of London. After 1710 Lowther's opponents also began lobbying the now heavily Tory Board of Trade and the SPG in hopes of securing the governor's dismissal.[76] Their complaints included the Tory 'Church in danger' rhetoric. Both Lowther and his opponents well understood the dangers of being a governor without the support of a friendly ministry at home. In a later description of the period printed in a pamphlet published in London in 1719 entitled *A representation of the miserable state of Barbadoes,* the governor's critics noted that Lowther had claimed during the Tory ascendency of 1710 to 1714 that 'this ministry are not my friends ... By God, if I had a Ministry that were my Friends, I would make you be glad to eat grass with your Cattle'.[77] The transition to an unfriendly Tory ministry at home, led by Robert Harley and Bolingbroke, meant that Lowther's defence of his conduct went unheeded, and in February 1714 orders for his recall were issued by Bolingbroke in his capacity as Secretary of State for the Southern Department.

Lowther was just one of many Whigs who were replaced in the colonies. William Sharpe briefly succeeded Lowther as head of the Barbados government and wrote to Bolingbroke of the previous governor's shortcomings. Employing Tory party rhetoric such as 'the Church in danger', Sharpe wrote that because of Lowther's antipathy to the Church, 'the Clergy had been of late very much discountenac'd'.[78] However, Sharpe's governership came to an abrupt end

---

[74]   Eveline Cruickshanks and Richard Harrison, 'Lowther, Robert (1681–1745), of Maulds Meaburn, Westmld', in D. Hayton, E. Cruickshanks and S. Handley (eds), *The history of parliament: the House of Commons, 1690–1715,* London 2002, iv. 703–4.

[75]   J. Harry Bennett, 'The SPG and Barbadian politics, 1710–1720', *Historical Magazine of the Protestant Episcopal Church* xx (1951), 190–206.

[76]   President William Sharpe to Henry St John, Lord Bolingbroke, 14 June 1714, CSPC, items 696, 697.

[77]   [Gordon], *State of Barbadoes,* 19.

[78]   Sharpe to Bolingbroke, June 1714, CSPC, item 697.

when the Hanoverian succession in 1714 and the proscription of the Tories the following year led to Lowther's reinstatement. As his opponents noted, Lowther had expertly exploited fears of Jacobitism and party divisions to regain his post by claiming to the Whig ministry that he believed 'the true reason of [his] recall was, that the then Ld. Bolingbroke might meet with no resistance in delivering up the Island to the Pretender'.[79]

The Lowther case further illustrates how the party political nature of appointments led to the alignment of colonial politics along transatlantic party axes. Lowther's brief recall and his past experience with British party politics prompted him to contextualise his dismissal in transatlantic party, rather than factional and local, terms. The links of the Barbados opposition to the now disgraced Tory party and their zealous support of the interests of the established Church provided the opportunity to charge them with disaffection to the Protestant succession. The Revd William Gordon claimed in a pamphlet printed in London in 1719 that 'it was spread all over the Island, that whoever would venture to oppose his [Lowther's] measures, must expect to be represented to his Majesty as a person disaffected to the present establishment'.[80] He was himself a recipient of the charge stating that 'I was not a little surprized to find, that I had been industriously and confidently represented as a furious Jacobite, and Pretender's Man'. He later noted that 'I would not be understood, as if I were surprized at being represented a Jacobite; for that is what every Man in Barbadoes, who has the misfortune to fall under his Excellency's frowns, expects to be.'[81]

After the proscription of the Tories and the Jacobite rebellion in 1715, opposition to Lowther was left bereft of political support from the ministry at home and stripped of much of its influence locally. Lowther was able to use his position to encourage the Grand Jury of Barbados to draft an address to the king assuring him that 'none but seditious, turbulent spirits find fault with his [Lowther's] conduct'.[82] Despite his good fortune, however, the governor's political battles were not over. Indeed, transatlantic issues relating to the Established Church, which had featured prominently in Lowther's debates with his leading opponents in the assembly, continued to plague him. His primary opponent and inveterate enemy was William Gordon, who although lacking the support of a friendly Tory ministry, which he previously had enjoyed, continued to make use of his connections in the SPG, as well as with the bishop of London. In 1716 he was appointed the bishop's commissary to the island of Barbados, but Lowther contested his authority and motives. In a letter to the bishop of London, later reprinted in the preface to a sermon

79   [Gordon], *State of Barbadoes,*, 32–3; CSPC, 30 Oct. 1719, item 436ii.

80   [Gordon], *State of Barbadoes*, 20

81   Idem, *A sermon preached before the governor and council, & general assembly of the island of Barbadoes*, London 1719, p. xli.

82   [Idem], *State of Barbadoes*, p. iii.

printed by Gordon, Lowther wrote that, due to the 'temper and principles of many of the clericks ... (in these Seditious and Rebellious times)', he would not allow Gordon to exercise his responsibilities and wondered if Gordon had been appointed to 'gratify the malignity of an expiring faction [Tories]'.[83] The bishop was not entirely convinced by Lowther's statements and sent a copy of the letter back to Gordon so the he might better answer the charges against him.[84]

Moreover, as Gordon recounted, after Lowther requested that Gordon preach a thanksgiving sermon on a day appointed to be observed for the 'happy suppression of the late unnatural rebellion', he accused Gordon of preaching disaffection in the form of a 'virulent satyr against the King's best friends and subjects' and of saying that the 'Whigs were the contrivers and fomenters of the late rebellion'.[85] In his complaints against Gordon's thanksgiving sermon, Lowther accused the minister of laying the blame for the rebellion at the feet of the Whigs as a means of ridiculing the 'solemnity of the day'.[86] Gordon sought to vindicate himself and had the entirety of the sermon printed in London with a preface demonstrating his loyalty to the Protestant succession and remarks detailing that the sermon made no mention of the Whigs.[87]

Gordon was also representative of Lowther's disputes with other clergymen on the island. The governor refused to appoint Dominick Langton and Mr Acourt, clergymen recommended by the bishop of London, to benefices in 1713 because, as he claimed, they were 'monstrous Toryes'. He defended his actions to the bishop by claiming that 'no party have shown so palpable, so groundless and so general dissatisfaction and malice to H.M. and the protestant succession as that wch goes under the denomination of Tory'.[88] He also stated that Mr. Acourt had 'resided here in my former government [1710–14] and behaved himself in such an extravagant and seditious manner both in and out of the pulpit'. In particular, he reported that 'some people applauded' him, a practice that Lowther thought appropriate as fit only for the 'Pretender's chappell'.[89] Langton too was suspect, having formerly been a Roman Catholic who converted to the Church of Ireland. A pamphlet printed in Dublin claimed that, even after his conversion, Langton supposedly encouraged others to continue as papists and was censured by the Irish House of Commons in 1711. Moreover, Langton was a High Church Irish Tory at a time when Irish clergymen were increasingly viewed with suspicion as

---

83   Idem, *A sermon*, pp. x, xi.

84   Ibid. p. viii.

85   Ibid. pp. iv, xiii.

86   Ibid. p. xiii.

87   Ibid.

88   Governor Robert Lowther to the bishop of London, 17 May 1717, *CSPC*, item 573ii.

89   Ibid.

Trinity College Dublin was seen as a Jacobite stronghold.[90] Furthermore he had reportedly railed against dissenters as rebels, a common High Church mantra, and was an associate of Francis Higgins, Ireland's Sacheverell.[91] Among Langton's books were numerous works by nonjurors and High Churchmen such as Charles Leslie, Francis Atterbury and others, further suggesting High Church if not Jacobite sympathies.[92] Lowther's complaints, therefore, were rooted in local realities. In light of the High Church Tory beliefs subscribed to by his opponents, Lowther's association with the Whig party in Britain stood him in good stead. In addition to the support that he received from many on the island, he was able to utilise the transatlantic political culture and his opponents' likely disaffection to maintain his position as governor until 1720.

A brief examination of a period in the career of Samuel Vetch provides a further instance of the way in which party rhetoric shaped politics, the currency of Jacobitism and the utility of accusations of Jacobitism in Britain's Atlantic empire. Vetch was the son of a covenanting Scottish Presbyterian minister, and he came of age during the party divisions of the reigns of Charles II and James II&VII.[93] He was a strong supporter of William of Orange's invasion of England, and his loyalty to the Protestant succession contributed to his rapid rise in the British Army. Eventually, with the assistance of his acquaintance Francis Nicholson, he secured the post of governor of Nova Scotia in 1710.

Vetch soon experienced disagreements with the ascendant Tory party, coming into conflict with the Tory ministry on a number of different accounts including religion and the economic future of Nova Scotia.[94] For example, as a Scottish Presbyterian, he was hostile to the resident Anglican chaplain John Harrison and turned the Anglican chapel into a barracks, surely a decision unlikely to win the support of the High Church Tories.[95] He was also at odds with the ministry over provision for the soldiers under his command and continually and unsuccessfully attempted to gain recompense for spending his own money and credit to provide for his garrison.[96]

In 1712 Vetch further alienated the Tory ministry when he accused George Vane, the engineer attached to the garrison protecting Annapolis Royal, of disaffection and Jacobitism. It was unlikely that the ministry would approve

---

[90]   Connolly, *Religion, law, and power*, 240–1.

[91]   *The report of the committee of the honble House of Commons: appointed to inspect the examinations given in by Dominick Langton, clerck, formerly a fryar in this kingdom*, Cork Hill 1711; Lowther to the bishop of London, 17 May 1717, CSPC, item 573ii; Hayton, 'Irish Tories and victims of Whig persecution', 90.

[92]   S. D. Smith, *Slavery, family, and gentry capitalism in the British Atlantic: the world of the Lascelles, 1648–1834*, Cambridge 2006.

[93]   George Waller, *Samuel Vetch, colonial enterpriser*, Chapel Hill 1960, 3–14.

[94]   Geoffrey Plank, *An unsettled conquest: the British campaign against Acadia*, Philadelphia 2001, 54–61

[95]   Ibid. 61.

[96]   Samuel Vetch to Montrose, 31 Mar. 1715, NAS, GD220/5/1910/13.

of being reminded of the associations of the Tory party with Jacobitism. Vane was a Jacobite who had served James II&VII in exile but returned to England in 1703 after parliament passed an Act of Indemnity. Vane provides a compelling example of the reintegration of Jacobites into English political life after the accession of Anne, as within four years he had been appointed engineer for St Johns, Newfoundland, a colony captured from the French during the War of the Spanish Succession. Yet his Jacobite sympathies continued to cause him trouble, and after the French recaptured St Johns, his fellow British officers accused him of conspiring with them. Held in captivity by the French from 1708 to 1710, he made his way back to England where, during the Tory ascendancy, he was assigned to Nova Scotia.[97] Vetch quickly took a dislike to Vane and his politics and, likewise, Vane was quick to disparage Vetch in letters to the Board of Trade.[98] Vane's suspected Jacobitism irked a number of other officers in the garrison in addition to Vetch. Lawrence Armstrong, a Protestant Irishman, was so incensed at what he regarded as Vane's Jacobitism that he smashed a decanter of wine over his head and almost killed him.[99] Vane was later court-martialled for other offences but reinstated at the behest of Vetch's High Church Tory successor Francis Nicholson.

By 1713 Vetch had alienated the Tory ministry in Britain to such a degree that it appointed Nicholson to replace him. Vetch believed that his removal was in part due to his antipathy towards the Jacobite Vane which, his biographer noted, marked him as 'no man to represent Bolingbroke in a colonial governorship'.[100] He also complained that the Tory ministry had been 'possessed with a character of him, as a partisan of the Whig Ministry' and were resolved 'to keep none in public posts but who were intirely in their interest'.[101] Though Nicholson and Vetch had once had an amiable working relationship, Nicholson was now such a polarising party figure that he acted only in the interests of the Tory ministry. Consequently, Vetch blamed much of his misfortune on him and claimed that 'His malice followed me home to the then ministry' and that 'he represented me as one violently opposite to the then government'.[102]

After the Hanoverian succession and the proscription of the Tories, Vetch exploited the notion that the Tory party was indistinguishable from the Jacobite interest. Between 1714 and 1715 he sent a number of petitions and letters to high-ranking Whigs including Montrose remarking on the reasons and motives for his dismissal. In them he attacked the Tory ministers mercilessly and

---

[97] F. J. Thorpe, 'George Vane', in *Dictionary of Canadian Biography Online*, <http://www.biographi.ca/EN/009004-119.01-e.php?id_nbr=1139>, accessed 9 May 2013.

[98] Captain George Vane to William Legge, 1st earl of Dartmouth, 1712, CSPC, item 403.

[99] Waller, *Samuel Vetch*, 248

[100] Ibid. 256.

[101] 'The case of Colonel Vetch', Dec. 1714, CSPC, item 122ii.

[102] Vetch to Montrose, 31 Mar. 1715, NAS, GD220/5/1910/13.

accused them of removing him from his post as a means of allowing the island to fall into the possession of the French, arguing that 'so far from meeting with a reward from the then ministry that for saving the garrison, I was turned out' for 'firmness to his present majesty's interest'.[103] He also claimed that Nicholson had informed him that 'preserving the garrison was his greatest crime' and that Nicholson's errand was to 'serve the Pretenders and French interest'.[104] Nicholson's cosy relationship with the previous Tory ministry probably encouraged the new Whig ministry to assume the worst, as the Tory party under Anne had flirted openly with the possibility of a Stuart restoration.

Vetch was also quick to attack Nicholson as 'not only a countenancer of Jacobites in general [i.e. Vane] but even those particularly who publickly drank the Pretender's health as King James the Third'. He also stated that Nicholson was a 'violent tool of the then ministry' who acted against Vetch for no other reason than his 'publickly supporting the right of the protestant succession in his present Majesty's house'.[105] Other statements that he attributed to Nicholson further represent the significance of party heats and passions and the association of Toryism with Jacobitism in Britain's Atlantic empire in 1714 and 1715. Vetch claimed that Nicholson publicly said that 'there was never such a damn'd nest of Whigs as in Cork and that they deserve to be extirpated' and that 'all that were not for indefeasible hereditary right were Whigs and Commonwealthmen'.[106] Vetch's complaints, like Lowther's, served him well and following the proscription of the Tories he was reappointed as governor of Nova Scotia. His Whig pedigree and his unfriendly relationship with the Tory ministry marked him out among Whigs in Britain as an excellent choice to represent the Whig interest in the British Atlantic.

Vetch's comments no doubt reflect a great deal of personal acrimony and animosity resulting from Nicholson's appointment and his own subsequent demotion. However, they, along with the examples of Bellomont and Lowther, are representative of the significance of party language in a developing and increasingly cohesive transatlantic political culture. Taking the three examples together, it is possible to trace the influence of important aspects of Britain's rage of party from imperial governance and appointments down to colonial political cultures. Colonial officials participated in the rage of party and consequently so too did colonists who opposed the governors. This, in turn, led colonial officials to interpret events in light of the rage of party.

Overt expressions of Jacobitism following the Revolution of 1688 illustrate elements of a transatlantic Jacobite subculture. Not only do these expressions elucidate features of Jacobite subculture, they point towards the evolution

---

[103] Ibid; Vetch to Montrose, 6 July 1715, NAS, GD220/5/577.

[104] 'The case of Colonel Vetch, Dec. 1714, CSPC, item 122ii.

[105] Vetch to Montrose, 31 Mar. 1715, NAS, GD220/5/1910/13.

[106] 'The case of Colonel Vetch', Dec. 1714, CSPC, item 122ii; Vetch to Montrose, 31 Mar. 1715, NAS, GD220/5/1910/13.

of a transatlantic political culture, an integral element of which was the division between the Whig and Tory parties. The rage of party created by the divisions shaped imperial appointments and developments, in turn enabling and encouraging colonists to participate in transatlantic party rivalries. This linked a number of disparate political cultures into a larger cohesive British Atlantic one, which in turn was both affected and shaped by understandings of Jacobitism. Following 1715 the transatlantic reverberations of the rage of party produced and encouraged a pervasive sense among Whigs in the colonies that the Tory party and Tory ministry were treasonous and sympathetic to the Jacobite cause. That this assumption was not entirely mistaken, and was further supported by the problematic relationship between politics and religion, is the subject of the next chapter.

2

Jacobitism and Religious Belief in the British Atlantic World

Religious belief provided much of the intellectual foundation for Jacobitism. In order to appreciate fully the extent, appeal and significance of Jacobitism throughout the British Atlantic world, it is necessary to understand its complex relationship with the variety of religious beliefs which nurtured it. Roman Catholics, members of the Church of England and Scottish Episcopalians each in their own manner held to notions of loyalty which helped to perpetuate Stuart claims to the kingdoms of England, Scotland and Ireland, and the empire throughout the Atlantic. Jacobitism was, for example, an integral aspect of Scottish Episcopalian belief from 1689 through to at least 1745. Similarly, it energised religious controversies that plagued the Church of England throughout the eighteenth century.[1] Older works on nonjurors have also illustrated the complex relationship between religious beliefs and Jacobitism.[2] English Catholic Jacobites also expressed Jacobitism in terms of both support for their co-religionist James and also an abiding royalism.[3] Religious beliefs, therefore, were integral to the ideological foundations of the Jacobite movement and thus bred, nurtured and inculcated Jacobitism at all levels of society.

Despite the relationship between Jacobitism and religious beliefs, little attention has been paid to the intriguing possibilities that this connection presents in the broader context of the British Atlantic. Scholars have only recently wrestled with the complexity of Jacobite ideology in a British context, and little of this scholarship has survived an Atlantic crossing.[4] This is partly because in the immediate aftermath of 1688 the ideology of Jacobitism was itself somewhat broad and ill-defined.[5] Initially, Jacobites in the three

---

[1] Tristram Clarke, '"Nurseries of sedition?": the Episcopal congregations after the Revolution of 1689', in James Porter (ed.), *After Columba, after Calvin: religious communities in North-East Scotland*, Aberdeen 1999, 61-9; Lenman, 'The Scottish Episcopal clergy', 36-48; Goldie, 'The nonjurors, episcopacy, and the origins of the Convocation Controversy', 15-35; Clark, *English society*, 83-105; Szechi, *The Jacobites*; Monod, *Jacobitism*, 126-58.

[2] Henry Broxap, *The later nonjurors*, Cambridge 1924.

[3] Glickman, *The English Catholic community*.

[4] For an example of this see Pestana, *Protestant empire*, 185-6.

[5] Gabriel Glickman, 'Political conflict and the memory of the revolution in England 1689-c. 1750', in Harris and Taylor, *Final crisis*, 243-71.

kingdoms of England, Scotland and Ireland had little to bind them together other than a belief in the hereditary right to the throne of James VII&II. If this were true for the various states of the British archipelago, it was equally if not more true for the entire British Atlantic.

Yet, over the next twenty-five years, as the process of anglicisation promoted a degree of ideological conformity among the various Episcopalian Churches, it also effected the development of a more coherent Jacobite ideology. Though possessing divergent goals following a restoration, various groups of Jacobites increasingly drew on a shared ideology. For example, although nationalism in Scotland following the Union of 1707 was a far cry from English nonjuring beliefs or High Church Anglican qualms about the accession of William of Orange or George I, throughout the British Isles in the two decades following 1689, Jacobitism was increasingly associated with a relatively coherent body of ideas and, consequently, Jacobitism became linked to a number of religious beliefs and controversies. This pattern, which was echoed across the Atlantic, has not received sufficient examination, although there was no shortage of religious controversies enabling the expression of Jacobitism or the eloquent articulation of anti-Jacobitism.

Recent works have begun to explore connections, including theology and politics, among religious groups in the Atlantic World, and both the Church of England and a pervasive anti-Catholicism have received notable attention.[6] In fact, accounts detailing the transatlantic integration of religious beliefs throughout the Atlantic are more informed than ever, and the importance of religion in the colonies and the British Atlantic world has been reasserted in a number of studies.[7] Yet Jacobitism, one of the major manifestations associated with certain religious beliefs during the period of intense religious and political conflict in the reign of Anne, is rarely mentioned.[8] In Britain and Ireland a pervasive Jacobite threat permeated political ideologies and religious beliefs of the late seventeenth and early eighteenth centuries, and by 1701 the political issues which were to undergird the ideologies of Jacobitism in England,

---

[6] James Bell, *The imperial origins of the king's Church in early America, 1607–1783*, Basingstoke 2004; Pestana, *Protestant empire*; Travis Glasson, *Mastering Christianity: missionary Anglicanism and slavery in the Atlantic world*, Oxford 2012; Clark, *The language of liberty*; Jeremy Gregory, 'Transatlantic Anglican networks, c. 1680–c.1770: transplanting, translating and transforming the Church of England', in Jeremy Gregory and Hugh McLeod (eds), *International religious networks*, Woodbridge, 2012, 127–42, and 'The later Stuart Church in North America', in Grant Tapsell (ed.), *The later Stuart Church, 1660–1714*, Manchester, 2013, 150–72; Kidd, *The Protestant interest*; Owen Stanwood, 'Catholics, Protestants, and the clash of civilizations in early America', in Chris Beneke and Christopher Grenda (eds), *The first prejudice: religious tolerance and intolerance in early America*, Philadelphia 2011, 218–40.

[7] Jon Butler, *Awash in a sea of faith: Christianising the American people*, Cambridge, MA 1990; Patricia Bonomi, *Under the cope of heaven: religion, society, and politics in colonial America*, Oxford 1986; Beneke and Grenda, *The first prejudice*; Pestana, *Protestant empire*.

[8] For an example see Pestana, *Protestant empire*, 185–6.

Scotland and the colonies, and feed the politics of the rage of party, were inseparable from religious opinions.[9]

This chapter seeks to contextualise religious controversy and denominational conflict within a larger Atlantic framework. It explores the relationship between Jacobitism and religious belief in the British Atlantic in order to illustrate the significance of Jacobitism and anti-Jacobitism in the British Atlantic World in the forty years following the Glorious Revolution. This in turn helps to make sense of accusations while also demonstrating the changing nature of Jacobitism, highlighting the shift away from its primary associations with Catholicism, nonjuring and (very early on) Quakerism and toward a more inclusive understanding which included its growing identification with High Church Anglicanism and Scottish Episcopalianism in the early eighteenth century.

One of the most striking aspects of the British Atlantic World in the early eighteenth century was the diversity of Christian beliefs. Quakers, Anglicans, Presbyterians, Scottish Episcopalians and Congregationalists battled for hegemony in regional conflicts both in Britain and throughout the British Atlantic World in a period that did not yet accept ideas of religious toleration. Ethnic tensions and political disagreements added elements of diversity which resulted in increasing religious discord; this was especially true in many of the colonies.[10] In Philadelphia, Quakers vied for supremacy against an emerging Anglican presence while in Boston and the surrounding towns Anglicans and Baptists undermined Congregational pre-eminence. Yet these conflicts were increasingly occurring within the orbit of British religious controversies, which in turn were infused with political significance, and thus were linked to political issues plagued by an ubiquitous Jacobitism.

The implications of such a fractured religious environment went well beyond the purely theological, for religious discord was often related to strikingly different political affinities. This is not at all surprising. Ever since the 1640s religious strife in Britain had been inextricably linked to political turmoil and this was also true for Britain's colonial possessions. As the colonies were drawn deeper into the ambit of British politics after the Glorious Revolution, religion and politics in the colonies became increasingly interconnected with ideas and events in Britain. The consequences of both British and colonial

[9]   Holmes, *British politics*; Bennett, *Tory crisis in Church and State*; Eveline Cruickshanks, 'Religion and royal succession: the rage of party', in Clyve Jones (ed.), *Britain in the first age of party, 1680–1750: essays presented to Geoffrey Holmes*, London 1987, 19–44; Goldie, 'The nonjurors, episcopacy, and the origins of the Convocation Controversy', 15–35; Brent Sirota, *The Christian monitors: the Church of England and the age of benevolence, 1680–1760*, New Haven 2014.

[10]   Ned C. Landsman, 'Roots, routes, and rootedness: diversity, migration and toleration in mid-Atalantic pluralism', in *Early American Studies: An Interdisciplinary Journal* ii (2004), 267–309; Chris Beneke, *Beyond toleration: the religious origins of American pluralism*, Oxford 2006.

religious controversies reverberated throughout the Atlantic and, as circumstances changed, so too did the controversies and beliefs related to them. This led to some interesting accusations.

Pennite Quakers, for example, are rarely associated with Jacobitism, but in the late seventeenth century they had had a curious relationship with Jacobitism.[11] Quakers settled throughout the colonies were often slandered as Jacobites or suspected of harbouring sympathies for the Stuarts. The primary reason for this was their association with William Penn. Penn was very likely a Jacobite; he was accused of Jacobitism, forced into hiding and arrested by the British government on at least four separate occasions between 1689 and 1691 for suspicion of Jacobitism.[12] There are many reasons why Penn was suspected of Jacobite sympathies: he was indebted to Charles II for the grant of Pennsylvania in 1684, and had supported his policy of toleration. He was also, arguably, a genuine friend of the exiled Stuart king.[13] Moreover, it was known that James II&VII had been kind to Quakers, releasing many of them from prison during his short reign. The questions raised by his known attachment to James reflected poorly not only on Penn himself but also on the Quaker sect as a whole. The most prominent Quaker in both the British archipelago and the colonies, Penn was influential in Quaker circles long before he was granted Pennsylvania. His ownership of Pennsylvania and the initiation of his 'Holy Experiment' only increased his prominence, especially among the Quakers who settled in that area.

Although it is unlikely that many Quakers in the colonies were Jacobites, the curious Quaker relationship with Jacobitism illustrates the transatlantic, yet decidedly local, understanding of Jacobitism. In 1698 a prominent local Anglican wrote that the Quakers in Pennsylvania were 'all Jacobites' because they were antagonistic towards the growth of the Church of England in Pennsylvania.[14] He based this accusation on the fact that a Quaker magistrate had told him that he was not worried about the defence of the colony because King James, who was in France, had ordered Jacobite privateers not to meddle with Quaker merchants in Pennsylvania because of James's loyalty to, and friendship with, Penn. While this accusation is seemingly unsubstantiated, it does indicate actual fears in the colonies of the malevolent influence wielded by the exiled Stuarts.

This is reinforced by the fact that the Quakers were slandered, not because of their vocal adherence to, and support of Penn, nor for any militant

[11]   See, for example, David William Voorhees, '"To assert our right before it be quite lost": the Leisler rebellion in the Delaware River Valley', *Pennsylvania History* lxiv (1997), 5–27.

[12]   Mary Geiter, 'William Penn and Jacobitism: a smoking gun?', *Historical Research* lxxiii (2000), 213–19; Monod, *Jacobitism*, 155–6.

[13]   Vincent Buranelli, *The king and the Quaker: a study of William Penn and James II*, Philadelphia 1962.

[14]   Mr [?] Suder to [Governor], 20 Nov. 1698, in *Historical collections relating to the American colonial Church*, ed. William Stevens Perry, ii, New York 1969, 10.

Jacobitism, but rather from their stated adherence to what was viewed as the Jacobite principle of non-resistance. This proved to be extremely controversial among their fellow colonists and colonial officials, especially with the constant threat of a French invasion as a consequence of King William's wars. Quaker antipathy towards supporting warfare of any kind, in any way, whether with money, men or supplies was construed as being support for the French, and therefore for the Stuart interest. The location of large numbers of Quaker settlers in Pennsylvania near the border with French Canada greatly alarmed those who already harboured suspicions or fears of Quaker loyalty. Mistrust of Quaker principles and the location of many of them, coupled with the associ-ation of Pennite Quakers with Jacobitism, led to accusations of Jacobitism. In 1691 Francis Nicholson, then lieutenant-governor of Virginia and a staunch Anglican, expressed this fear and questioned Quaker loyalty, writing to the Lords of Trade and Plantations that 'if they be of William Penn's pernicious principles they may hold correspondence with the French and Indians by land and with the French by sea'.[15] Similarly, following the declaration of war with France in 1689, Quakers in Pennsylvania declared that they would not fight if invaded by the French. This led the council of Virginia to order in 1691 that 'no Quakers hold meetings without giving due notice as required by Act of Parliament, and that they receive no strangers and publish no strange news without informing a justice of the peace'.[16]

It was not only in the mainland colonies that distrust of Quakers resulted in accusations of Jacobitism. In 1693, during the Nine Years War, James Kendall, governor of Barbados, echoed his fellow colonial governors when he stated that 'the Quakers indeed are very numerous here and a great weakness to the island, for they are wholly useless to its defence'.[17] He went on to argue that 'it is most certain that they are all Jacobites ... the heads of them holding correspondence with William Penn, who governs them as absolutely as the King of France'.[18]

Many colonists in the late seventeenth century perceived Quakerism to be inherently disloyal, and therefore, as tantamount to Jacobitism. This was confirmed by the Quakers' expressed non-resistance in the face of the French threat. To many colonists their association with Penn marked them as questionable and placed them squarely in the Jacobite camp. None the less, Charles Petrie's claim that the 'Quakers in Pennsylvania were Jacobite to a man' seems largely unsubstantiated and misleading.[19] Quakers scattered throughout the British Atlantic may not, in fact, have been Jacobite to a man. However, the identification of Pennite Quakers with Jacobitism in England helps to explain the assumption in the colonies that Quakers either favoured

[15] Nicholson to the Lords of Trade and Plantations, 10 June 1691, *CSPC*, item 1583.
[16] Minutes of the Council of Virginia, 18 Feb. 1691, *CSPC*, item 1324.
[17] Kendall to the Lords of Trade and Plantations, 10 July 1693, *CSPC*, item 442.
[18] Ibid.
[19] Charles Petrie, *The Jacobite movement: the first phase, 1688–1715*, New York 1948, 73.

or were favoured by the exiled Stuarts, thus demonstrating the significance of religious beliefs as a key component of political identification.

Perhaps the most obvious example of the interplay between religious contro-versies and Jacobitism is the nonjuring schism in England which, as Mark Goldie observed, was the 'clerical counterpart of Jacobitism'.[20] Despite strong Anglican support for the revolution in 1688, in 1689 the Church of England experienced a traumatic schism. The political settlement reached after the invasion of William of Orange proved unsatisfactory to a number of prominent clerics. The fact that the throne, instead of a regency, was offered to William put many of the clergy in a difficult position regarding oaths that they had sworn to James II&VII. Many refused to swear oaths of allegiance to William and Mary because to do so would deny the sanctity of the oaths that they had sworn to James. Those who refused to swear – more than 400, perhaps, 4 per cent, of the clergymen of the Church of England – were known as nonjurors.[21] They were considered to be 'Jacobites by definition'.[22] Even if not all of those who refused the oaths were active plotters in the Jacobite interest, their unwill-ingness to recognise the new king as *de jure* denied the legitimacy of William and Mary's reign and thus upheld the claims of the exiled Stuarts. This created what Murray Pittock has called the 'dangerously thin line' between a passive refusal to swear an oath and active attempts to alter the succession.[23] This is especially true after 1701 when a new oath explicitly abjuring the Stuart prince of Wales was required. A refusal to swear this oath was a clear indication that the nonjuror in question supported the legitimacy of the exiled Stuarts' claims to the throne. Whether nonjurors were active plotters makes little difference. They provided the religious and intellectual foundation for continued support and sympathy for James II&VII and his son.

The influence of the nonjurors over the next fifty years far outweighed their numbers. Many of the most prominent clerics and scholars between 1688 and the accession of George I were nonjurors, including Henry Dodwell, a nonjuring polemicist, Archbishop Sancroft and five other bishops. In the mid-1690s a number of nonjurors broke away from the Church of England to set up what they considered to be the true Church of England, thus creating a nonjuring schism. Not only did the nonjurors provide the core ideological support for the exiled Stuarts' claim to the throne, the debates in which Dodwell and others engaged had a profound influence on the theology and politics of those High Churchmen who were willing to swear the oaths to William and Mary.[24]

---

[20]   Goldie, 'The nonjurors, episcopacy, and the origins of the Convocation Controversy', 15.

[21]   Monod, *Jacobitism*, 142

[22]   Ibid. 139

[23]   Murray Pittock, 'Treacherous objects: towards a theory of Jacobite material culture', *Journal for Eighteenth-Century Studies* xxxiv (2011), 39–63.

[24]   Sirota, *The Christian monitors*, 149–222; Goldie, 'The nonjurors, episcopacy, and the

The beliefs of nonjurors, therefore, were often indistinguishable from their conforming High Church brethren, excepting only their committed refusal to swear the necessary oaths. The origins of the Convocation Controversy, for example, which was instrumental in the division of the Church of England into High and Low Church parties, and often attributed to Francis Atterbury, can be found in the writings of the nonjurors.[25] Furthermore, many clergymen followed the example of Nathaniel Crewe, bishop of Durham, and swore the necessary oaths with mental reservation.[26] This created a pool of men sympathetic to Jacobitism and nonjuring, but unwilling to suffer the penalties of outspoken disaffection. Moreover, it was also possible for nonjurors to return to regular communion as laymen of the Church of England while still declining to take the oaths. For example, Henry Dodwell and Thomas Ken, bishop of Bath and Wells, left the nonjuring church and re-joined the juring communion in 1710 but continued to refuse to subscribe the oaths.[27] The scholarship of the nonjurors and their passage in and out of the High Church helped to stimulate many of the conflicts between the High and Low Church during the reigns of William III & II and Anne. This ambiguous relationship between a High Church party willing to swear the oaths, and their sympathy for, and association with, the scholarship and practice of nonjurors connected them with disaffection and made it easy for their opponents to question their loyalty to the Protestant succession.

The nonjuring schism was not the only divisive or polarising issue facing the Church of England, even if it was the most extreme. The political and religious climate created by the Revolution settlement drove many High Church clergy and laity towards support or sympathy for the exiled Stuarts and High Church Anglicanism became entangled with the politics of the succession crisis. As Brent Sirota has observed, 'irreconcilable visions of Anglican confessionalization' contributed to 'political and religious polarization'.[28] The toleration act of 1689, which allowed Trinitarian dissenters freedom of worship, led many churchmen to bewail the increase in dissent and heresy.[29] The seemingly unchecked growth of dissent and unorthodox beliefs stirred up fears among many churchmen that the Church of England was in danger. From the mid-1690s through to 1716, the cry of 'the Church in danger' was the clarion call which drew concerned clergymen and laymen to its banner and would continue to serve as a rallying cry of the High Church party throughout the period.

origins of the Convocation Controversy', 15–35.

[25] Goldie, 'The nonjurors, episcopacy, and the origins of the Convocation Controversy', 15–35.

[26] Monod, *Jacobitism*, 147, 151.

[27] Ibid. 140.

[28] Sirota, *The Christian monitors*, 15.

[29] Harris, *Politics under the later Stuarts*, 152–3.

Thus, High Church became both a descriptive and proscriptive term in the early eighteenth-century British Atlantic. Precise meanings have proved elusive because it possessed both religious and political connotations, but the term remains instrumental to understandings of early eighteenth-century accusations of Jacobitism. Beyond its rather slippery meaning, it was often a pejorative term of abuse which incorporated either or both political and religious aspects. It does, however, designate a preference for certain devotional practices, often pointing towards a religious inclination to stress the divine necessity of episcopacy, an elevated view of the sacraments and a respect for patristic scholarship. Low Church Anglicans on the other hand, often supported the toleration of dissent, minimised the importance of the apostolic succession, tended towards latitudinarianism, and supported liberty of conscience and an international Protestant interest which often drove them towards an alliance with the Whig party.

The differing levels of importance placed on elements of belief and practice had practical political consequences. The religious meanings of High Church and Low Church were often entangled with political ones.[30] Fearing for the Church of England, many High Church clergy and laity supported the Tory party and consequently, High Church Anglicanism became entwined with Tory politics. The Whig party found much of its support among dissenters and those Low Church Anglicans sympathetic to dissent. Because of their antipathy towards the Whig pillars of dissent and latitudinarianism, High Church Anglican Tories sought to suppress the growth of these invasive threats. These efforts were often inextricably linked to party political manoeuvres, including acts banning occasional conformity. Leading Tories, such as Daniel Finch, 2nd earl of Nottingham, were devout High Church Anglican laymen, devoted to supporting the Church of England and were instrumental in pursuing bills limiting the power of dissent. Despite some exceptions, High Church Anglicanism became almost inseparable from the Tory party: the 'Tory party at prayer'.[31]

Religious controversies became an instrumental element of British party politics. In the early eighteenth century Toryism was increasingly aligned with High Church Anglicanism. For example, in three consecutive years from 1702 to 1704, the Tory party in England sought to end the practice of occasional conformity, by which dissenters would take communion in the Church of England once a year in order to qualify for public office. Similar efforts were

---

[30] John Walsh and Stephen Taylor, 'Introduction: the Church and Anglicanism in the "long" eighteenth century', in John Walsh, David Hayton and Stephen Taylor (eds), *The Church of England, c. 1689–1833*, Cambridge 1993, 1–66; Donald Spaeth, *The Church in an age of danger: parsons and parishioners, 1660–1740*, Cambridge 2000; Pasi Ihalainen, 'Preaching in an age of party strife, 1700–1720: contributions to the conflict', in Peter McCullough, Hugh Adlington and Emma Rhatigan (eds), *The Oxford handbook of the early modern sermon*, Oxford 2011, 495–513.

[31] Walsh and Taylor, 'Introduction', 34.

pursued by High Churchmen in Ireland. Tories also supported the High Church Anglican preacher Henry Sacheverell after he was impeached by the Whig ministry in 1709 for preaching and printing a sermon which celebrated the doctrines of passive obedience and non-resistance.[32] His sermon was viewed as an attack on the Revolution Settlement of 1689 and a tacit reminder that the Stuarts were the rightful heirs of the kingdom. Although not all High Church Tories were Jacobites, the conflation of Toryism and High Church Anglicanism, epitomised by Sacheverell, brought about by fears of 'the Church in danger' from dissent and an unsupportive monarch, drew High Church Anglicans ever closer to supporting the exiled Stuarts as the succession of the Lutheran Hanoverians approached.

The High Church Tory drift toward Jacobitism was not confined to England. In Ireland, too, High Church Tories, influenced by events and disputes in England, were increasingly associated with Jacobitism. Just as in England there was an increasingly 'militant High Church Party' among the Irish clergy. As S. J. Connolly has noted, 'the Irish High Church party was in some respects a direct extension of the English'.[33] Consequently, just as in England, observers often assumed that the political allegiance of Irish clergy was less certain after 1714 than between 1688 and 1691.[34] Furthermore, educational institutions, such as Trinity College Dublin, were seen as Jacobite strongholds, eliciting another parallel between Ireland, Scotland and England.[35] All of this contributed to the emergence of a 'small but raucous Irish Protestant Jacobite interest' during the final years of Anne's reign.[36]

If the nonjuring schism in England was distressing, an even more traumatic division occurred in 1689 in Scotland where all Scottish Episcopalians were forced into nonjuring following the refusal of the Scottish bishops to swear the required oaths of allegiance. As a result William was forced to support the removal of bishops from the Scottish Church by a majority of Presbyterians in the Revolution Convention, thus creating a Presbyterian establishment. This was uncompromising towards the Jacobitism of Episcopal ministers, and hundreds of forced evictions followed.[37] Almost two hundred Episcopalian

---

[32] For the most comprehensive account of Sacheverell see Geoffrey Holmes, *The trial of Dr. Sacheverell*, London 1973; for more recent discussions of the importance of the Sacheverell trial see Mark Knights, 'Introduction: the view from 1710'; W. A. Speck, 'The current state of Sacheverell scholarship'; Brian Cowan, 'The spin doctor: Sacheverell's trial speech and political performance in a divided society'; and, for Irish parallels, David Hayton, 'Irish Tories and victims of Whig persecution: Sacheverell fever by proxy', all in *PH* xxxi (2012), 1–15, 16–27, 28–46, 80–98.

[33] Connolly, *Religion, law, and power*, 172.

[34] Ibid. 241.

[35] Ibid. 240; O'Ciardha, *Ireland and the Jacobite cause*, 173–6.

[36] O'Ciardha, *Ireland and the Jacobite cause*, 115.

[37] On this see Jeffrey Stephen, *Defending the revolution: the Church of Scotland, 1689–1716*, Burlington, Vt 2013.

ministers were deprived of their parishes and over the next thirty years, as the new Presbyterian establishment worked to oust their Episcopal antagonists, further deprivations continued.[38] This created a sizable pool of potential Jacobite support not only amongst clergy but amongst the Episcopalian laity as well.[39] Bruce Lenman has argued that in Scotland the Episcopal clergy were 'the most significant single group of men creating and transmitting articulate Jacobite ideology'.[40] Moreover, despite the deprivations, at least 110 Episcopalians, of whom eleven were listed specifically as nonjurors, continued to enjoy their benefices as late as 1710 and were probably instrumental in the continuing dissemination of Jacobite ideology in Scotland.[41] For example, one magistrate in the notoriously Jacobite-friendly city of Aberdeen noted that 'besides being educated under Jacobite masters, [at the Colleges] they [the gentry] had an episcopal minister who they heard preach. To these in a great measure the Jacobite spirit which prevails ... is owing'.[42] Episcopalians provided the backbone of support for the rising in 1715. After its failure, a further thirty-six Episcopal clergymen were evicted from their parishes on charges of Jacobitism.[43] Throughout the period there were not only active Episcopalian clergymen propagating Jacobite ideology from the pulpit, but King's and Marischal Colleges in Aberdeen continued to instil conservative, episcopal and Jacobite ideas into their students until at least 1717.[44]

After the Union of 1707, Scottish Episcopalian complaints of persecution, despite their overt Jacobitism, fed into the British Tory politics of 'the Church in danger'. Many Anglican High Churchmen had initially refused to support the Union of 1707 because it would perpetuate the establishment of the Presbyterian Church in Scotland at the expense of an Episcopal Church, whose members the Church of England increasingly viewed as co-religionists.[45] After the Union, High Church Tories supported their Episcopal brethren in Scotland and pushed through the Toleration Act of 1712 which allowed for the toleration of juring Scottish Episcopalian worship in Scotland, though not many were willing to subscribe the oaths, and Scottish

---

[38] Manuscript biographical accounts of Episcopal clergy deprived of their parishes by the committee of the estates, 1689, NAS, CH/12/12/202.

[39] Clarke, 'Nurseries of sedition?', 61-9.

[40] Lenman, 'The Scottish Episcopal clergy', 36.

[41] NAS, CH/12/12/202. See also Clarke, "Nurseries of sedition?', 61-9.

[42] [?] to Adam Cockburn of Ormiston, 13 June 1715, NAS, GD220/5/455/4.

[43] Clarke, 'Nurseries of sedition?', 62; Lenman, 'The Scottish Episcopal clergy', 46.

[44] [?] to Cockburn, 13 June 1715, NAS, GD220/5/455/4; Clarke, 'Nurseries of sedition?', 64.

[45] For the relationship between Anglican and Scottish Episcopalian worship see Alisdair Raffe, 'Presbyterians and Episcopalians: the formation of confessional cultures in Scotland, 1660-1715,' *English Historical Review* cxxv (2010), 570-98, and Stephen, *Defending the revolution*, 153-246.

Episcopalians increasingly associated their cause with the successes of High Church Anglicans.[46] Toleration lasted until 1715 when Episcopalians joined the Jacobite rebels in large numbers. Political victories were fleeting as the death of Anne brought an end to a brief High Church ascendancy which flourished in the years 1710 to 1714. Moreover, this brief alliance reinforced notions that High Church Anglicans were sympathetic to Jacobitism. The proscription of the Tory party following the accession of George I, and his reliance on Low Church Whig allies in 1715, increased the disaffection of High Church Tories and drove them ever further towards Jacobitism.

The threat of a Stuart restoration, especially in the years between 1689 and 1745, meant that theology became a politicised battleground as religious controversies contributed to a growing High Church attachment to Jacobitism. Throughout the early eighteenth century, debates about the *jure divino* nature of episcopacy brought Scottish Episcopalians into the confessional culture of the Church of England, but similar debates also encouraged Anglican schemes for a possible union with the Gallican Church in France.[47] This was advocated by a number of different Anglican divines including William Wake and Charles Leslie, but motivations varied.[48] In the case of nonjurors like George Hickes and Leslie, a union with the Gallican Church would have paved the way for a Stuart restoration by bringing the Catholic Stuarts back into a more universal Anglican establishment. Derogatory accusations of Gallicanism, therefore, are not simply anti-Catholic, they are, at the core, anti-Jacobite.[49]

Similarly, the High Church advocacy of the *jure divino* nature of episcopacy led to debates about the validity of baptism and ordination outwith the presence of a bishop. If lay baptism were invalid, as many High Churchmen and nonjurors claimed, then dissenters outside an Episcopal Church were not legitimately Christians. Thus, according to many Jacobites, the previously Lutheran Hanoverians, though accepted into the Church of England upon accession, lacked a proper Christian initiation and were essentially dissenters and incapable of serving as the head of the Anglican Church.[50] In effect, Jacobitism 'lingered not far below the surface' of debates about the divine nature of episcopacy, potentially providing the intellectual rationale for a Stuart restoration.[51] Yet this also provided those who were antagonistic to the growth of the Church of England with a justification for accusing those who argued for bishops in the colonies of Jacobitism and disaffection.

[46] [?] to Cockburn, 13 June 1715, NAS, GD220/5/455/4.

[47] Raffe, 'Presbyterians and Episcopalians', 570–98; George Every, *The High Church party, 1688–1718*, London 1956, 70.

[48] For a different interpretation of the Gallican Union see William Gibson, *The Church of England, 1688–1832: unity and accord*, London 2001, 182–216

[49] Every, *The High Church party*, 70.

[50] Bennett, *The Tory crisis in Church and State*, 151.

[51] Sirota, *The Christian monitors*, 180.

The religious controversies undergirding the politics of the rage of party were not confined to the British archipelago. Rancorous partisan debates about issues such as occasional conformity had parallels in the colonies; but too often the parallels are viewed as distinct colonial issues rather than as issues spanning the Atlantic. Historians studying the pressure for an American episcopacy, however, have noted the High Church propensity for *jure divino* understandings of episcopacy, and have built a solid foundation for exploring the Atlantic context and implications of those beliefs.[52]

The bishop of London served, *de officio*, as the diocesan for the Church of England in the colonies but this never proved to be adequate. Although the absence of local bishops in the colonial Church of England is important, and the Church operated in an environment very different from that in Britain, the Church of England in the colonies was not distinct or set apart from the mother church, nor was it disassociated from the controversies engulfing the Church in Britain. Much of the misunderstanding surrounding the importance of the interaction of politics and theology is based on the assumption that the Church of England in America was somehow separated from the mother Church in England because it lacked an identically defined episcopal structure or government support. This is certainly true to a degree. The absence of a resident bishop created the need for commissaries, clergymen appointed by the bishop of London to exercise aspects of his authority, and enhanced the importance of colonial governors in the administration of the Church. It also made it difficult for colonials to seek ordination because ordination at the hands of a bishop required a trip to London.[53] Moreover, the large numbers of dissenters in the colonies, including Quakers, Independents and Presbyterians, created a religious diversity unparalleled in England. The dominance of dissent went almost unchecked, especially in the absence of a local bishop who could ordain and discipline clergymen.

Despite the obvious variations and difficulties caused by the differing institutional aspects of the government of the Church of England in the Atlantic empire, many elements of the Church remained unchanged. The liturgy and the festival calendar created a transatlantic communion which increasingly included Scottish Episcopalians,[54] while the political inheritance of the Church's previous hundred years remained unaltered. However, the lack of a resident bishop had profound effects. With the bishop of London acting as diocesan, colonial ministers were required to send regular reports back to Britain either to the SPG or to the bishop. This kept the colonial

[52]   James Bell, *A war of religion: Dissenters, Anglicans and the American Revolution*, Basingstoke 2008; Carl Bridenbaugh, *Mitre and sceptre: transatlantic faiths, ideas, personalities, and politics, 1689–1775*, Oxford 1962; Nancy Rhoden, *Revolutionary Anglicanism: the colonial Church of England clergy during the American Revolution*, Basingstoke 1999; John Woolverton, *Colonial Anglicanism in North America*, Detroit 1976.

[53]   Bell, *Imperial origins*, 142–65.

[54]   Raffe, 'Presbyterians and Episcopalians', 570–98

ministers attuned to political and religious developments which were affecting the Church in Britain. An increasingly active transatlantic Anglican network also supplied ministers with books and pamphlets intended to instruct and inform both ministers and laity in the traditions and beliefs of the Church of England.[55] These clergymen, serving in their various capacities, were an important vehicle in facilitating the circulation and transmission of beliefs, experiences and ideologies rooted in the party politics and religious controversies which engulfed the British Isles.

Through these connections, belief and ideology were transported across to the colonies. Thousands of miles of Atlantic Ocean could not quench High Church zeal. Nor did it miraculously wash away beliefs about the taint of rebelliousness associated with Presbyterianism. Immediate political contexts might not be identical but ideology often was. Beliefs which divided the High Church and Low Church factions in Britain spanned the Atlantic, even if the manifestation of those beliefs were not always analogous. Nonjuring was often problematic in the colonies just as it was in Britain. Noting the divisions between High and Low Church beliefs is significant because High Church attitudes were often tinged with a pro-Stuart dynastic inclination, which shaped relationships between differing political and religious groups.

Throughout the British Atlantic, political parties were associated with specific religious traditions. As in Britain, those colonists who dissented from the Church of England or those Anglicans who maintained a more latitudinarian approach to dissent were closely associated with a transatlantic Whig party. Conversely, the aims of the Tory party were at times almost inseparable from the colonial High Church Anglican interest. This is clearly seen in a manuscript list from 1722 noting the political leanings of Maryland's twenty-two Anglican clergymen. The descriptions, probably drafted by a Whig, are both colourful and insightful. One clergyman, James Williamson, is listed as 'an idiot & Tory', while two others, John Donaldson and Thomas Robinson, are listed as 'grand' Tories. The implications of 'grand Tory' were certainly a contrast to Giles Rainford who was listed as 'a stickler for the present happy establishment' and William Machonchie, a 'mighty stickler for the present establishment'.[56] The political implications of religious identifications directly affected the relationship between the growing Church of England and dissenters and, just as in Britain, this would shape opinions on the Protestant succession. In order better to understand and appreciate the conflicts involving the Church of England in the colonies and the accusations of Jacobitism that resulted, it is necessary to keep these religious controversies in their proper Atlantic context.

It was against the background of religious and political conflict in Britain that the Church of England in America experienced a period of rapid expansion.

---

[55] Gregory, 'Transatlantic Anglican networks', 127–42
[56] FP, Lambeth Palace Library, London, iii. 20–1 (microfilm).

In the years between 1688 and 1727 the Church became legally established, at least in part, in four colonies, despite concerted and even transatlantic resistance from Quakers and other dissenters. Acts establishing the Church were passed in 1693 in New York, 1702 in Maryland, 1706 in South Carolina and 1715 in North Carolina. The strength of the Church grew rapidly even in colonies where legal establishment remained elusive. Furthermore, the SPG, a missionary organisation designed to support Anglican missions to the colonies, was incorporated in 1701. One of its many goals was to provide ministers, paid by SPG funds, to the many vacant parishes throughout the colonies, especially those where establishment proved elusive. It was also responsible for sending countless books and pamphlets to its ministers. In the early eighteenth century a growing Anglican population, with the assistance of the SPG, contributed to the building of numerous churches. Between 1688 and 1727 over 180 ministers were sent either as missionaries by the SPG or licensed and sent to parishes as curates by the bishop of London. There were also numerous chaplains who served on the ships which plied the waters of the Atlantic.[57] The proliferation of Anglican ministers and religious and political literature help to spread aspects of the religious controversies that were plaguing political debates in Britain.

An appreciation of the nature of the divisions in the Anglican Church in the reigns of Anne and George I is essential for a proper understanding of Jacobitism and anti-Jacobitism in the British Atlantic world. Often in studies of the colonial Anglican Church, terms such as High Church, Low Church and nonjuring are used without explanation of their meaning,[58] even though, in early eighteenth-century Britain and its colonies, they were laden with significance. It is problematic to assume that arguably lay-controlled Low Church establishments, such as those in Virginia or South Carolina, can always be conflated with widespread, Low Church sentiment among clergy and laity;[59] likewise that members and clergy of the Church of England in the different colonies were inherently Low Church in ideology and practice because the local church establishments lacked the episcopal government so often celebrated by High Church advocates of the divine right of episcopacy. A consequence of this has been the marginalisation of discussions about High Church ideology and Jacobitism in the colonies. Jacobitism was so deeply woven into the fabric of the debates engulfing the Church of England that a misunderstanding of the Church in the colonies necessarily leads to a misinterpretation of the significance of Jacobitism.

One often overlooked aspect of the Church of England in America was the ethnic and political diversity of its clergymen. Men from different educational

---

[57] James Bell, *Colonial American clergy of the Church of England database*, <www.Jamesbbell. com>.

[58] Woolverton, *Colonial Anglicanism*, 95. According to Woolverton, High Church represented an imperial church.

[59] John Nelson, *A blessed company: parishes, parsons, and parishioners in Anglican Virginia, 1690–1776*, Chapel Hill 2002.

backgrounds and nations contributed to the wide variety of beliefs propagated throughout the colonies. The Anglican clergymen sent to the colonies, either by the SPG or the bishop of London, included many Scottish Episcopalians who, unable to find employment in Scotland, accepted ordination in the Church of England. This added an interesting element of ethnic and ideological diversity to the colonial religious setting. At least sixty-one clergymen sent to the colonies were Scottish by birth and sixty-three had attended Scottish universities.[60] Many of these men had witnessed, participated in or, at the very least, had opinions on the divisive political climate in Britain. This was equally true for those English or Irish clergymen who were educated during a period of intense religious and political controversy. In fact, at least eight clergymen in the colonies during the period were known Jacobites and one had even fought with the Jacobites at the Battle of Prestonpans prior to his ordination.[61] This number included prominent English nonjurors such as Richard Welton as well as Scottish Jacobites like William Skinner, but it also represented less overt Jacobites like John Talbot.

The number of Scottish Episcopalians who, with little prospect of gainful employment at home after the establishment of a Presbyterian church order, were ordained in the Church of England is especially significant because many of them had experienced the persecution of Episcopalians at first hand. Not only had they witnessed religious controversies, but many had been educated in Jacobite principles. At least thirty colonial ministers had been educated prior to 1727 at one of the Aberdeen colleges, bastions of Jacobitism through the first three decades of the eighteenth century. This suggested, at the very least, a possible sympathy with Jacobitism. James Honeyman, for example, a High Church man and an SPG missionary in Rhode Island, was educated at Marischal College in the 1690s, and was the son of an Episcopalian minister in Scotland deprived in 1689.[62] Although there is no direct evidence that Honeyman was a Jacobite, the circumstances are certainly suggestive and would have been seen as such by contemporaries; in fact he was accused by contemporaries of disaffection.[63] Similarly, George McQueen, a minister in Virginia, had been driven out of Scotland by Presbyterian persecution after 1689 and likely possessed little love for William and Mary and the revolution settlement.[64] Moreover, in 1699, two Scottish ministers in Virginia, Samuel Gray and John Gordon, published and distributed a 'certain scandalous, false, malicious and seditious libel, wherein were contained several wicked and malicious reflections and aspersions on his Most gracious Majesty'

---

[60] Bell, *Colonial American clergy of the Church of England database.*

[61] 'William Skinner', ibid..

[62] 'James Honeyman', ibid; NAS, CH12/12/202.

[63] James Honeyman to the Secretary, *FP* iii. 212–13.

[64] 'George McQueen', Bell, *Colonial American clergy of the Church of England database.*

further suggesting a strain of disaffection among Scottish clergymen in the colonies.[65]

Regardless of origin, the colonial clergy were serving during a period of intense political and religious controversy which reverberated throughout the British Atlantic world. The growing strength of the High Church party in the first decade of the eighteenth century had parallels in the colonies. Indeed, High Church clergymen were often warned to moderate their zeal in order to avoid alienating dissenters. This was especially true in colonies with a large or active dissenting population such as Rhode Island or New Jersey, but such warnings often went unheeded by clergymen who viewed dissenters as enemies. James Chamberlain, secretary of the SPG wrote in 1707 to a leading layman in New York asking him to 'qualify' the zeal of the young missionary from 'North Briton', George Muirson.[66] John Talbot, a missionary in New Jersey, was repeatedly reprimanded for his immoderation by the secretary of the SPG who wrote that it would be in the interest of the Church and nation to send those of too warm a spirit to the 'Frozen poles'.[67] Unchecked High Church fervour was an increasingly active component in the growth of the Church of England in the colonies.

High Church passions were often regarded by the authorities in Britain as an unwelcome aspect of missionary work. The SPG had a diverse membership in Britain, ranging from White Kennett, a leading Whig propagandist, to the respected nonjuror Robert Nelson, creating potential for disagreements regarding the direction and role of the society. Leading Whigs in the society, including Chamberlain, were conscious of the implications of religious and party divisions and sought to squash what they considered a misdirected High Church fanaticism, leading to resentment among High Church clerics in the colonies. In 1711 Honeyman complained that Chamberlain was too quick to 'foster divisions between missionaries and the society' regarding moderation.[68] This sentiment was seconded by James Henderson, a missionary in Pennsylvania, who was not surprised that 'my zeal should put me under the displeasure of the enemies of our holy church, yet I hoped for better things from our patrons at home'.[69] Clearly, High Church zeal was not restricted to Britain.

The transatlantic nature of religious fervour was evident in the years following the Sacheverell trial, particularly after the Tory party won a decisive parliamentary majority in 1710. Its victory solidified the High Church ascendancy in Britain and provided High Churchmen in the colonies with

---

[65]   Cited in George McClaren Brydon, *Virginia's mother Church and the political conditions under which it grew*, Richmond, VA 1947.

[66]   Secretary to Colonel John Heathcote, SPG papers, LPL, xiv. 111.

[67]   Secretary to Talbot, ibid. xii. 239, 251

[68]   James Honeyman to Stubbs, 19 Oct. 1711, SPG papers, RHL, ser. A, vii. 543.

[69]   James Henderson to the Secretary, 9 July 1713, ibid. vii. 478.

an administration friendly to the cause. As a result, High Church zeal in the colonies became more pronounced. After 1710 accusations of persecution of Anglicans echoed the previous complaints of Episcopalians from Scotland. Although with the recent Tory parliamentary victories, the established Church may have been in less danger in England, the Church of England was still on a precarious footing in the colonies and the cry of 'the Church in danger' sprang up across the Atlantic. High Church clergymen, aware that they had a sympathetic ministry in London, sent accounts to Britain crying up the danger to the Church. SPG records reveal that stories of the persecution of Anglicans also began to make their way to Britain in far greater numbers. For example, in 1712 the church in Stratford, Connecticut, complained that they were prey to the Independents who sought 'all opportunities to destroy the church both root and branch'.[70] Similar accounts came from Pennsylvania and New York. In 1712 Evan Evans, the rector of Christ's Church in Philadelphia, accused the governor of the province of failing adequately to support the Church after the governor appointed a Presbyterian to the office of sheriff.[71] Vestries and clergymen echoed complaints previously heard in Britain, protesting that they were oppressed and persecuted and that 'any encouragement given to any other society different from us is a discouragement to our church'.[72]

Local religious controversies galvanised both laymen and clergymen, precipitating the development of nascent church parties in New York, New Jersey, Pennsylvania, South Carolina and Barbados in the years between 1701 and 1727. In each colony clergymen were leaders of the parties and were supported by local laymen who subscribed to High Church beliefs. These parties cultivated Tory alliances throughout the British Atlantic World. In 1714 church parties in New York and New Jersey turned to Francis Nicholson, appointed by the Tory administration as governor of Nova Scotia and as a spiritual inspector by the bishop of London, for support and guidance. In Barbados, a local party led by William Gordon, an Anglican clergyman, relied on prominent local planters to develop relationships with the Tory administration and the SPG in Britain.[73] In both cases the Hanoverian succession quickly ended any hopes that the parties harboured of securing a High Church ascendancy in their respective colonies. After their Tory allies were removed from office in 1715, any semblance of power that they had managed to secure locally slipped out of their grasp, clearly illustrating the demise of High Church Tory hopes that had spanned the Atlantic.

Many High Churchmen in the colonies had pinned their hopes and futures on the success of the 1710–14 Tory administration. The death of Queen Anne

---

[70] *An account of the sufferings of the members of the Church of England at Stratford, Connecticut,* ibid. vii. 350–5.

[71] Governor Charles Gookin to the Secretary, 21 Jan. 1712, ibid. vii. 506.

[72] Henderson to the Secretary, 12 Dec, 1712, ibid. viii. 97.

[73] Bennett, 'The SPG and Barbadian politics', 190–206.

and the Hanoverian succession dashed these expectations. Just as the failure of a High Church programme following the proscription of the Tories pushed many clergymen in England inexorably toward Jacobitism, so many clergymen in the colonies followed much the same path. In 1716 a number of clergymen in South Carolina were accused of drinking the health of the pretender,[74] while clergymen in New York and New Jersey were thought to have created a local Jacobite party.[75] In Barbados the governor was concerned that 'the *Jure divino* Clergy, zealous Romanistes, and high-flown (indefeasible) Church-men have held a very strict correspondence of late, and have made more frequent visites to each other than are agreeable to the rules of common civility, hospitality, or friendship'.[76] He also wrote of one clergyman that 'he behaved himself in such an extravagant, turbulent, and seditious manner' and was only 'fitt to officiate in the Pretender's Chapell'.[77] In fact, after Tory proscription and the Jacobite rebellion of 1715–16, the SPG had received so many complaints about its missionaries that it was deemed necessary to write to all clergymen and governors, asking them to report any clergymen who were disaffected to the Protestant succession.[78]

Religious controversies occasionally pitted parishioners against their clergymen. One layman in Philadelphia in 1722 went so far as to author and advertise a pamphlet against his Jacobite preacher. The advertisement, printed in the Philadelphia *American Weekly Mercury*, claimed that the pamphlet, 'A discourse upon *Heb. 13, ver. 17*', was 'occasioned by an incomprehensible sermon' about the obedience due the clergy. The pamphlet was also to include an appendix demanding a reason why the clergyman could demand obedience while '*those excellent prayers of the Church, for his Majesty, the Prince and the Royal Family, ought not to be read with as much Fervency and Devotion, as the Prayer for the Clergy and People?*' He continued, complaining that the clergyman prayed for the royal family with 'Indecent Hastiness' and 'Confused Muttering'.[79]

Jacobitism and High Church zeal were not exclusively the domain of Church of England clergy. It was occasionally the laity who, often contrary to the inclination of a minister, favoured the Stuarts. In 1724 a clergyman in Virginia complained that he suffered the 'displeasure of my friends or relations' for his duty and deference to King George.[80] Similarly, in 1716, a clergyman in South Carolina reported, to his distress, that the people of Charleston regularly drank the health of the duke of Ormonde and that 'the Pretender and his friends'

---

[74]   Ebenez Taylor to the Secretary, 18 Apr. 1716, SPG papers, RHL, ser. A, xi. 163–205.

[75]   See chapter 5 below.

[76]   Lowther to the CTP, 30 Dec. 1715, *CSPC*, item 715.

[77]   Lowther to the bishop of London, 17 May 1717, *CSPC*, item 573 ii.

[78]   3 May 1716, SPG journals, iii.

[79]   *AWM*, 8 Nov. 1722, no. 152.

[80]   *Papers relating to the history of the Church in Virginia, 1650–1776*, ed. William Perry, n.p. 1870, 253.

health are drank regularly' in the town.[81] John Checkley, a Boston Anglican layman, printed pamphlets trumpeting passive obedience and non-resistance, generating a good deal of displeasure amongst some Anglican clergymen.

It was not only High Church sympathies that spoke of the Atlantic context of disaffection in the colonies. Outright nonjuring also had an immediate impact on the Church of England in the colonies. The Church of England was a minority Church in most of the colonies but this did not preclude the existence of problems identical to those in Britain. For example, in 1689 a number of clergymen in the colonies, like their brethren in England, questioned whether or not to take the oaths necessary to demonstrate their loyalty to William and Mary. One of the Anglican clergymen in New York refused the oaths and ceased officiating in any official capacity.[82] In Barbados, during the celebrations in honour of the accession of William and Mary, the clergy absented themselves 'on some mistake or scruple of conscience as to their oath of allegiance to King James' and the colony did not have sermons for a few weeks.[83] Their clerical Jacobitism was short-lived as, after some cajoling from the governor, the clergy laid aside their 'mistaken sentiments' and followed the clergy and laity of England in 'securing the Protestant religion'.[84] The governor attributed their decision to doubts about the validity of new oaths rather than a stubborn refusal to support the Protestant succession but he understood well that an obstinate group of clergy might have quickly become a 'menace to peace on the island colony'.[85] Others were more conscientious than the Barbados clergymen. In Jamaica, in 1692, Thomas Scrambler, a 'beneficed minister', refused to take the oaths, was deprived of his living and later arrested.[86]

After the initial confusion of 1689, nonjuring became less of an immediate problem in the colonies, where the organisational structure of the Church of England made it less of a threat. All of the clergy who were licensed by the bishop of London to officiate in the colonies were required to subscribe to the necessary oaths prior to ordination or licensing.[87] This meant that all the clergymen sent by the SPG or the bishop of London were willing to take the oaths. This does not, however, imply that all of them remained steadfast in their juring beliefs. For example, John Talbot, a clergyman in New Jersey, became increasingly sympathetic to the nonjuring position following the Hanoverian succession. Thirteen years after he was sent as a missionary by the SPG, he refused to take the oaths when prompted. His only defence was that

---

[81] Taylor to the bishop of London, 18 Apr. 1716, SPG, RHL, ser. A, xi. 163–205.

[82] Nelson R. Burr, *The Anglican Church in New Jersey*, Philadelphia 1954, 14

[83] Stede to Shrewsbury, 30 May, 1689, CSPC, item 155.

[84] Ibid.

[85] Ibid.

[86] Minutes of the Council of Jamaica, 9, 19 May 1692, CSPC, items 221, 236.

[87] Bell, *Imperial origins*, 159.

he had been 'williamite from the beginning' and, for evidence, he pointed his detractors towards the oaths that he had sworn during the reign of William and Mary.[88] Old oaths did not guarantee static beliefs and Talbot's evolving beliefs led him to accept consecration as a bishop in the nonjuring communion in 1721 which he exercised quietly in the colonies until his activities were reported to the bishop of London in 1725.[89]

If the neeed to swear oaths prior to ordination and licensing prevented a good deal of nonjuring amongst ministers sent by the bishop of London or the SPG, it could not stamp it out altogether. Nonjurors could easily move across the Atlantic and serve in an unofficial capacity. The distance between London and the colonial parishes, and the time it took to receive information, meant that many colonial parishes were for long periods without a settled minister. This was in part due to the daunting obstacles which had to be overcome by colonists in order to be ordained, including crossing the Atlantic. Often the vestries of vacant parishes would resort to accepting unlicensed, nonjuring ministers rather than do without a preacher. In 1716, for example, the vestry of Oxford parish in Pennsylvania wrote to the secretary of the SPG informing him of their need for a new minister. They also informed him that a 'nonjuring itinerant has been filling in' following the death of their settled missionary.[90] Although the identity of the itinerant minister remains unknown, his presence demonstrates the existence of an anonymous nonjuring minister. Moreover, it illustrates the willingness of the vestry to allow a nonjuror to officiate without a licence if it were necessary to maintain the church. This could lead to interesting problems.

The most fascinating nonjuror in the colonies by far was Richard Welton. A High Church cleric who, after refusing to swear the necessary oaths in 1715 following the accession of George I, had been deprived of his position as rector of Whitechapel in London, he was by no means a moderate. Even nonjuring bishops were unhappy with Welton's morals and controversial attitudes and objected to his consecration as one of their number.[91] He was an active author in London, writing works extolling the virtues of the nonjuring Church and claiming that the juring church was schismatic. He attacked the bishop of London anonymously for his lack of support during the persecution of the nonjuring Church in 1715, and he argued that the oath of abjuration was 'contrary to all the Laws of Truth, of Righteousness, and the Gospel of Jesus Christ' and that if 'it be possible for your Lordship to trim and to comply in these cases, either out of Fear or Interest, we [the clergy] must renounce our Obedience to You, as a perfidious and false Bishop'.[92]

[88]   Talbot to the bishop of London, 21 Oct. 1715, FP vi. 128–9.

[89]   Broxap, The later nonjurors, 87; Talbot to Bishop Gibson, 2 July 1725, FP vi. 130–1.

[90]   Vestry of Oxford parish to the Secretary, [c. 1716], SPG, RHL, ser. A, xi. 234.

[91]   Thomas Brett to Archibald Campbell, 24 Oct. 1724, NAS, CH12/15/109,180–5.

[92]   [Richard Welton], The clergy's tears; or, A cry against persecution: humbly offered in a letter to the bishop of London, in our present great distress and danger, London 1715.

Despite the publication of numerous nonjuring polemics, Welton was best known for the altarpiece set up in his church at Whitechapel which contained a picture of the last supper portraying Judas, the betrayer of Jesus, in the 'habit of a clergy-man'.[93] It was indeed said that the figure of Judas was painted to look like White Kennet.[94] News of Welton's antics with regard to the altarpiece reached as far as Boston.[95] His antipathy towards Low Churchmen and those who were willing to swear the oaths of abjuration knew few, if any, bounds.

In 1721 Welton was consecrated in Britain as a bishop in the nonjuring communion along with John Talbot.[96] His arrival in the colonies was noted in June 1724. He was soon voted in and employed by the vestry as the rector of Christ Church in Philadelphia, which a contemporary estimated had eight hundred communicants. This was in spite of the fact that the local newspaper, the *American Weekly Mercury*, reported the year before that 'Dr. Welton, the nonjuror' had been taken into custody in Britain.[97] Church of England ministers in the area surrounding Philadelphia denied having anything to do with Welton and stated that he professed 'to have come into these parts only to see the countrey', though this belated defence seems a bit self-serving.[98] While many have taken at face value the assertion of Peter Evans, a vestryman of Christ Church, that the vestry employed Welton not knowing that he was a vocal and prominent nonjuror, such ignorance seems unlikely. In an attempt to defend the appointment, Evans disingenuously claimed in a letter to the bishop of London that he had read in London prints that Welton had sworn the necessary oaths.[99] Commissary Henderson of Maryland, however, had heard by August 1724 that both Talbot and Welton were in episcopal orders. He claimed that Welton's parishioners in Philadelphia were equally aware that Welton was a notorious nonjuror but were so fond of him that they 'would have him right or wrong'.[100] Regardless, Welton's appearance in the colonies caused quite a stir. Henderson wrote to the bishop of London stating that 'the nonjuring schism has reached thither'.[101] Another Church of England minister, in New Haven, Connecticut, feared that with the arrival of

---

[93] [Anon.], *The whole tryal and examination of Dr. Welton, rector of White-Chapel and the church-wardens, on Monday last, in the bishop of London's court*, London 1714.

[94] G. V. Bennett, *White Kennett: bishop of Peterborough: a study in the political and ecclesiastical history of the early eighteenth century*, London 1957, 127-31.

[95] Jeremiah Dummer to Benjamin Colman, 15 Jan. 1714/15, Benjamin Colman papers, Massachusetts Historical Society, Boston, Massachusetts (microfilm).

[96] Broxap, *The later nonjurors*, 88.

[97] Peter Evans to Bishop Gibson, [c. 1725], *FP* vii. 121-2. For the number of communicants see Patrick Gordon to the bishop of London, 19 July 1726, ibid. vii. 126-7; AMW, 16 May 1723, no. 178.

[98] Clergy of Pennsylvania to the bishop of London, *FP* ii. 5-6.

[99] Evans to Bishop Gibson, [c. 1725], *FP* vii. 121-2.

[100] Henderson to the bishop of London, 16 Aug. 1724, *FP* iii. 41-2.

[101] Ibid.

two nonjuring bishops, Welton and Talbot, some of his parishioners, recently brought into the Anglican fold, would wander 'out of one schism into another and with all into disaffection to the King'.[102] Equally important, the governor of Pennsylvania, William Keith, a member of Christ Church and a former Jacobite, knew of Welton's principles. In a self-justifying letter to the bishop of London, Keith claimed that for the sake of peace, he 'was obliged to be passive in things which are both indecent and disorderly, such as suffering some of the clergymen to read prayers and preach without mentioning the King, Prince, or Royal family'.[103] How much of Keith's passivity was necessary is questionable, as it was charged against him that he also allowed Welton to officiate at the wedding of his daughter-in-law.[104]

Not only were Welton and Talbot nonjuring bishops in the colonies, they were also active propagandists for the nonjuring cause. One antagonistic clergyman in Maryland claimed that Talbot had 'poisoned all the neighbouring clergy with his rebellious principles'.[105] Moreover, a clergyman in New England wrote to the bishop of London that 'it is certain that the nonjurors have sent over two Bishops into America' and noted that 'one of them has travelled through the country ... to promote their cause'. He also expressed concern that 'my well meaning people otherwise well enough affected will be in great danger of being imposed on and led aside' and was 'sensible that their [the nonjuring bishops] powers of persuasion are very considerable'.[106] Perhaps even more important was the fact that Welton and Talbot had each brought to the colonies numerous tracts and pamphlets espousing the nonjuring cause. Talbot was noted as having come 'fraught from England' with scandalous pamphlets including one referred to as 'The Case Truly Stated'. Although this pamphlet cannot be identified, the person mentioning it certainly viewed it as nonjuring propaganda.[107] Furthermore, Welton was accused of bringing printed reproductions of his famous altar-piece to which he had added a scroll coming out of the mouth of White Kennet, saying 'I am not he who betrayed X^t though as ready to do it as ever Judas was'.[108]

Word of such activity was certain to reach London. The nonjuring bishops in England had been aware that Welton and Talbot had been ordained and sent to the colonies as early as 1724. In October 1724 Thomas Brett noted that 'I suppose in about a years time we shall have an acct. in our public newspapers of these new Bps appearing in America ... and what encouragement they

---

[102] Joseph Browne to the bishop of London, 15 Mar. 1725, FP i. 210–11.

[103] Governor William Keith to the bishop of London, 24 July 1724, FP vii. 114–15.

[104] Charles P. Keith, 'Sir William Keith', *Pennsylvania Magazine of History and Biography* xii (1888), 1–33.

[105] Mr [?] Urmston to [?], 29 July, 1724, SPG papers, RHL, ser. C, box 7, item 67.

[106] Browne to the bishop of London, 15 Mar. 1725, FP i. 210–11.

[107] Urmston to [?], 29 July, 1724, SPG papers, RHL, ser. C, box 7, item 67.

[108] Stubbs to the bishop of London, 16 Apr. 1725, FP vii. 117–18.

find there.'[109] This news in fact arrived as early as February 1725. The Revd J. Berriman wrote to his acquaintance in Connecticut that 'We hear of two Nonjuring Bishops (Dr. Welton for one) who are gone into America.'[110] Upon hearing of the activities of Welton and Talbot, the bishop of London and the king acted quickly to end what one critic described as Welton's 'chimerical prospects'.[111] In Pennsylvania, Governor Keith, under the authority of the bishop of London, served Welton with a writ of privy seal, commanding him to return to Great Britain.[112] Welton never made it back to Britain for he died *en route*, but before he left the church in Philadelphia, he preached and printed a final sermon entitled *The certain comforts of God the Holy Ghost*, which he advertised in the local paper.[113] The new commissary in Philadelphia wrote to the bishop of London that Welton's sermon attacked the established clergy in a 'scurrilous manner' and entreated his audience to reject any minister sent amongst them.[114] In his sermon Welton made a final plea for the case of the nonjuring Church. He exhorted his 'sorrowful congregation' to find comfort in religion but, more important, he charged his 'Dear Lambs' to beware of the 'IMPOSTORS, and FALSE PROPHETS' who would come amongst them.[115] Throughout the sermon Welton continued to lambast not only the Church of England, but the bishop of London as well. He reminded his congregation, without much subtlety, that the bishop had treated them not as a 'Tender Father' but as a 'STEP-FATHER'. He continued by mocking the SPG and praying that his parish would be secure from 'the PROPAGATIONS of those wolves'.[116] He prayed that his flock would not be seduced to 'Betray the FAITH and UNITY in Christ's Holy APOSTOLICK CHURCH'. Referring again to the bishop of London, he warned his auditors of the danger of the 'Wolf' who would send his 'IMPS' among them and finally exhorted them to 'enter not into their secrets, whose prayers are an abomination to the righteous God!'[117] After venting his spleen against the juring Church, he urged his people to remember his 'sacred Brother Jonathan [Talbot]' who was the partner of his afflictions and 'fellow labourer'. This is the only evidence from either Welton or Talbot of the connection between them. It is fascinating to note that Welton claimed that if he was at all successful in his labours in Philadelphia, it was

---

[109] Brett to Campbell, 24 Oct. 1724, NAS, CH12/15/109, 180–5.

[110] Eben Edwards Beardsley, *Life and correspondence of Samuel Johnson, D.D.*, New York 1874, 55.

[111] Mr [?] Cummings to the bishop of London, 19 Oct. 1726, FP vii. 128–9.

[112] BL, MS Add. 36125, fos 370, 372; Keith to the bishop of London, 8 Apr. 1726, FP vii. 124–5.

[113] [Richard Welton], *The certain comforts of God the Holy Ghost, &c, preached at the Episcopal Church in Philadelphia*, Philadelphia 1726; AWM, 5 Feb. 1725/26, no 321.

[114] Cummings to the bishop of London, 19 Oct. 1726, FP vii. 128–9.

[115] Welton, *The certain comforts*, 3, 10, 20.

[116] Ibid. 21.

[117] Ibid. 22.

owing to Talbot's previous work serving that church when he was not needed at his own church in Burlington, New Jersey and the fact that he made Welton 'Love, and Pity' the church even before he settled there.[118] Although this is the only sermon that Welton had printed in Philadelphia, it was probably not the only such sermon that he would have preached: spoken sermons were a significant element in the public sphere and an effective means of influencing audiences' beliefs without being subject to the same level of detailed scrutiny as in a printed publication.[119]

Roman Catholicism, too, contributed to the persistence of Jacobitism throughout the British Atlantic. Roman Catholics in England, Scotland and Ireland remained an important source of support for their co-religionist James Stuart and his heirs, and the same was often true of their fellow Catholics in the colonies. As in England and Scotland, Roman Catholicism was a minority faith in the colonies, even in Maryland, which was in some respects a Catholic sanctuary. In the uncertain aftermath of the revolution of 1688, and its various manifestations in the colonies in 1689, accusations of Jacobitism were as common as they were confused and Catholics often bore the brunt of the vitriol, although not without reason.

In 1689, as word of the invasion of England by William of Orange reached the colonies, colonial governors appointed by James II&VII were caught unprepared. Unsure of how to proceed in the absence of orders from England, their administrations in Boston, New York and Maryland prevaricated and failed to act decisively for either James or William. Simultaneously, rumours of war and of a French and Indian conspiracy were circulating throughout the British Atlantic, stirring fears of a larger Catholic conspiracy.[120] Eventually, settlers in Boston, New York and Maryland rose up against their governors and established new interim governments which promptly proclaimed the accession of William and Mary. Fears of Catholic supporters of the Stuarts and France proved a rich mixture and in the wake of the revolution of 1688, these governments regularly accused their opponents of popery and Jacobitism. For example, in Maryland, the popish party was accused of distributing pamphlets and arguing that 'King James will be restored'.[121] But accusations were not rooted in an 'imagined' threat; Catholics were legitimately associated with Jacobitism throughout the British Atlantic.

In the 1690s Roman Catholics in the colonies were regularly associated with the threat posed by an antagonistic Catholic French imperial state. Colonial participation in the Nine Years War (1688–97) with France, including failed

---

[118]   Ibid, 23.

[119]   Jennifer Farooq, *Preaching in eighteenth-century London*, Woodbridge 2014, 108.

[120]   Owen Stanwood, 'The Protestant moment: antipopery, the Revolution of 1688–1689, and the making of an Anglo-American Empire', JBS xlvi (2007), 481–508.

[121]   Representatives of Maryland to the king and queen, 25 Apr. 1691, CSPC, item 1427.

attacks on Quebec, increased confessional antipathy. Fears that French-supported Catholics posed a threat to the colonies gained credence in 1689 when Irish Catholic servants in the Leeward Islands, aided by the French, rose in rebellion and declared themselves for King James.[122] The possibility of similar revolts by Irish Catholics supported by French forces encouraged governors in the Caribbean to disarm the local Catholic population.[123] French action against the English continued to plague the colonists. In 1689 the French captured the island of Anguilla and installed as governor an Irish Catholic who required the populace to take oaths of allegiance to James VII&II.[124]

More troubling for some, it was possible for Catholic Jacobites to be protected rather than denounced by officials. In Pennsylvania in 1689 a justice of the peace complained that when he attempted to seize two Catholic gentlemen he was discouraged by his fellow justices who said 'they were very honest persons' and 'after drinking King James's health with them, allowed them to go'.[125] Similarly, in Jamaica, the interim governor, who took counsel from a 'popish' priest, was censured by his council for refusing to hear charges against a papist who spoke seditious words against King William.[126] Although it was uncommon, official sanction of Jacobitism provided a means of perpetuating loyalty to the Stuarts among Catholics. Colonists were also fearful that Jacobitism among indentured servants might go unpunished by sympathetic owners. In 1706 Governor Seymour of Maryland wrote of the 'growing mischief' of importing Irish servants who were mostly papists and noted that the Jacobite Charles Carroll had imported two hundred such people.[127]

Catholics in the colonies also participated in the rituals associated with Jacobitism, such as drinking the health of King James – reportedly practised regularly in some Catholic homes – and celebrating Jacobite holidays. In Maryland, in 1698, a group of men were accused of being at the home of Walter Smith when King James's health was drunk. The accused denied that they participated but did admit that several others did.[128] Also in Maryland Benjamin Hall was required to pay £1,000 as a security for good behaviour for drinking King James's health. Similarly, in Antigua in 1718, one critic complained that 'in the evening of St. Patrick's Day since H.M. accession 50 or 60 of them [Catholics] got together in St. John's at midnight and drank ye

[122] Lieutenant-General Christopher Codrington to the Lords of Trade and Plantations, 31 July, CSPC, item 312; John Netheway to the king and queen, 9 July 1689, CSPC, item 237.

[123] Codrington to the Lords of Trade and Plantations, 31 July 1689, CSPC, item 312; Netheway to the king and queen, 27 July 1689, CSPC, item 212; Order of the King in Council, 2 May 1689, CSPC, item 102.

[124] Codrington to the Lords of Trade and Plantations, 19 Sept.1689, CSPC, item 444.

[125] Deposition of Jehan Forat, 4 Oct. 1689, CSPC, item 469

[126] Extract from the minutes of the Council of Jamaica, May 1689, CSPC, item 874v; 'A short account of the state of affairs in Jamaica, July 1689, CSPC, item 299.

[127] Governor John Seymour to the CTP, 8 Mar. 1706, CSPC, item 160.

[128] AOM xxiii. 461-2.

Pretender's health several of them with drawn swords and roved about ye town in a riotous manner'.[129] Drinking the health of James VII&II was a communal ritual which reinforced the relationship between Catholicism and Jacobitism for a number of colonists, especially in Maryland.

Catholic Jacobite activity increased in the years before the rebellion in 1715 as some Catholics eagerly anticipated a Stuart restoration. After the news of the '15 reached the colonies, Catholics were suspected of showing their disaffection to the monarch by 'spreading sundry false rumours' about the 'advantage gained by His Majesty's enemies' and 'drinking or offering to drink, the Pretender's health'.[130] On 10 June 1716, the birthday of the 'Old Pretender', two Catholics in Maryland drank James's health and spoke 'contemptibly' of King George. They were tried, found guilty and imprisoned until they could pay the £100 fine for their actions.[131] On the same day to the 'extreme Surprize Dread & Disquiett of all his said Majesty's good & faithful Subjects of this Province ... four of the Great Guns on the Court House Hill in the City of Annapolis where loaden And two of them fired off by some wicked disloyal & Traiterous Persons [two Irish Catholic servants]' in order to celebrate the birthday of the exiled Stuart king. The government responded swiftly. After notice of a reward of twenty pounds sterling was advertised, one of the servants, no doubt to the chagrin of his companion, 'confessed himself' and received a pardon while his companion was tried, convicted and received a whipping and time in the pillory.[132]

Jacobitism survived among Catholic gentry in the colonies, primarily in Maryland. As with the Jacobite gentry of Scotland, England and Ireland, religion, associational rituals and family ties perpetuated Jacobite loyalties for generations.[133] The Carroll family of Maryland provides a clear example. They maintained a family loyalty to the Stuarts over a period of almost thirty years. Charles Carroll immigrated to Maryland from Ireland in 1688 as an appointee of Lord Baltimore but soon after he arrived, his appointment was made null by the accession of William and Mary and the loss of Baltimore's charter. Carroll was a member of a staunchly Jacobite Irish Catholic family: some of his immediate family who had remained in Ireland fought and died for King James at the Battle of the Boyne.[134] Carroll himself was temporarily imprisoned for 'discourses against the government' in 1689.[135] He remained a Jacobite throughout his life, and in 1716 the government of Maryland, upon receiving

---

[129] 'Affidavit by Col. Valentine Morris of Antique, 29 Jan. 1718, CSPC, item 335.

[130] AOM xxv. 334.

[131] AOM xxx. 373-4.

[132] AOM xxx. 373.

[133] Monod, Jacobitism, 132-8.

[134] For the Carroll family in Ireland see Ronald Hoffman, Princes of Ireland, planters of Maryland: a Carroll saga, 1500-1782, Chapel Hill 2000.

[135] Richard J. Purcell, 'Irish colonists in colonial Maryland', Studies: An Irish Quarterly Review xxiii (1934), 279-94 at p. 282.

notice that Carroll had acquired an appointment from the proprietor, required that he take the oaths of allegiance, supremacy and abjuration. Although he was willing to subscribe the oaths of allegiance and supremacy, he refused to swear the oath of abjuration.[136] Nor was he the only Jacobite in his family in Maryland; his nephew was imprisoned and fined for drinking the health of the pretender in 1716.[137] Outside the Carroll family, Richard Smith suffered fines after he refused to swear the oaths of allegiance and supremacy in 1698 due to his religious beliefs.[138]

Catholic association with Jacobitism led to numerous laws and anti-Catholic declarations. After news of the attempted Jacobite rebellion of 1708 reached the colonies, Governor Seymour of Maryland noted that 'the Roman Catholicks in this province discourse of the late designed invasion by the Pretended prince of Wales, and were listning after the success'. Seymour consequently thought it best to 'take the number of them' in each county.[139] Also in Maryland in 1716 Governor Hart attempted to temper perceived Catholic Jacobite intrigues by issuing a declaration 'against papists and nonjurors spreading false rumours about the victories of the rebels and drinking the health of a popish pretender'.[140] In addition sheriffs in Maryland were instructed to make lists of all the Roman Catholics in their respective counties. In Antigua, a law was passed which one contemporary noted was intended to 'prevent the increase of papists and non-jurors in this island' and to better govern those already settled there. This was passed in 1718 after complaints about 'the extraordinary misbehaviour of the papists and their disaffection to His Majesty and the Protestant succession'.[141]

Jacobitism, a vital aspect of the religious and political controversies gripping Britain from 1689 to 1727, had transatlantic repercussions. Confessional groups, such as nonjurors, Scottish Episcopalians, Catholics, High Church Anglicans and High Church clergy in Ireland provided the ideological foundations for a transatlantic Jacobite subculture, and these confessional groups had colonial analogues. There were a number of nonjurors in the colonies. Nonjurors even managed to send bishops to America, a feat that the juring Church of England was never able to accomplish. Similarly, many Scottish Episcopalians were men educated in Jacobite principles at Aberdeen who were later ordained and sent to the colonies as ministers of the Church of England. They constituted a small but influential pool of men who were probably

---

[136] AOM xxx. 374.
[137] Beatriz Betancourt Hardy, 'A papist in a Protestant age: the case of Richard Bennett, 1667–1749', *Journal of Southern History* lx (1994), 203–28 at p. 215 n. 51.
[138] AOM xxv. 21.
[139] Seymour to the CTP, 7 Sept. 1708, *CSPC*, item 131.
[140] AOM xxv. 335.
[141] 'Journal, April 1718: Journal Book T', *JBTP* xxx. 358–72.

sympathetic to the exiled Stuart dynasty. Many Catholics also maintained a sympathy for the Stuarts despite the penalties and suspicions that they laboured under. The religious controversies dividing the High Church and Low Church parties in the Church of England were also replicated throughout the British Atlantic: disputes dividing the Church of England such as occasional conformity, lay baptism, and 'the Church in danger' all had parallels in the colonies. Such controversies fostered transatlantic party alignments. The Tory ascendency of 1710–14 drew High Church Anglicans in the colonies into the orbit of a Tory party increasingly susceptible to Jacobite sympathies. This in turn affected the perception of Anglicans and Jacobites in the colonies. Thus, the religious foundations of Jacobite ideology were an instrumental component of both Jacobitism and anti-Jacobitism in the British Atlantic world.

3

Jacobitism and Anti-Jacobitism in the Atlantic Public Sphere

Religious controversies, the operation of imperial politics and the appointments system provided a mechanism for public and private expressions of both Jacobitism and anti-Jacobitism. Moreover, these religious and governmental systems served as institutional networks of communication, connecting colonists to the religious controversies and party politics of mainland Britain. However, the communication of a political culture deeply imbued with Jacobitism was not limited to institutional links. Ideas, images, news and attitudes also circulated *via* extra-institutional means such as newspapers, material culture, personal letters and family networks. Jacobitism, therefore, was as much a cultural phenomenon as it was a political or religious movement, thus proving to be a significant and enduring aspect of a transatlantic political culture. Indeed, it permeated nearly every aspect of British culture, including print, religion, poetry, architecture, medicine and politics.[1]

Cultural conflicts did not dissipate after emigrants left Britain's shores nor did they evolve beyond recognition. Informal personal networks and an increasingly vibrant print culture provided a means of transmitting and sustaining multi-faceted and contested elements of British culture throughout the British Atlantic. Contested religious and political beliefs circulated around the Atlantic. So too did the news, pamphlets and broadsides which triggered or inflamed the disputes. In the colonies, as well as in Britain, both Jacobitism and anti-Jacobitism were important components of news and print culture primarily because they were deeply rooted elements of British society. Informational and cultural exchanges were communicated to and throughout the colonies via a migration of peoples and a lively print network, which together fed a shared extra-institutional Atlantic public sphere. This effectively knit together a transatlantic British public, thus creating a keen awareness among Whigs in the colonies of the perils posed by Jacobites, while simultaneously contributing to a transatlantic Jacobite subculture.

The British Atlantic was a dynamic world of cultural and information exchange. Ian Steele's unsurpassed study of communication and community in the English Atlantic demonstrates the extensive communication networks which

---

[1] Pittock, *Jacobitism*, and *Material culture and sedition*; Monod, *Jacobitism*, 45–94; Parrish, 'A party contagion', 41–58; Guthrie, *Material culture*; Nicholson, '"Revirescit"', 25–48.

connected the Atlantic world.[2] Thousands of people from England, Scotland and Ireland crossed the Atlantic to settle in Britain's colonies. Thousands more connected the disparate regions together through an extensive and aggressive pursuit of trade and commerce. After their arrival in the colonies, colonists or merchants were kept apprised of British news by correspondence with friends and family or through interaction with the multitude of traders who dealt in both news and material goods. Packet boats, newspapers, postal routes and merchants all contributed to the growing integration of a transatlantic communications network.

The transatlantic public sphere was suffused with elements of Jacobitism and anti-Jacobitism. Recently, an extensive body of literature has detailed the development of the English press and print culture and touched on the relationship between Jacobitism and this efflorescence of the printed word. While illustrating the increasing prominence of newspapers in late seventeenth- and early eighteenth-century political culture, these studies have also shown the symbiotic relationship of press and party in the party conflicts of the early eighteenth century. Jacobites exploited partisan presses to propagate Jacobite materials, thus enabling their participation in a contested, transatlantic public sphere.[3] In England, for instance, from 1714 to 1760 Jacobite works outnumbered the publications of both republicans and the 'country' opposition. In fact, according to Michael Harris, the primary public opposition to George I was Jacobite.[4]

The explosion in British print culture in the late Stuart era, therefore, provided a vehicle for partisan political discussion during a period of massive political unrest and division.[5] Texts often had a number of meanings, and words, ideas and images were all contested entities, a confusion effectively exploited by Jacobites. Yet this print culture was not confined to London. This period also witnessed the remarkable growth and impact of British provincial newspapers, which were tied to and reliant on various London publications.[6] Moreover, recent works have also documented the relationship between Scottish and Irish public opinion and events in London, thereby extending understanding of the impact of a burgeoning, politicised print culture and illustrating the development of a 'British' press and an increasingly 'British' public.[7]

---

[2]   Steele, *The English Atlantic*.

[3]   Paul Chapman, 'Jacobite political argument in England, 1714–1766,' unpubl. PhD diss. Cambridge 1983; Michael Harris, *London newspapers in the age of Walpole*, London 1987; Bob Harris, *Politics and the rise of the press: Britain and France, 1620–1800*, London 1997; Monod, 'The Jacobite press and English censorship', 125–42; Jeremy Black, *The English press, 1621–1861*, London 2001; Joad Raymond (ed.), *News, newspapers, and society in early modern Britain*, London 1999.

[4]   Chapman, 'Jacobite political argument', 23–4; Harris, *London newspapers*, 14.

[5]   Knights, *Representation and misrepresentation*.

[6]   G. A. Cranfield, *The development of the provincial newspaper, 1700–1760*, Oxford 1962.

[7]   Karin Bowie, *Scottish public opinion and the Anglo-Scottish union, 1699–1707*, Woodbridge 2007.

There was a simultaneous rapid expansion of print in Britain's colonies. Colonists had a voracious and growing appetite for the printed word. In the eighteenth century newspapers, pamphlets and almanacs were printed in ever larger quantities throughout the British colonies, and increasing numbers of books, tracts and pamphlets were imported from Britain.[8] Yet even with the rapid growth of a transatlantic print culture, there remained in both the colonies and Britain a mixed print and manuscript culture, reminding us that the open discussion of ideas was far more complex than can be accounted for by a print culture alone.[9] Thus, through various channels, colonists and colonial officials were able to participate in an increasingly comprehensive transatlantic public sphere.

Taverns, coffee houses and other public spaces in the colonies were integral components of an increasingly active and complex public sphere.[10] By 1710 Boston, a town with a population of around 10,000 people, had at least eighty-one people engaged in the inn and tavern business and by 1720 there were four well-established coffee houses which served as important cultural and mercantile centres.[11] This was, of course, a fraction of London's tally, yet there is broad agreement that, just as in London, these public spaces often complemented a flourishing print culture by stocking up on recent local imprints for their clientele. They also served as a place where mariners might leave mail or hang up mail bags, and they operated as important centres of information exchange.[12] Although there is debate about the democratising effect of such spaces, most scholars agree that they were an essential component of an increasingly active political public. Contemporaries in the British colonies remarked on 'coffee-house news'.[13] As in the British Isles, colonists effectively used these places as a source of news gathering and

---

[8]   Charles Clark, *The public prints: the newspaper in Anglo-American culture, 1665–1740*, Oxford 1994; Hugh Armory and David D. Hall (eds), *The colonial book in the Atlantic world*, Cambridge 2000; Phyllis Whitman Hunter, 'Transatlantic news: American interpretations of the scandalous and heroic', in Leslie Howsam and James Raven (eds), *Books between Europe and the Americas: connections and communities, 1620–1860*, Basingstoke 2011, 63–82; Uriel Heyd, *Reading newspapers: press and public in eighteenth-century Britain and America*, Oxford 2012; David S. Shields, *Civil tongues and polite letters in British America*, Chapel Hill 1997, and *Oracles of empire: poetry, politics, and commerce in British America, 1690–1750*, Chicago 1990.

[9]   Shields, *Civil tongues and polite letters*, and *Oracles of empire*.

[10]   Cowan, *The social life of coffee*; Steve Pincus, '"Coffee politicians does create": Coffeehouses and restoration political culture', *Journal of Modern History* lxvii (1995), 807–34; David Conroy, *In public houses: drink and the revolution of authority in colonial Massachusetts*, Chapel Hill 1995; Peter Thompson, *Rum punch and revolution: taverngoing & public life in eighteenth-century Philadelphia*, Philadelphia 1999; Sharon Salinger, *Taverns and drinking in early America*, Baltimore 2002.

[11]   Carl Bridenbaugh, *Cities in the wilderness: the first century of urban life in America, 1625–1742*, New York 1955, 265.

[12]   Ibid. 266; Olson, *Making the empire work*, 64,

[13]   Daniel Leeds, *The second part of the mystery of Fox-Craft*, New York 1705, 22.

politicking. In 1714 Samuel Sewell, a Boston judge, noted that he had read the Schism Act in Thomas Selby's Crown Coffee House soon after a copy of the act arrived.[14] Similarly, in 1698, Governor Bellomont of New York remarked upon 'a paper which was very industriously dispersed' and was left in 'the coffy house in this town'.[15] Regardless of whether these places preserved a traditional hierarchical culture or democratised cultures by bringing diverse patrons together, these spaces undoubtedly provided a place for public engagement and contributed to the emergence of an informed and curious provincial public.

The developing print culture and the growth in the number of public spaces in the colonies contributed to the emergence of a transatlantic public sphere, the term used in its broadest, post-Habermasian sense. Although the value of the Habermasian model is contested, if tempered it provides a useful framework for analysing the relationship between Jacobitism, anti-Jacobitism and public discourse in the British Atlantic World.[16] If the public sphere is not encumbered by the need for a politically active rising bourgeoisie, an idealised rational discourse, or a specific date of emergence, the term becomes a useful means of encapsulating the rising importance of public opinion and action, the growth of a print culture – especially newspapers – and the role of public spaces such as coffee houses and taverns as places where the public and private intersected.

Numerous critiques of Habermas's public sphere have deconstructed or reinterpreted elements of his theory, yet have at the same time reinforced the utility of the term and given it a more complex and nuanced meaning.[17] Mark Knights has tempered the idealist impulses of the Habermasian model, noting that contemporaries, though engaging in misrepresentation, continued to believe that public discourse would point readers towards the truth.[18] Moreover, studies of Jacobitism, while often not engaging directly with the public sphere, have reminded us of the restrictions imposed on the public sphere, even after the lapse of the 1695 Licensing Act, through prosecution for sedition and libel.[19]

---

[14] *Diary of Samuel Sewell* (Collections of the Massachusetts historical society vii, 1882), 18.

[15] Coote to the CTP, 27 Apr. 1698, *CSPC*, item 317.

[16] Jurgen Habermas, *The structural transformation of the public sphere: an inquiry into a category of bourgeois society*, trans. Thomas Burger, Boston 1989; Brian Cowan, 'Geoffrey Holmes and the public sphere: Augustan historiography from the post-Namierite to the post-Habermasian', *PH* xxviii (2009), 166–78.

[17] Bowie, *Scottish public opinion*; Knights, *Representation and misrepresentation*; Brian Cowan, 'Geoffrey Holmes and the public sphere', in Peter Lake and Steven Pincus (eds), *The politics of the public sphere in early modern England*, Manchester 2007.

[18] Mark Knights, 'How rational was the later Stuart public sphere', in Lake and Pincus, *The politics of the public sphere*, 252–67.

[19] Monod, 'The Jacobite press and English censorship', 125–42; Chapman, 'Jacobite political argument'; Guthrie, *Material culture of the Jacobites*; Pittock, *Material culture and sedition*.

The mechanics of expressing public opinion differed according to locale – Scotland, Ireland, England; their differing institutions and disparate political cultures ensured that this would be so. Yet, despite their differences, these individual spheres were all shaped by London influences and thus necessarily functioned within a larger British sphere.[20] The problem of different public spheres is exacerbated when looking at the British Atlantic. England, Scotland, Ireland and each separate colony all possessed a unique government and local political culture, yet overlap was inescapable. The component parts and disparate political cultures were tied together by events, shared publications and overlapping networks into a larger, more nebulous public sphere. Scholars of the American colonies who have examined public discourse and the public sphere have rightly shown that a colonial public sphere or public spheres in individual colonies in the early eighteenth century were most certainly less developed than their counterparts in England and Scotland.[21] However, when grouped together they both created and were enveloped within a complex Atlantic public sphere, contributing to 'a consciousness of the status of colonials as provincial citizens in an extended empire'.[22]

The public sphere, therefore, provides an excellent foundation and framework for understanding the communication of both Jacobitism and anti-Jacobitism in the British Atlantic. The increasing amount of scholarship examining disparate print cultures and public spheres has demonstrated the mechanics of political and religious discourse and the integration of ideas into local societies. This allows for a more specific study of the communication of Jacobitism and anti-Jacobitism – or Jacobite and pro-Hanoverian political cultures – in a larger geographical context than England, Scotland or Britain alone. This chapter explores the communication of Jacobitism and Jacobite political culture alongside a corresponding – if antithetical – anti-Jacobitism throughout the British Atlantic World. This process is two-fold. First, it examines how news about Jacobitism was transmitted and disseminated throughout the colonies. Such news was a vital ingredient in the emergent public sphere as it was encapsulated in debates regarding foreign policy, religion and political economy which were hallmarks of English public discourse. It kept various colonists, including merchants, clergymen and political officials, apprised of the threat that the Jacobites posed to Britain. It also informed colonists about party divisions and the relationship between Jacobitism and the Church of England

---

[20] Bowie, *Scottish public opinion*, 7–11; Joad Raymond, 'The newspaper, public opinion, and the public sphere', in Raymond, *News, newspapers, and society*, 109–40; Toby Barnard, 'The impact of print in Ireland, 1680–1800: problems and perils', in Eve Patten and Jason McElligott (eds), *The perils of print culture: books, print, and publishing in theory and practice*, Basingstoke 2014, 96–117; O'Ciardha, *Ireland and the Jacobite cause*, 115.

[21] Michael Warner, *The letters of the republic: publication and the public sphere in eighteenth-century America*, Cambridge, MA 1990; Christopher Grasso, *A speaking aristocracy: transforming discourse in eighteenth century Connecticut*, Chapel Hill 1999.

[22] Landsman, *From colonials to provincials*, 34.

and the Tory party. In fact, the news or print culture was predominantly anti-Jacobite, and thus prone to exaggerate any extant Jacobite threat in Britain and to flag up with great anxiety any Jacobitism evident in the colonies. Yet, even if it might alarm many colonists, this news might also serve the secondary purpose of encouraging identification either with or against the Jacobites. For example, news of the problematic relationship between the Church of England and Jacobitism might encourage some colonists to associate High Churchmen in the colonies with disaffection while simultaneously driving those very same High Churchmen towards Jacobitism as they engaged with transatlantic political and religious cultures. Thus the news and information that colonists received about Jacobitism shaped public opinion and individual attitudes towards Tories, High Churchmen and Jacobitism. Colonial participation in local manifestations of British debates on party politics and religious beliefs, both of which possessed a potent infusion of Jacobitism, drew them into a transatlantic public sphere. Finally, this chapter explores how elements of Jacobite culture were communicated and practised in the British Atlantic public sphere. There are examples in the colonies of printed Jacobite material and openly spoken disaffection. Furthermore, there are notable cases where disaffection is couched in veiled terms, thus giving Jacobite ideology or sentiment access to the nascent Atlantic public sphere.

At the outset, it must be noted that the communication of Jacobitism did not require a positive declaration of support for the Stuarts. Jacobite sympathies ranged from a nostalgic toast to open celebration of Stuart birthdays and anniversaries or declarations of their right to the throne. Equally Jacobite was a denial of the legitimacy of William or the Hanoverians. Such a denial might take the form of a refusal to pray for the king by name, a celebration of the Tory virtues of passive obedience and non-resistance, or even an outright declaration that George I was a usurper or had no right to the throne. Of course, Jacobite participation in the public sphere was limited as open sedition was censored or, after 1695, prosecuted as sedition or libel. Even a veiled Jacobitism was dangerous as Nathaniel Mist, the Jacobite printer, and others discovered.

Explicit Jacobite ideas were largely excluded from being expressed in a 'free' and rational public sphere. In order to participate in the public sphere, Jacobites were necessarily forced to couch their beliefs and sentiments in more palatable and appropriate language, and even this only allowed access to the fringes of public debate. This necessitated the creation of a subculture in which ideas could be communicated to an audience literate in the language of sedition and sentiment.[23] In some respects this created a 'counter public sphere' in which Jacobites self-consciously acted publicly yet set themselves apart from the larger public. This is exemplified by the use of material objects such as drinking glasses, art and architecture, which demonstrated a loyalty to the Stuarts and

---

[23] Monod, *Jacobitism*, 10.

was intended to be understood only by a select audience.[24] However, despite the exclusion of explicit expressions of Jacobite sentiment and the creation of a counter public, many Jacobites sought to engage in public debate. While their core beliefs often forced them to the fringes of a public sphere, because it was dangerous to discuss them openly, they entered into public discourse by veiling disaffection in acceptable terms. This use of language designed to avoid prosecution, which the Jacobites' relationship with the Tory party made possible, allowed Jacobite ideas and ideology to enter the wider public sphere. Ideas were 'disguised in satire, allegory, ironical eulogies of the Hanoverians and their ministers, or parallel history'.[25] Jacobite publications, therefore, became possible 'under a disguise of metaphor, allegory, and ambiguity'.[26] That state authorities was unable to stamp out veiled disaffection, despite repeated attempts, promoted continued Jacobite involvement in the public arena.[27] One of the most notable examples of this is provided by the sermon, prosecution and trial of Henry Sacheverell. Sacheverell was impeached before the House of Lords because a sermon that he preached on the 5 November was viewed as attacking the intellectual rationale for the revolution of 1688.[28] While the sermon itself was a celebration of Toryism, many Whigs rightly viewed it as intended to undermine the Protestant succession. Sacheverell's light punishment demonstrates the success of his charade, but the furore arising from his sermon and trial shows the very real obstacles placed before Jacobites wanting to engage in public discourse.

Communicating Jacobitism, however, was not restricted to those who sympathised with, or supported the Stuarts. Moreover, it is often difficult to discern the difference between news about Jacobitism and Jacobite propaganda. News about Jacobitism or the Jacobite rebellions might effectively communicate Jacobite ideas and support as could anti-Jacobite polemics, all of which tied the colonies to the politics and culture of Britain. News, rumours and information about the Jacobites could encourage some to entertain a growing sympathy for them. For others, it exaggerated an extant, if minimal, threat. Even the publication of tracts or newspapers expressing anti-Jacobite sentiments might dimly reflect the existence of Jacobite sentiments or a Jacobite community, as they were likely printed and employed by those antagonistic to the claims of the exiled Stuarts in order to combat a local Jacobite presence, thus making Jacobitism a shadowy, elusive element in a public sphere. Thus, the communication of Jacobitism in the British Atlantic public sphere is a helpful reminder that the Atlantic world was a dynamic and contested space of cultural and

---

24   Pittock, 'Treacherous objects', 39–63, and *Material culture and sedition*.

25   Chapman, 'Jacobite political argument', 29.

26   Clark, *English society*, 142.

27   Cowan, *The social life of coffee*, 209–22.

28   Monod, *Jacobitism*, 147–8; Knights, 'How rational was the later Stuart public sphere', 252–67.

ideological exchange, a fact crucial to understanding both the perception and reality of Jacobitism in the Atlantic world.

This chapter focuses its attention on the relationship between Jacobitism and print culture in the emerging Atlantic public sphere, but first it is necessary briefly to consider whether there was a potentially receptive audience. It is an inescapable fact that migration was a vitally important means of cultural diffusion in which Jacobitism was a crucial ingredient. In fact, the most explicit manner in which Jacobitism was transferred around the Atlantic was *via* the migration of Jacobites. Hundreds of Jacobite prisoners were forced migrants, transported to the colonies in the years between 1716 and 1746 following the failure of Jacobite risings in 1715, 1719 and 1745.[29] Communities from the Scottish Highlands with close ties to Jacobitism were relocated to colonial outposts in Georgia in the 1730s as a means of colonial defence.[30] Yet, migration necessitates the movement of more than people: they carried with them their cultural practices, ideologies and religious beliefs.[31] This would be equally true for individual Jacobites and for Jacobite communities who either through forced or voluntary migration settled in the British colonies.

Jacobite prisoners were the most significant element. More than 639 Jacobite prisoners were transported to the colonies after the failed rising of 1715. According to the records, 176 of them were sent to South Carolina while over 200 were sent to Virginia and Maryland. It is likely that many of the prisoners maintained their Jacobite beliefs. For example, John Dunbar, an unrepentant Jacobite prisoner sent to the colonies wrote to a correspondent in Scotland that 'I'm very farr from thinking that the almighty God will impute rebellion to my charge whatever other sins I'm guilty of.'[32] Dunbar eventually moved to Rhode Island and settled near two of his brothers, who were probably sympathetic to his plight.[33]

Although many of the prisoners were sold as indentured servants, purchasers had the right to free them so long as they were willing to put up bonds for good behaviour.[34] When freed (if they were lucky enough to be freed, or better yet, never sold for indenture) Jacobite prisoners often sought out communities that shared their beliefs. Edward Hunt provides a notable example of this. He was one of the many Jacobite rebels captured after the battle of Preston in 1715. One of ninety-six rebels transported on the *Scipio*, which was originally bound

---

[29]   Dobson, *Scots banished to the American plantations*.

[30]   Anthony Parker, *Scottish highlanders in colonial Georgia: the recruitment, emigration, and settlement at Darien, 1735–1748*, Athens, GA 1997.

[31]   Alison Games, 'Migration', in Armitage and Braddick, *British Atlantic world*. The most provocative statement of this is David Hackett Fischer, *Albion's seed: four British folkways in America*, Oxford 1989.

[32]   John Dunbar to James Erskine, Lord Grange, 26 June 1716, NAS, GD298/379/1.

[33]   Dunbar to Grange, 9 July 1717, NAS, GD298/379/3.

[34]   Sankey, *Jacobite prisoners*, 59–75.

for Antigua but instead sailed to Virginia, by 1720, only four years after being transported, he was living in Philadelphia, a member of Christ Church, the local Anglican Church pastored by the High Church minister John Vicary. That Christ Church vestry invited the nonjuror Richard Welton to serve as rector only two years later suggests the existence of a community of High Churchmen sympathetic to nonjurors and Jacobites. Hunt did not stay out of trouble for long: he was executed in 1720 for counterfeiting coins. But Vicary wanted to give Hunt a proper burial and intended to raise a 'high church mob' to see it accomplished.[35] It is apparent that despite his participation in the rebellion of 1715, or perhaps because of it, Hunt was welcomed warmly into the High Church culture fostered in Philadelphia. Thus it is possible to connect him to a larger community likely to be receptive to Jacobite, or at the very least, High Church Tory propaganda. Although Hunt provides the best example, Margaret Sankey shows that numerous other prisoners were purchased by men in the colonies harbouring similar political opinions or by men with family connections to the prisoners.[36]

There are other noteworthy examples of Jacobite migration. A number of Scottish ministers educated in Aberdeen migrated to the colonies in search of employment and many of them settled in New York, New Jersey and Rhode Island. Each pastored a church and as the leader of the church likely inculcated Jacobite sentiments amongst some of their congregation. Similarly, individual Jacobites who came from largely Jacobite families, such as Charles Carroll of Maryland or Alexander Skene of South Carolina, settled in the colonies and ensconced themselves within a friendly environment, whether that be Catholic or High Church Anglican.[37] Others such as Colonel Mackintosh in Rhode Island, who was closely related to many prominent Jacobites and referred to by a participant in the rebellion of 1715 as an 'honest hearty gentleman', created friendly communities, both opening his home to Jacobites and donating land and money for the construction of an Anglican church.[38]

In addition to prisoners and clergymen, other small-scale communities of Jacobites were established in the colonies. In Georgia in the 1730s James Oglethorpe and the trustees of the colony recruited 163 Scots from families which were well represented in the 1715 rising and of which thirteen had been transported as prisoners to South Carolina to settle on Georgia's border with Spanish Florida. That settlement, renamed Darien, served as a means of providing protection for the Carolina colonies from the Spanish colony of

[35] For news about Hunt see *AWM*, 20 Oct., 24 Nov. 1720, nos 44, 49. For the quotation about the mob see Wendel, 'Jacobitism crushed', 58–65 at p. 60.

[36] Sankey, *Jacobite prisoners*, 59–75.

[37] See chapter 2 above.

[38] TNA, SP 35, xxvi, fo. 33b

Florida but it also clearly demonstrated the development of Jacobite communities in the British colonies.[39]

Jacobites in Britain were aware of the possibility of extant communities of like-minded sympathisers in the colonies. Many Jacobites in Britain viewed Maryland as a potential haven, and they imagined that if they relocated to the colony, they would be among a sympathetic populace.[40] Thomas Brett, the nonjuring clergyman, considered moving to South Carolina as he thought it might be an amiable environment for a nonjuror, but he was dissuaded by a friend.[41] However, Brett's daughter and son-in-law did move to Charleston and wrote to Brett complaining that 'All our company are either Whigs or dissenters' and commented on the fact that they were 'to settle among the Bangorians', or supporters of the ideas of Benjamin Hoadly, bishop of Bangor, a champion of the Whig party and a leading latitudinarian. Nevertheless, she still hoped 'we shall find friends amongst those unfortunate gentlemen who were transported on the Preston Account'.[42] Her comment illustrates both knowledge of a potential community of Jacobites and the desire to settle amongst it. Perhaps more important, there is evidence that the British government was aware of influential Jacobites in the colonies and intercepted letters written to prominent Jacobites.[43]

The migration of Jacobites to the colonies, therefore, enabled the development of local, albeit small, Jacobite communities often displaying the subcultural behaviours prevalent in England that have been described by Monod. Moreover, the continued importance of Jacobitism in Britain and the existence of Jacobites in the colonies amplified extant fears of Jacobitism, making news and information about Jacobitism all the more important to colonists. This, in turn, reminds us that fears of Jacobitism, expressed within a dynamic public sphere, were not solely rooted in distant realities, but were instead deeply rooted in a transatlantic cultural discourse made possible in part by the movement of people.

In addition to migration, the early eighteenth century witnessed the increasing circulation of news and information. The development of posts and the printing of newspapers transformed Atlantic communications. Ian Steele has described newspapers as 'the most powerful and extensive public communications innovation that developed within the English Atlantic' in the early eighteenth century. Newspapers were a transformative vehicle of communication. The importation of British papers tied the provinces tightly to London and encouraged a consistent and reliable exchange of information undreamed

---

39   Sankey, *Jacobite prisoners*, 73.

40   Ibid. 68.

41   Brett to Campbell, [c. 1723], NAS, CH12/15/109.

42   Brian J. Enright, 'An account of Charles Town in 1725', *South Carolina Historical Magazine* lxi (1960), 13–18, quotation at p. 14.

43   TNA, SP 35, xxvi, fo. 33b

of by prior generations. The role of the newspapers in creating a transatlantic public sphere was remarkable. The timely and largely accurate information about Jacobitism printed in the papers made certain that colonists were aware of the threats posed by the Jacobites. This development can be seen in the contrast between the uncertainty of 1688 and the proliferation of news in 1722 regarding the Atterbury plot. The ability to transmit an accurate and consistent account of Atterbury's Jacobite conspiracy in a timely manner contrasts greatly with the confusion created by the lack of reliable news following the revolution of 1688, which was untimely, sporadic and confused.[44]

Although not rapid by modern standards, the distribution of news and information to and in the British colonies was transformed over the almost forty-year period between 1688 and 1727. Both the quality and speed of communications increased dramatically. Newspapers printed throughout the colonies or imported from Britain provided their readers with dependable and consistent information about British politics and European events. They encouraged colonial participation in a shared political culture. The 'public prints', as Charles Clark has explained, engaged readers in a larger mental world in which readers saw European and London news through London eyes. Indeed, newspapers embodied and diffused inherited traditions and shared beliefs which created a coherent culture and a transatlantic public sphere.[45] This, of course, included ideas about Jacobitism. News stories about Jacobite rebellions and conspiracies were prominent features in many news prints, connecting the populace of the colonies to ideas and events in Britain. Papers printed in Boston and Philadelphia were distributed throughout Britain's colonies, providing their readers with fresh information about Jacobite developments and, in doing so, ensured an awareness of Jacobitism throughout the Atlantic world.

The first English language newspapers, or *courantos*, were imported from Amsterdam in the 1620s and in turn encouraged the publication of news in London.[46] The news in these early prints focused primarily on foreign affairs, but the government was wary of their influence and regulated their printing. The civil wars of the 1640s led to a breakdown in government regulation and an increase in news prints, but the Commonwealth government of the 1650s reinstated regulatory measures. Following the restoration of the monarchy in 1660, the government of Charles II established a licensing system to oversee pre-publication censorship. This was fairly effective, excepting during periods of major controversy such as the Exclusion crisis in 1679, until 1695 when the Licensing Act expired and parliament was unable to agree on a new act. Soon after the act lapsed, three newspapers, *The Flying Post*, *Post Boy* and *Postman*,

---

44   Steele, *The English Atlantic*, 94–112.
45   Clark, *Public prints*, 221.
46   Black, *The English press*, 4.

appeared and the first successful daily newspaper arrived on the scene in 1702.[47]

The first colonial newspaper, *Public Occurrences, Both Foreign and Domestic,* was printed in Boston by Benjamin Harris in 1690. Although it was intended to be a regular digest of news, it was quickly suppressed by the local authorities because of Harris's ill-advised decision to print local news without the prior approval of the local government.[48] The paper was premature in other respects. Private newspapers had yet to establish themselves in Britain and would not do so until after 1695. Harris's project proved no exception to the English norm. When the English parliament allowed the lapse of the Licensing Act in England, resulting in the shift from pre-publication to post-publication censorship in 1695, the publication of newspapers and other forms of print rapidly expanded. This in turn led to a dramatic increase in the amount and type of news and print available throughout the British empire.

In 1704 John Campbell, the Boston postmaster, successfully launched the *Boston News-Letter.* Campbell's role as postmaster gave him a number of advantages. First, he had quick access to an ever-increasing amount of news and papers coming off the boats in Boston's harbour. Second, he was able to distribute his paper using the recently developed postal routes without cost. New York and Boston were connected by postal routes as early as May 1693 and Pennsylvania was connected to New York soon after.[49] The new routes and a locally published newspaper demonstrate the hunger for fresh and reliable information. The colonial development of a successful newspaper is best understood in the larger context of developments in the British Isles.[50] Campbell's *News-Letter* was one of the earliest provincial newspapers printed in the British Atlantic, preceded only by the English newspapers in Norwich, Bristol and possibly Exeter.[51] In Scotland, the privy council licensed the first regular newspaper, *The Edinburgh Gazette* in 1699, followed by the *Edinburgh Courant* in 1705.[52] By 1723 there were about twenty-eight English-language provincial newspapers, four of which were printed in the colonies. This allowed for an increased level of public engagement in metropolitan events. Prior to publishing the *News-Letter,* Campbell had sent news to privileged correspondents by means of a manuscript newsletter, a practice common in England, Scotland and other colonies.[53] Following its initial printing in 1704, the *News-Letter* remained the only printed colonial newspaper until 1719 when

[47]   Ibid. 5–8.

[48]   Clark, *Public prints*, 57–9.

[49]   Steele, *English Atlantic*, 123.

[50]   Charles Clark, 'Periodicals and politics: part one: early American journalism: news and opinion in the popular press', in Hugh Amory and David D. Hall (eds), *A history of the book in America, I: The colonial book in the Atlantic world*, Chapel Hill 2010, 347–65.

[51]   Ibid. 352, and *Public prints*, 57.

[52]   Steele, *English Atlantic*, 143–4.

[53]   Clark, 'Periodicals and politics', 352.

both the *American Weekly Mercury* and the *Boston Gazette*, in Philadelphia and Boston respectively, began publication. A mere two years later, Boston, a provincial town with a population of around 10,000 people, was home to a third newspaper, the *New-England Courant*, printed by James Franklin.

The publication of competing newspapers encouraged the dissemination of an increasing diversity of news, and the politically partisan nature of London papers influenced colonial counterparts, tying the colonies to a British Atlantic more politically and religiously heterogeneous than some scholars have suggested.[54] In addition to connecting colonials to a Protestant interest, newspapers and broadsides remarked upon important divisions among Protestants. For example, during the crisis caused by the Atterbury plot, the *New England Courant* printed a letter attacking the untimely, anti-Catholic narrative about the pope published by its competitor, the *News-Letter*, and requested that the *Courant* reprint an interesting article, previously appearing in London's *Flying Post* which detailed Atterbury's crimes; an attempt to focus the audience's attention on British politics and religious disputes rather than on European Catholicism.[55] Furthermore, the *New England Courant*, rather than focusing primarily on foreign news, gave a great deal of attention to domestic and local news, often directly related to British events, and encouraged reader participation by printing unsolicited letters to the author or printer of the paper.

The three Boston newspapers competed for both a local and regional audience. This is clearly evidenced by the advertisements in the papers as well as letters written directly to the papers. The *New England Courant* received letters from subscribers in Boston as well as the neighbouring town of Canterbury. The *Courant* printed advertisements for products and people in Boston, Marblehead and Newport, Rhode Island, a town over seventy miles away.[56] John Winthrop of New London, Connecticut, noted that a number of people along the postal road from Boston through the Massachusetts hinterland were subscribers to the paper.[57] Moreover, certain subscribers would be likely to share the news, such as ministers who were interested in the local controversies related in the prints. In response to accusations of divisiveness, James Franklin mentioned in his *Courant* that several ministers 'both in town and country constantly take the *Courant*, which I believe they wou'd not do, if they thought it publish'd on purpose to bring their Persons into Disesteem'.[58] The *American Weekly Mercury*, published by Andrew Bradford in Philadelphia, was intended for a much wider audience than its New England peers. Even the name of the paper suggests the scope of the audience sought by Bradford. An advertisement in the first issue

---

54 Kidd, *The Protestant interest*, 51–73.

55 *NEC*, 17 June 1723, no 98.

56 *NEC*, 24 June 1723, no. 99.

57 Steele, *English Atlantic*, 122–3.

58 *NEC*, 4 Dec. 1721, no 18.

stated that subscriptions were available from Boston to Virginia indicating Bradford's ambitious intentions.[59] In fact, although Bradford did not enjoy the inherent advantages of being a postmaster, such as free delivery, two of his subscription agents were, and this dramatically extended the geographical scope of his distribution.[60] By the time of his third issue, Bradford was already advertising for a slave-owner in Virginia, suggesting a level of success for his ambitious distribution.[61] Within a few years the paper was also being printed and sold in New York by Bradford's father, likewise a printer.[62]

Accurate distribution figures for newspapers remain elusive but Campbell's *News-Letter* had a print run of 200–300 each week in its earliest years.[63] Subscriptions do not reveal the entirety of a newspaper readership. The *New-England Courant* printed advertisements for the Crown Coffee House, suggesting a symbiotic relationship in which the coffee house would have subscribed to the paper and provided a public venue for discussion of its contents, thereby further increasing the number of persons engaging with the news. The same was true for Bradford's *American Weekly Mercury* which also printed advertisements which implied knowledge of local public spaces including the local coffee house.[64]

In order to attract an audience, competing newspapers used a number of different London prints and regularly printed exact copies of articles from London papers. Articles were primarily drawn from Whig-leaning papers such as the *Flying Post*, the *London Journal* and *Political State*, allowing colonists a remarkable glimpse of British politics and an opportunity to interact in a transatlantic culture shaped by news and politics. The colonial prints do not exhibit the same clear Whig or Tory partisan divisions as were evident in London, and the *New England Courant* made the point that it was not designed as a 'Party paper'.[65] The fact that articles were more regularly drawn from Whig papers suggests a general sympathy towards the Whig party, although the High Church opinions of some of the *Courant's* Anglican authors suggest that they probably sympathised with the politics of British Tories.[66] Despite the largely one-sided perspective, the expanding number of London papers being used by colonial papers broadened engagement in the British political realm and expanded public debates. The greater diversity of news presented was caused, in part, by the increasing number of colonial

---

[59]   *AWM*, 22 Dec. 1719, no 1.

[60]   Clark, *Public prints*, 105.

[61]   *AWM*, 5 Jan. 1720, no. 3.

[62]   *AWM*, 9 June 1720, no. 25.

[63]   Clark, 'Periodicals and politics', 354.

[64]   *AWM*, 28 July 1720, no. 32.

[65]   *NEC*, 4 Dec. 1721, no 18.

[66]   David Sloan, 'The *New England Courant*: voice of Anglicanism, the role of religion in colonial journalism', *American Journalism* viii (1991), 108–14.

papers. As the ubiquity of the papers increased, their diverse materials reached an ever widening audience.

Colonial newspapers regularly printed stories relating to Jacobitism, reflecting both the importance of Jacobitism in Britain as well as the desire for this sort of news in the colonies, a desire highlighting the integration of political cultures. From 1704 to 1719 there was only one colonial newspaper and, as a result, important events during the reign of Anne, such as the trial of Henry Sacheverell in 1710 and the Jacobite rebellion of 1715, received less newspaper coverage than did later conspiracies or rebellions. The *News-Letter*, however, did provide its readers with a number of reports on the Jacobites in Britain. For example, in 1708, the paper reported in multiple issues on the attempted invasion of Scotland by the Jacobites and also provided its audience with reprints of addresses of loyalty to the queen from a number of Scottish towns and presbyteries.[67] The paper also reported on the tensions building in the wake of the Tory election victories following Sacheverell's trial in 1710.[68] By reading about and participating in shared anxieties, colonists were acting within an Atlantic public sphere as provincial Britons and, as such, were participating in elements of a predominantly Whig transatlantic political culture haunted by the spectre of Jacobitism. Moreover, news about Jacobitism did not remain confined to the printed page, but also informed local street theatre. As early as 1702 anti-Jacobitism merged with the anti-Catholic Pope's Day celebrations in Boston, during which the burning of effigies of the exiled Stuarts was a central feature.[69]

Newspapers and broadsides supported the appropriation of party language and partisanship in the colonies. Although establishing exactly who the readers were or exactly how many readers might have read such ephemeral literature is notoriously difficult, it is clear that that even a passing engagement with ideas might influence opinions. Contemporaries noted that familiarity with title pages was itself an act of reading. One author compared reading title pages to knowing a person by sight.[70] Thus, even seeing the titles of recently published books or pamphlets could increase awareness and influence understandings of current debates.

Following the failed rebellion of 1715, Benjamin Green, a printer in Boston, printed a copy of George I's 1716 speech to parliament decrying the Jacobite rebellion and its pernicious consequences.[71] Similarly, in 1715, Thomas Fleet reprinted a broadside, originally printed in London, instructing George's parliament to look into the treasons committed by previous parliaments, including the payment and arming of Jacobite clans in Scotland and the

---

[67] *BNL*, 7, 14 June 1708, nos 216, 217.
[68] *BNL*, 22 May 1710, 27 Dec. 1714, nos 319, 558.
[69] McConville, *The king's three faces*, 58–9.
[70] Nathaniel Mist, *Collection of letters*, i, London 1722, pp. v–vi.
[71] *His majesty's most gracious speech to both houses of parliament*, Boston 1716.

preparation for the return of the Pretender.[72] Though couched in ambiguous terms, this was clearly an attack on the Tory parliament in the last years of Anne's reign and reminded its readers of the Tories' open flirtations with Jacobitism. In 1716 a Boston paper printed an article on the Jacobite rebellion laying responsibility for the uprising at the feet of those who cried 'the Church in danger'. This paper reported on the outcome of the rebellion and, equally important, the involvement of high-ranking Tories such as Henry St John, Bolingbroke and Ormonde, further implicating the Tory party.[73] A broadside printed in Boston in 1715 entitled *An abstract of the French king's will* noted the Jacobite activities of the exiled Tories Bolingbroke and Ormonde in France, again reinforcing the notion that the previous Tory parliament and ministry had been, and continued to be, treasonous.[74] Moreover, in a reprint of the king's speech, George I was noted as having said that the crying out of 'the Church in danger' was the 'main artifice employed' in carrying out the rebellion.[75] Within another two months the paper was explaining in greater detail that what Tories meant when they claimed the Church was in danger was that the Church was to be governed by the formerly Lutheran George I. In March 1716 it informed its readers that 'had we been at a loss before to know what the faction [Tories] meant by their noise of the Church's being in Danger, they have now explained it, and boldly told us, that 'tis the excluding of the Pretender and fixing King George upon the throne', a commentary easily accessible to many colonists.[76]

Nor did the dangers associated with Toryism and Jacobitism apply only to events in Britain. Colonial officials parroted the king's speech, while applying it to the local context. In a speech printed first in New York and later in Boston's *News-Letter*, Robert Hunter, governor of New York, praised King George's defeat of his rebellious subjects. Hunter claimed that the rebels hid their disaffection in 'a pretended danger to the church' which 'created a real danger to the state', clearly drawing transatlantic parallels, to which colonists in New Jersey and New York could easily relate since Hunter was locked in a struggle with a High Church party. Hunter's speech would also have resonated with well-informed colonists in Boston like Cotton Mather, who was very aware that Hunter was 'encumbered by his enemies, who were all of the high church party'.[77] The continued publication of news about the rebellions and conspiracies along with the reprinting of Hunter's speech, in addition to tying

---

[72]   *Instructions by the citizens of London, to their representatives for the ensuing parliament*, Boston 1715.

[73]   BNL, 2 Jan 1715, 30 Jan 1716, nos 612, 615.

[74]   *An abstract of the French king's will*, Boston 1715.

[75]   BNL, 2 Jan 1716, no. 612.

[76]   BNL, 26 Mar. 1716, no 624.

[77]   BNL, 23 Apr. 1716, no. 628; Cotton Mather to Robert Hunter [c.1714], in *Selected letters of Cotton Mather*, ed. Kenneth Silverman, Baton Rouge, LA 1971, 205. For a fuller discussion of New York see chapter 5 below.

the colonists to Britain, also knit together disparate colonial political cultures. The printing of anti-Jacobite stories in the *News-Letter* hints at a local interest in Hunter's speech and provides evidence of a Boston community eager to participate in a trans-colonial and transatlantic public sphere.

Even after the 1715 rebellion, colonists continued to receive updates concerning Jacobite conspiracies. The Swedish plot of 1717 received mention in the papers with the *News-Letter* reporting that 'the Swedish envoy's papers were seized and it was discovered that there were thoughts of descending on Scotland'.[78] The regularity of news stories commenting on serious conspiracies after the '15 reinforced Whiggish fears of a Stuart restoration for many Britons, including those across the Atlantic, reminding them that disaffection was often masked in High Church Tory principles.

The emergence of a further three weekly newspapers by 1722 and the maturation of the press in Britain and the colonies meant that the Atterbury plot received significantly greater and more varied attention than had previous Jacobite conspiracies and rebellions. Information about a conspiracy against the crown began to filter into the colonies by October 1722. For example, on 11 October 1722 George I informed parliament of the discovery of a recent conspiracy designed to subvert his government in favour of a 'popish pretender'. A print of his speech was available in London that same day. Within two days, the speech was being published in London newspapers, including the *London Gazette*, the official government paper.[79] Two months later a copy of the speech was printed in Philadelphia's *American Weekly Mercury*. Not long after that, *The New England Courant* reproduced the speech with the brief disclaimer that although the speech had already been published in Boston, it 'may perhaps be new to many of our Country Readers'.[80] Further south, although there was no locally printed newspaper, Francis Nicholson, the governor of South Carolina, had received news of the plot by early January 1723, if not sooner, from his correspondents in Boston who had forwarded copies of Boston's newspapers.[81] The papers were soon full of reports relating a number of different arrests and discoveries. The *American Weekly Mercury* reported on the arrest of a Jacobite conspirator, a Captain Kelly, in London and by 1 November informed its readers of the arrest of Francis Atterbury.[82] Similarly, the *News-Letter* testified to Atterbury's arrest and confinement in the Tower of London.[83]

The huge variety of papers printed in London and imported into Boston also contributed to the diversity of news reports printed in the colonial papers. For

---

[78]   *BNL*, 22 Apr. 1717, no. 679.

[79]   *His Majesty's most gracious speech to both houses of parliament, on Thursday October 11, 1722*, London 1722.

[80]   *NEC*, 11 Feb. 1723, no. 80.

[81]   Nicholson to the Secretary, 11 Jan. 1722/23, SPG papers, RHL, ser. A, xvi. 95-9.

[82]   *AWM*, 11 Oct., 1 Nov. 1722, nos 148, 151.

[83]   *BNL*, 29 Oct. 1722, no. 978.

example, the *News-Letter* reprinted a satire about Atterbury originally printed in London's *Flying Post*,[84] while both Philadelphia's *American Weekly Mercury* and Boston's *News-Letter* reprinted from the *London Journal* some of the 'British Cato's lucubrations on the conspiracy'. The Cato publications were written by John Trenchard and Thomas Gordon, two staunch and outspoken Whigs. Bradford's *Weekly Mercury* went so far as to carry Cato's letters reflecting on the conspiracy for four consecutive weeks.[85] Colonists were also made privy to Atterbury's speech before the House of Lords during his trial for treason which was given seven consecutive weeks of coverage in Bradford's Philadelphia paper.[86]

News reporting the reality of Jacobitism or activities of Jacobites was not restricted to British figures. Local Jacobites also received attention in the press. In Philadelphia in 1721 the *American Weekly Mercury* recounted a speech by a local judge of the Admiralty given in judgement of 'two Persons, who were tried before him for Contempts against the King'.[87] The long-winded speech related their crimes including denying the king's title to the crown and 'compassing his death'.[88] One of the prisoners confessed and received the rather light punishment of standing 'under this court-house for the space of one hour on two Marked-Days, with one paper fixed on your Breast, and another on your back' marked with the words 'I stand here for speaking contemptuously against my sovereign Lord King George' and was fined twenty marks sterling. His more stubborn (or principled) compatriot refused to confess and was forced to stand 'in the pillory in this market-place, for the space of two hours on two market days' and after his time in the pillory he was to 'be tied to the tail of a cart and drawn round two of this city squares' and finally was to be whipped on his bare back with forty-one lashes and imprisoned.[89] This clearly demonstrates the existence of local Jacobitism in the public sphere both in print and street theatre. Moreover, the publication of the seditious words and the sentencing, along with the public punishments, illustrates the authorities' intention to discourage similar expressions of sedition while also suggesting that authorities suspected the existence of a larger community sympathetic to Jacobitism. Equally important, the punishments assigned provide reminders of the dangers faced by Jacobites who dared openly to express their views. Three weeks later, an abbreviated version of the judge's speech was printed in the *Boston News-Letter*, informing even more readers that Jacobitism and disdain for the Hanoverians was not confined to the British mainland and confirming the increasingly trans-colonial and transatlantic nature of the public sphere.[90]

---

84   *BNL*, 16 May 1723, no. 1007.

85   *AMW*, 11 Feb. 1723/4, 12 Mar. 1724, nos 217, 1050.

86   *AWM*, 10 Oct. 1723, nos 199, 200, 201, 202, 203, 204, 205.

87   *AWM*, 23 Mar. 1721, no. 66, 1.

88   Ibid.

89   Ibid. 3.

90   *BNL*, 10 Apr. 1721, no 891.

Readers did not simply receive the news. Through prints, they could participate in debates about Jacobitism sparked by news reports. In some ways partisan debates were encouraged by the colonial papers. For example, the *American Weekly Mercury* in Philadelphia devoted seven weeks to printing Francis Atterbury's speech during his trial for treason. It dedicated the following two weeks to British Whig responses to the bishop's speech, both taken from the *London Journal*. This provided readers with an opportunity to engage in debates roiling in Britain.[91] Similarly, a letter printed in the *American Weekly Mercury* in 1723, directly engaged with questions of loyalty when the author wrote 'as to the profession of loyalty, they are like those of friendship: what a multitude of them have our counties made in address to their sovereign ... when rebellion has been their intention?'[92] The *New England Courant* printed a letter reflecting on the doctrines of passive obedience and non-resistance which contested that 'upon the whole, it is much to be desired, that that [High Church] Party who have appropriated all Loyalty to themselves, would take care to shew it in something besides words' and hoped that they would 'practice according to the principles they profess and not pretend to believe that which in works they deny'.[93] In one of the most notable examples, the *American Weekly Mercury* advertised a discourse written by 'Philobangor' which attempted to harness public opinion by declaring itself printed on 'behalf of the Laity of Pennsylvania' against a minister who did not properly pray for the royal family in 1722. This demonstrates a keen colonial understanding of the recent religious debates dominated by Benjamin Hoadly, who was viewed as a menace to the High Church and Jacobites. It is worth noting that, in both cases, the minister and the author were keen to exploit the growing public sphere and find support amongst a broader audience.[94] Furthermore, that this pamphlet was written as a direct response to a sermon provides a helpful reminder that sermons were an integral part of a politicised and contested public sphere both in London and the British Atlantic world.[95]

As this advertisement suggests, sermons, broadsides and pamphlets, a staple of British Atlantic print culture, played a key role in disseminating controversies beyond the readership of newspapers. Such vehicles – especially spoken sermons – often aired more controversial ideas because they were less tractable to government influence than serial publications like newspapers.[96] If this is true of controversial pamphlets printed in the colonies, it is all the more true of British imports, which having been printed in Britain were all the more difficult to control in the colonies. Reprints of controversial British pamphlets

91   AMW, 10, 17 Dec. 1723, nos 211, 212.
92   AWM, 17 Mar. 1723/4, no. 221.
93   NEC, 24 June 1723, no. 99.
94   AWM, 8 Nov. 1722, no 152.
95   Farooq, *Preaching in eighteenth-century London.*
96   Shields, *Oracles of empire,* 100.

tied the colonists to metropolitan disputes. Thus, the New England controversialist John Checkley's publication in 1719 of Charles Leslie's *The religion of Jesus Christ the only true religion* (1697), sparked a fierce debate about Jacobitism in Boston which lasted over five years and spawned a number of pamphlets, countless newspaper articles and vehemently antagonistic sermons despite attempts by the Massachusetts authorities to end the debates through prosecution. Similarly, a 1714 pamphlet by Richard Steele (of *Tatler* and *Spectator* fame), entitled *The crisis; or, A discourse representing from the most authentick records, the just causes of the late happy revolution*, which discussed the succession crisis and the 'danger of a popish successor', was reprinted in Philadelphia in 1725, no doubt as a response to the aggressive High Church presence in the city.[97]

Residents of the colonies authored pamphlets intended to address local issues which were tied to transatlantic events. For instance, in 1724, terrified by the spectre of High Church Anglicanism, an anonymous author in Boston printed an attack on Anglicans and Jacobites entitled *The madness of the Jacobite party*.[98] The author used transatlantic events and ideas to great effect in his attack on a local High Church party linked in his mind to a transatlantic Jacobite threat. Similarly, an anonymous author identified only as 'a lover of the present happy constitution' printed, in Boston in 1723, a pamphlet titled *Gloria Britannorum*. It has been argued that the pamphlet was written by a young local Boston man, which suggests a vibrant, inclusive public sphere.[99] The poem celebrated George I's government

> Religious Truths in Purity shall shine,
> Tho' Rome in bloody league with *High-Church* join,
> To root them out, they firm as Heaven remain,
> whilst giddy Zealots spend their rage in vain,
> Unable to answer *Hoadly's* nervous strain.[100]

Furthermore in an 'ode on His Majesty's [George I] coronation' the poet wrote

> How did the palace ring with Joy!
> Sad Omen to the Rival Boy [James III],
> And all the Tory crew,
> Tho' forc'd some of 'em to proclaim
> Great Brunswick's Title and his Name,
> And swear Allegiance too.

---

[97] Richard Steele, *The crisis; or, A discourse representing from the most authentick records, the just causes of the late happy revolution*, Philadelphia 1725.

[98] Anon., *The madness of the Jacobite party, in attempting to set a popish pretender on the British throne*, Boston 1724.

[99] J. A. Leo Lemay, 'Francis Knapp: a red herring in colonial poetry', *New England Quarterly* xxxix (1966), 233–7.

[100] [Anon.], *Gloria Britannorum; or, The British worthies*, Boston 1723, 23.

The self same Faction that before
Had south th' Impostor to Restore,
And overturn the State;
Now perjur'd and the publick Scorn,
Yet serv'd his Triumph to adorn, Such was the Will of Fate.

Thus Heaven that orders humane things,
That governs States, and sets up Kings,
The Sovereigns Title own'd;
Baffled the ill Designs of those
That did his Settlement oppose,
And all their Schemes confound.[101]

The timing of this publication suggests that it was written in part as a response to the growth of a High Church party in Boston, thus providing a helpful reminder that local debates were all taking place within an Atlantic public sphere dominated by events in London.

Authors also consciously accepted the growth of public engagement and tried to harness or direct public opinion. Many of the pamphlets demonstrate a desire to engage with and involve the public. A number of the prints were addressed as 'recommended as proper to be put in the hands of the Laity' or written as a dialogue in which one of the characters is more plebeian so that a greater number of readers might sympathise with the argument.[102] David Shields has shown that Governor Robert Hunter's satirical play *Androboros* reflects a keen understanding of the value of the printed word in shaping transatlantic disputes. Shields suggests that the actual date when the play was printed is unknown and that the date provided on the publication, 1 August, the day of Queen Anne's death, is itself meant to be read as satire as it portrays the antagonist, the High Church Tory Francis Nicholson, as the walking dead, illustrating Hunter's understanding of the fall of the Tory party in the wake of Anne's death and the accession of George I.[103]

Almanacs too, were hugely popular. Prior to and concomitant with the growth and importance of newspapers, almanacs served as vehicles of information and entertainment.[104] In part because of their popularity, they were pulled into the orbit of party politics and Jacobitism, especially during the reign of

[101] Ibid. 26.

[102] Anon. *A modest proof of the order and government of the Church as settled by Christ and his Apostles*, Boston 1723; AWM, 8 Nov. 1722, no 152; John Checkley, *Choice dialogues between a godly minister and an honest countryman concerning election and predestination*, Boston 1720. For the helpful point about plebeian characters see Shields, *Oracles of empire*, 102.

[103] Shields, *Oracles of empire*, 143. For the play see Robert Hunter, *Androboros: a biographical* [sic] *farce in three acts, viz. The senate, The consistory, and The apotheosis*, New York 1714.

[104] Marion Barber Stowell, *Early American almanacs: the colonial weekday Bible*, New York 1977.

Anne.[105] Yet despite their popularity, almanacs have not featured prominently in many discussions of the public sphere, nor have they been examined as part of a Jacobite subculture. Almanacs provided readers with information about politically meaningful dates, such as a monarch's birthday or 5 November (Gunpowder Plot and William of Orange's invasion). Most almanacs in the British Atlantic were decisively Whig in tone and sympathy, decrying popery and the Jacobites and praising the Protestant succession. Many did not provide detailed commentary but they served as participatory voices in a larger public sphere by reinforcing certain contested holidays and histories. There were, however, notable exceptions to the Whig domination of almanacs. These propagated Tory principles and a thinly veiled Jacobitism by celebrating Tory holidays such as Restoration Day (29 May), the anniversary of the death of the 'royal martyr' Charles I (30 January), and wildly praising the firebrand cleric Henry Sacheverell.

In England, in the early years of the eighteenth century, John Gadbury and George Parker, two prominent almanac authors in London, used their almanacs to serve Tory party interests.[106] Parker attacked Whigs and celebrated Tory holidays. In his *Ephemeris* of 1707, he celebrated January as the 'month the Whigs have stained with such a blot' and in a chronology noted Archbishop Laud's sacrifice at the hands of 'fanatic fury', while refusing to mention 5 November. Parker also complained that his work had been censored by the Company of Stationers because he wanted to note the anniversary of the Rye House Plot.[107] In his preface to his 1711 *Ephemeris*, Parker praised the Tories and celebrated the parliamentary victory of 1710, stating that 1710 was the reverse of 1641 and that designs against the Church had been defeated.[108] He also exclaimed in verse 'but all that love the church their party fly,/ honour the Queen, on her success rely,/ stand to our text, and proudly own we're High'.[109] In this edition he listed Sacheverell's sermon of 5 November as a public holiday along with the Gunpowder Plot.[110]

The blurred lines between high Tory and Jacobite and the Jacobite undertones in any celebration of Sacheverell are suggestive of Parker's intentions. Contemporaries certainly believed that his loyalty was suspect. He was accused of disaffection, a claim that he vehemently denied.[111] Even more suggestive was the response of some of Parker's audience. There are handwritten notes on a copy of Parker's *Ephemeris* of 1712, which include an elegy to King James VII&II,

---

[105]   Bernard Capp, *Astrology and the popular press: English almanacs, 1500–1800*, London 1979, 238–55.

[106]   Ibid. 240–3.

[107]   George Parker, *Parker's Ephemeris for the year of our Lord 1707*, London 1707, 8, 17, 3.

[108]   Idem, *Parker's Ephemeris for the year of our Lord 1711*, London 1711.

[109]   Ibid. 6.

[110]   Ibid. 20.

[111]   Idem, *Parker's Ephemeris for 1707*, 3.

and the 'last dying prayer and words of John Matthews', a printer executed for printing Jacobite propaganda. Furthermore, in a copy of his 1713 *Ephemeris* there is a handwritten query on the birth of James, the Old Pretender. The notes in both of these almanacs suggest that Jacobites were a key demographic of Parker's audience.[112]

Party divisions are significant because similar distinctions between Whig and Tory almanacs are evident in colonial prints. New England almanacs were very much Whiggish in tone and often copied their English counterparts. Samuel Clough, an almanacker in New England, borrowed from the prominent English Whig almanacker John Partridge.[113] No almanacs published in Boston from 1702 to 1722 mentioned the Tory holidays 30 January or 29 May. However, they did celebrate 5 November and, after 1714, commemorated and memorialised George I's birthday (28 May) and accession (1 August).[114] In light of the Gunpowder Plot and William of Orange's invasion, Daniel Travis in 1716 celebrated November as a 'month of deliverance and month of praise'.[115]

Like Parker in London, Daniel Leeds, a prominent almanac author in New York, was the Tory counterpoint to a largely Whig-dominated field. Leeds's almanacs were written specifically for the mid-Atlantic market but he maintained that they would be useful from 'Newfound-Land to Carolina'.[116] The size of the audience for these almanacs is unknown but in 1707 Leeds mocks a competitor for printing 5,000 but not selling a quarter of them, suggesting that a print run of 5,000 was not unusual.[117] Leeds authored almanacs from 1687 to 1714 and there is a steady intensification in Tory thought and High Church views in those published between 1705 and 1714. This is due primarily to his conversion from Quakerism in the early 1700s

[112] Idem, *Parker's Ephemeris for the year of our Lord 1712*, London 1712; *Parker's Ephemeris for the year of our Lord 1713*, London 1713. Both copies are held at the British Library and are available through the electronic database *Eighteenth Century Collections Online*.

[113] Kidd, *The Protestant interest*, 74.

[114] For a representative selection of almanacs see Samuel Clough, *The New-England almanack for the year of our Lord, MDCCII*, Boston 1702; *The New-England, almanack for the year of our Lord, MDCCIII*, Boston 1703; and *Clough's farewell, 1708: an almanack for the year of our Lord (according to the common account) 1708*, Boston 1708; Nathaniel Whittemore, *An almanack for the year of our Lord MDCCVI*, Boston 1706; Daniel Travis, *An almanack of the coelestial motions for the year of the Christian epocha 1707*, Boston 1707, and *An almanack of the coelestial motions & aspects, for the year of the Christian aera, 1716*, Boston 1716; Edmund Holyoke, *An almanack of the coelestial motions, aspects and eclipses, &c. for the year of the Christian aera, 1713*, Boston 1713, and *An almanack of the coelestial motions, aspects and eclipses, for the year of the Christian aera, 1715*, Boston 1715; and Thomas Paine, *An almanack of the coelestial motions, aspects and eclipses, &c. for the year of the Christian aera 1718*, Boston 1718.

[115] Travis, *An almanack of the coelestial motions* (1716).

[116] Daniel Leeds, *The American almanack for the year of Christian account, 1705*, New York 1705, 1.

[117] Idem, *The American almanack for the year of Christian account, 1707*, New York 1707, 2.

and his association with John Talbot, the High Church and later nonjuring minister. In his almanac for 1705, Leeds makes clear that because 'the Church of England has made a good progress in these parts of America', his purpose for the almanac is, in part, to inform his readers of the practices and holidays of that Church.[118] He provides lengthy descriptions of the purposes and practices of the Church of England and of church festivals. He also commemorates 30 January as the day of King Charles I's martyrdom and 29 May, demonstrating a hyper-loyalty common to both High Church Tories and Jacobites. These are regular features in his almanacs, but in 1710 Leeds mentions in his timeline the birth of the 'pretended Prince of Wales'. Although at face value, this does not lend itself to a Tory or Jacobite celebration, the fact that Leeds mentions the date at all is significant. Not even Parker, a rabid English Tory, went so far as to mention the Pretender.[119] Moreover, Leeds had mentioned that his almanac would include the birthdays of successive heirs to the British throne, which makes his mention of the 'pretended' prince all the more intriguing especially in light of the fact that Leeds had stated the same aim in previous almanacs without mentioning him. Moreover, Leeds was a vestryman at St Mary's Church, Burlington, pastored by John Talbot. At the very least, Leeds's almanac served as a means of introducing a Tory political calendar into colonial political discourse and provides a helpful reminder of the numerous discourses shaping the transatlantic public sphere.

Despite the rapid growth of newspapers and an expanding print culture, a large proportion of communication undoubtedly remained personal in nature. The transatlantic public sphere was fuelled in part by private discourse. Cotton Mather, the eminent Congregationalist minister, was not content to receive news only from the newspapers, which he called a 'thin sort of diet'.[120] He received regular updates about Jacobitism in Scotland and England from his correspondents, Robert Wodrow and John Maxwell. In 1710 he was surprised by the arrival of a Captain Wentworth who carried 'a large cargo of intelligence' including fresh information about Sacheverell's trial and the consequent High Church mob riots and demonstrations in London. He quickly passed the information on to a friend stressing the value of the news by remarking that he offered 'nothing that you may expect from our public News-Letter'.[121] Benjamin Colman, a Presbyterian minister in Boston, also received valuable news from distant correspondents. In 1714, before the death of Queen Anne and the accession of George I, a friend wrote to Colman that 'the public affairs, here, look but darkly at present'. The friend was of the opinion that 'the number of those persons who wish well to the P——er [pretender] are lately

[118]   Idem, *The American almanack, 1705*, 2.
[119]   Idem, *The American almanack for the year of Christian account, 1710*, New York 1710, 10.
[120]   Cotton Mather to Stephen Sewall, 30 Jan. 1706, *Selected letters of Cotton Mather*, 70.
[121]   Mather to Samuel Penhallow, 22 May 1710, ibid. 86.

very much increased'.[122] In 1715 the Massachusetts agent Jeremiah Dummer sent to Colman copies of the nonjuror polemicist Richard Welton's 'sermon & preface' about the altar-piece which mocked White Kennett.[123]

In addition to illustrating the transmission of news, the letters exemplify the expectation that information concerning debates on party politics and Jacobitism would be of great interest to provincial Britons in the colonies. The former governor of Nova Scotia, Samuel Vetch, wrote to his father-in-law Robert Livingston of New York in 1714 that 'I can say nothing as yet of my business I came over upon, the violence of partys taking up every bodys time here.' Vetch also made certain to enclose a number of public prints relating to party controversies.[124] Similarly, a letter sent by James Heath, a Maryland merchant trading in London, to Elizabeth Bennett in Maryland in 1715 provided detailed information about the recent rebellion. Heath, a Catholic, noted that the 'Lords Derwentwater and Widdrington' had risen and that numerous other figures had been arrested in London, and also remarked upon the 'contagious distemper' which had disturbed the Tories after their proscription following George I's accession. Yet Heath was also concerned that he would be thought a 'Whig Papist' for wishing Catholics 'at all times would sit down quiet'.[125]

News about Jacobitism, although often transatlantic, also circulated throughout the colonies in the form of conversation. Of course conversation is an almost impossible source to recover but it is worth considering what little has survived in recorded form. In 1725, following the controversy and accusations of Jacobitism stirred up by John Checkley, Anglican ministers in New England planned to meet in order to send an address of loyalty to George I. Prior to the meeting, one of the ministers, George Pigot, engaged in a conversation with two of his fellow preachers who had been antagonistic to Checkley and his party. Pigot recorded the conversation as a dialogue in a letter to the bishop of London, thus providing a rare glimpse of a conversation which may suggest other like conversations taking place throughout the colonies:

> M[ossom]: What do you intend to do at your convention?
> P[igot]: We will agree on that when we come there. But however, I think it is our
> duty loyally to address his Majesty King George in a body...
> H[arris]: It is a contrivance of you and your party!
> P: I am no party man...
> M: What have they been doing at the westward?
> P: You will know better when you see Mr. Johnson [An SPG missionary to
> Connecticut]

---

[122] Samuel Bannister to Colman, 15 Feb. 1713/14, Colman papers.

[123] Jeremiah Dummer to Colman, 15 Jan 1714/15, ibid. For Welton and the altarpiece see chapter 2 above.

[124] Vetch to Robert Livingston, 7 June 1714, Livingston family papers, microfilm, reel 3.

[125] James Heath to Elizabeth Bennett, 18 Oct. 1715, Tilghman-Lloyd collections, Maryland Historical Society, Baltimore, Maryland 2001.

H & M: Why, what is the matter?

P: Gentlemen; I do not question but that you know better than I; especially since the society [SPG] have withdrawn their pension from one of their missionaries.

H: Who is that?

P: As if you do not know. Mr. Talbot. [Accused of having been ordained as a nonjuring bishop]

H: What were they doing?

P: What you would call Jacobitism. Why, gentlemen, we must take care to act nothing against the King's supremacy.[126]

One of the most notable features of this dialogue is the fact that it illustrates the verbal transmission of news over hundreds of miles. News of events in New York and New Jersey had travelled to Boston through a number of channels and was being discussed by interested parties. Not only was it being discussed, but the news had important ramifications for a group of clergymen in New England who had aligned themselves with a transatlantic Tory and High Church interest and were contemplating a political act as a direct response to events. News of a nonjuring bishop in the colonies and accusations of disaffection against some New England clergymen drove them to send an address of loyalty to the king.[127]

The prominence of party language in the incipient Atlantic public sphere indicates the significance of Jacobitism as an item of public interest. Yet Jacobitism and party divisions were not simply distant curiosities or interesting news. Although Jacobitism in Britain was on multiple occasions expressed openly in the form of rebellion or outspoken disaffection, it was in the interest of Jacobites to communicate and propagate their principles primarily through other, more subtle means. Due to the sedition inherent in Jacobite beliefs or behaviours, which were increasingly equated with treason, the penalties against them were severe. Consequently, explicit Jacobite sentiments were not often given a public airing.[128] The fact that Jacobite expressions were seditious negated their open inclusion in the public sphere. However, if explicitly Jacobite ideas could not be openly discussed in a rational-critical public sphere, they had to be disseminated by other means. Symbols, phrases and stories were appropriated by Jacobites in order to share messages and beliefs with fellow Jacobites.[129] This was equally true for those in the colonies. The governor of Maryland accused one official of 'visiting none but men of his own stamp, and drinking "to the man that should have his mare again,"

[126] George Pigot to the bishop of London [1725], *FP* iv. 157–8.

[127] 'Address of most of the clergy of Massachusetts, Connecticut, and Rhode Island, assembled in Newport, 21 July 1725, to George I', *FP* iv. 161–2.

[128] Pittock, 'Treacherous objects', 40–4.

[129] Monod, *Jacobitism*, 15–92.

a phrase used here to signify King James'. This provides, at the very least, a helpful example of the perception of associational language among Jacobites in the colonies.[130]

Nevertheless, there was a tension between the existence of a Jacobite subculture and an evangelical desire to draw as many people into the fold as possible. Many Jacobite items, words and symbols, intended to be understood by a select audience might also serve as veiled propaganda and were intended for public consumption as Jacobites hoped to convert those who might not share their political beliefs but could not do so in the context of an open debate. In Britain, Jacobite medals engraved with '*Reddite*' meaning 'return, render, restore or give back', served both as associational items and propaganda that could be passed around.[131] There were explicit Jacobite images and motifs which served the Jacobites well by veiling disaffection; those propagating such motifs often avoided prosecution by maintaining a harmless secondary meaning. The Stuart symbol of the Oak was a common Jacobite motif but it might also refer to Charles I or Charles II: illustrations of a restored oak might point the audience toward a future restoration of the exiled Stuarts or hearken back to the Restoration of Charles II in 1660.[132] Similarly, Latinate poetry was often appropriated by Jacobites but was usually safe because it referenced a classical author. Themes of regeneration and virility were all arrogated by the Jacobites in order to communicate with each other and proselytise outwith their community.[133] The press, material culture, art, poetry and architecture were all reflective of a communicative subculture. Jacobitism therefore existed both on the fringes of a legitimised public sphere and also as a counter-public estranged from participation in the public sphere.

The printing presses in Britain provided a constant source of Jacobite material. Broadsides, pamphlets and newspapers such as Charles Leslie's *Rehearsals* and Nathaniel Mist's *Weekly Journal* were Jacobite papers. According to Paul Monod, known Jacobite papers like Mist's spoke in a language which was easily decoded by those well versed in the subtext.[134] Mist's paper advocated passive obedience and non-resistance as a means of propagating the Jacobite ideology of legitimacy but he couched his disaffection in the well-worn terms favoured by High Church Anglicans. Thus, when a colonial pamphlet or sermon celebrated these virtues, opponents rightly viewed it with suspicion and hostility. Colonists were not averse to employing other Jacobite cant as Daniel Leeds did in his 1710 almanac in which he noted the birth of the Pretender and celebrated in verse the 'Golden Age yet to come'

---

[130] Governor and Council of Maryland to the Lords of Trade and Plantations, 1691, CSPC, item 2706.

[131] Monod, *Jacobitism*, 75.

[132] Guthrie, *Material culture of the Jacobites*, 44

[133] Pittock, 'Treacherous objects', 52-3; Guthrie, *Material culture of the Jacobites*, 22-6, 63-4.

[134] Monod, *Jacobitism*, 28.

by quoting Virgil's *Aeneid*. As Murray Pittock explained, the *Aeneid* 'became virtually a Jacobite document' due to the themes of restoration and exile.[135] Leeds writes 'from the hard Oak there shall, sweet Honey sweat forth and fall. The Sea shall then be quiet, no Ship shall range Abroad, her wares with others to exchange: Then every Land shall every thing produce, And then to plow the Earth they shall not use'.[136] Leeds's quotation incorporates a number of Jacobite themes including the Oak, regeneration and virility while simultaneously celebrating the Christian religion and the Latinate tradition, suggesting familiarity with a Jacobite subculture.[137] Yet Leeds's 1711 almanac contains what appears to be a virulently anti-Jacobite satire.[138] In his preface, Leeds states that he has 'presented you with the satirical verses ... upon the pretended Prince of Wales'.[139] However, given Leeds's connections to Talbot, it is possible that the anti-Jacobite rhetoric is simply an ironic means of propagating information about Jacobitism.[140] Similarly, the dissemination of Jacobite themes through sermons was commonly practised by preachers who veiled their disaffection in metaphor, as was demonstrated by Welton's farewell sermon in Philadelphia. Such veiled language allowed Jacobite ideas entry, even if only onto the fringes, into an increasingly expanding Atlantic public sphere.

Colonists directly engaged with Jacobitism and anti-Jacobite rhetoric through the exchange of information facilitated by an Atlantic public sphere. An emergent public sphere encouraged colonists to participate in transatlantic religious controversies and party political disputes associated with Jacobitism. The migration of Jacobites, either forced or voluntary, meant that there were communities well-versed in and receptive to expressions of a Jacobite subculture. Furthermore, these Jacobites were integrated into communities which shared many of their sympathies. The existence of such communities and the friendly reception of Jacobites within them increased fears of the threat posed by a transatlantic Jacobitism.

The emergence of newspapers further connected colonists to an Atlantic public sphere. Information about the increase and expression of Jacobitism in mainland Britain served to reinforce colonists' fears of the prevalence and significance of the Jacobite threat. In response to emerging local threats, colonists participated in religious and political debates as a means of combatting

[135]   Leeds, *The American almanack*, *1710*, 20; Murray Pittock, *The invention of Scotland: the Stuart myth and the Jacobite identity*, *1638 to the present*, London 1991, 58.

[136]   Leeds, *The American almanack*, *1710*, 20.

[137]   Guthrie, *Material culture of the Jacobites*, 63–4.

[138]   Daniel Leeds, *The American almanack for the year of Christian account*, *1711*, New York, 1711.

[139]   Ibid. 1

[140]   Howard Erskine-Hill, 'Twofold vision in eighteenth-century writing', *ELH* lxiv (1997), 903–24.

Jacobitism locally, but also in order to demonstrate loyalty to the Protestant succession. The emerging Atlantic public sphere did not, however, create a homogenous, Whig, transatlantic political culture, but rather tied colonists into complex British political and religious debates played out in varying ways in the individual colonies.

PART II

CASES

4

Occasional Conformity in Miniature: The Rage of Party, Jacobitism and Anti-Jacobitism in South Carolina, c. 1702–1716

South Carolina provides an intriguing case study of the significance of the relationship between party politics, Jacobitism and anti-Jacobitism in the British Atlantic world. Party-inspired imperial appointments, religious controversies and the diffusion of party political conflicts shaped a variety of local political conflicts and religious debates. Consequently, both Jacobitism and anti-Jacobitism, important elements of British political culture during the rage of party, were significant features of South Carolina's social and political culture in the early eighteenth century. Although there were no Jacobite-led or -inspired rebellions in the colony, there is sufficient evidence of Jacobite political culture to warrant further consideration and explanation. This in turn suggests the transatlantic scope of the rage of party. An examination of political and religious controversies in South Carolina therefore provides a fuller understanding of the development of Britain's transatlantic political culture.

South Carolina possessed a distinct history, society and practice of politics that differentiated it from the Mid-Atlantic colonies, New England, England, Scotland and Ireland. First, South Carolina was a proprietary colony: it was the private possession of a group of individuals. The crown therefore had little influence over political appointments, which were almost exclusively the preserve of the proprietors, most of whom were located in England. Thus the political inclinations of the proprietors had great impact on political life in the colony. South Carolina was also a plantation society, dominated by a handful of elites. Moreover, early in the eighteenth century it lacked the vibrant, local print culture which was coming to fruition in New England and the mid-Atlantic colonies. In some respects this encouraged a more insular development, and yet, despite its unique attributes and the absence of an indigenous print culture, the colony was assimilated into a larger transatlantic political culture dominated by party political disputes imbued with the rhetoric of Jacobitism and anti-Jacobitism.

There are numerous examples of accusations of Jacobitism in early eighteenth-century South Carolina. Jacobitism, however, does not usually feature prominently in the historiography. The few mentions of Jacobitism and the colony together in historical works are usually with reference to the importation of Jacobite convicts at the request of, and purchased by, the lieutenant governor Robert Daniell in 1715–16 as a means of enlisting manpower in the

Yamassee war of 1715.[1] The other significant association of Jacobitism and South Carolina was made by Charles Petrie in his rather bold and somewhat misleading claim that all of the clergy in South Carolina in 1715 were Jacobites or harboured Jacobite sympathies.[2] These claims invite closer attention.

In South Carolina, evidence of a Jacobite political culture and accusations of Jacobitism against the governors and Anglican clergymen during periods of intense political conflict reflect elements of a contested, transatlantic language of party politics shared among Britons in the Atlantic world. This chapter argues that expressions of Jacobitism and anti-Jacobitism in the increasingly party-infused political language of South Carolina, especially in debates surrounding the role of the Anglican Church and beyond, reveal an important aspect of political and cultural cohesion with England, Scotland and Ireland. It first examines the transatlantic context of South Carolina's religious and political controversies, focusing primarily on the political debates surrounding the passage of acts establishing the Church of England in South Carolina in the early eighteenth century. It then explores how these debates were instrumental in extending the rage of party across the Atlantic, thereby fostering Whig and Tory political cultures in the colony. Accusations of Jacobitism and evidence of a Jacobite political culture were fundamental to these developments and provide a compelling lens through which to view the development of transatlantic politics.

South Carolina in the late seventeenth and the early eighteenth century was a religiously diverse and severely fractured political polity. Charleston, the capital, was a hotbed of conflict. Arguments over the validity and legality of differing forms of religious worship divided the populace in Carolina and the proprietors in London. A succession of governors, who sought both to further the aims of their patrons, the proprietors, and individual profit, came and went with a rapidity that only aggravated existing conflicts, decreased stability and increased political animosity. There were no less than eleven different governors during the seventeen-year period from 1685 through 1702, and many of them left office in disgrace after having unsuccessfully navigated Carolina's dangerous political waters. The rise of opposing local factions in the late seventeenth century played a major role in destabilising the government: factions were quite adept at working towards the removal of political opponents. For many years no single issue dominated the political landscape and factions were divided over questions as diverse as religion, trade with Native Americans and proprietary quitrents.[3] Gideon Johnston, the bishop of London's commissary in South Carolina from 1707 to 1715, demonstrated the depth and rancorous

---

[1]   Sankey, *Jacobite prisoners*, 70–1.

[2]   Petrie, *The Jacobite movement*, 73.

[3]   L. H. Roper, *Conceiving Carolina: proprietors, planters, and plots, 1662–1729*, New York 2004; Eugene Sirmans, *Colonial South Carolina: a political history, 1663–1763*, Chapel Hill 1966.

nature of the political conflicts when in 1708 he expressed his distaste for the people of South Carolina, caustically describing them as 'the most factious and seditious people in the whole world'.[4]

Factional conflict has been explained variously as a result of the lack of strong proprietary control, a progressive march towards religious freedom, or even as an entrenching of the power of the local landed elites.[5] Recent studies have placed it within an Atlantic framework, providing a reminder that understanding the transatlantic context is essential for understanding local colonial politics.[6] The prevailing view is that the primary transatlantic direction came from Whig archetypes like Daniel Defoe, John Locke or Anthony Ashley Cooper, 1st earl of Shaftesbury, an early proprietor of the colony and author of the Fundamental Constitutions. Any apparently Tory influence is characterised as the meddling of British Tory magnates who were putting 'the best interest of the colony behind metropolitan political interests'.[7] Others have noted that 'imperial concerns drove local politics only intermittently' or that imperial interactions involved little more than factious Carolinians using 'transatlantic connections to local effect'.[8] Studies of the Anglican Church in the colonies assert that 'partisans of the Proprietors' (rather than ideological adherents of Whig and Tory parties) sought establishment.[9] It is arguable that such statements downplay the viciousness of Britain's party politics and the transatlantic implications of the ideological divisions undergirding them, thus providing an incomplete picture of the transatlantic nature of South Carolina's politics. From 1702 to 1716 colonial factions were not mere satellites, but were completely absorbed into Britain's rage of party.

The political discourse in South Carolina, and the specific language used in local political controversies, underscore a much clearer contemporary understanding of English and Scottish politics than has previously been identified. Analysis of Jacobitism, nonjuring and Toryism amongst colonists and church officials over the period from 1702 to 1716 indicates a considerable degree of political and cultural integration with the British Atlantic world, especially among elites. Moreover, responses to Jacobitism and nonjuring in Carolina

---

[4] Gideon Johnston to the bishop of Sarum, 20 Sept. 1708, SPG papers, RHL, ser. A, iii. 67.

[5] Robert Weir, *Colonial South Carolina: a history*, Millwood, NY 1983; John Brinsfield, *Religion and politics in colonial South Carolina*, Easley, SC 1983; Roper, *Conceiving Carolina*.

[6] Weir, *Colonial South Carolina*, 75–104; Brinsfield, *Religion and politics in colonial South Carolina*, and 'Daniel Defoe: writer, statesman, and advocate of religious liberty in South Carolina', *South Carolina Historical Magazine* lxxvi (1973), 107–11; L. H. Roper, 'Conceiving an Anglo-American proprietorship: early South Carolina history in perspective', in L. H. Roper and B. Van Ruymbeke (eds), *Constructing early modern empires: proprietary ventures in the Atlantic world, 1500–1750*, Leiden 2007, 389–410.

[7] Roper, *Conceiving Carolina*, 131.

[8] Weir, 'Shaftsbury's darling', 385; Roper, *Conceiving Carolina*, 121.

[9] Bell, *Imperial origins of the king's Church*, 39.

illustrate the lasting significance of Jacobitism throughout the British Atlantic world while simultaneously demonstrating both change and continuity within Jacobite political culture. A clear link with the English political scene in the early eighteenth century, which necessarily involves an appreciation of Jacobitism, allows a much fuller understanding of politics in South Carolina and illustrates another aspect of the multi-faceted nature of the British Atlantic world.

There was, in South Carolina, a definite lack of consistent, organised control or direction from England. Due in part to the existence of differing spheres of authority, the Church of England, the Crown and the proprietors all initially lacked the ability to effectively exercise their power to the fullest in Carolina, although the Church and Crown increased their influence and control over time. The proprietors, of course, exerted a great deal of influence over appointments in the colony and were instrumental in shaping its political development. However, proprietors were not a politically homogenous group: the proprietary board included both Whigs and Tories. The diversity of their views on party politics and religious controversies in England directly influenced and shaped the political climate in South Carolina.

The succession of Queen Anne in 1702 brought a staunch Anglican, who was more in sympathy with High Church position within the Church of England, onto the political scene. During the latter years of William's reign and the early years of Anne's, questions about the established Church's role in society became increasingly important: the position of the Church and the potential danger of dissent were major points of contention between the Tory and Whig parties.[10] Fears of the spread of atheism, heresy and the growth of dissent in the wake of the Toleration Act of 1689 caused general unease among High Church Tories, an unease which led them to rally around cries of 'the Church in danger'. High Church Tories were determined to protect the Church from dissent and what were perceived as the Low Church attitudes of the Whig bishops. Such attitudes were believed to assist and encourage the spread of atheism and heresy by weakening the established Church. This resulted in attempts in 1702, 1703 and 1704 to pass bills against occasional conformity (taking holy communion in the Church of England once a year for the sole purpose of qualifying for office). High Church Tories viewed dissenters as rebels in waiting and thought that the practice of occasional conformity was little more than a Trojan horse; a means of destroying the established Church of England and encouraging heresy and atheism.[11] To prevent this, they were prepared to use controversial methods to force the passage of the act including tacking it on to an appropriations bill. The debates about occasional conformity in England illustrate an important aspect of the philosophical divide between High Church Tories and their Whig opponents. Tories advocated an ecclesiology in which the Church

10   Holmes, *British politics*; Harris, *Politics under the later Stuarts*.
11   Harris, *Politics under the later Stuarts*, 152–3.

and the State were interdependent and believed that dissent and schism in the Church would ultimately destroy both Church and the State.[12] Moreover, the Tory impulse to strengthen the Established Church as a means of combating irreligion and possible dissenting sedition was not confined to England. The Irish parliament, controlled by High Church Tories, passed a Test Act in 1704 barring dissenters from qualifying for office: a clear imitation of what was going on in England.[13] In many respects, the rancorous divisions caused by competing views regarding the relationship of the Anglican Church with the British state reverberated throughout the British Atlantic.

Religious controversies in South Carolina, therefore, fit comfortably within a larger Atlantic context. There were two obvious parallels. First, the colonies, like England, Scotland and Ireland were influenced by a resurgent High Church zeal which also witnessed the increased importance of the Society for the Propagation of the Gospel in Foreign Parts. The Society had received its royal charter from William in 1701 and throughout the reign of Anne received considerable support from the monarchy. Its aim was to provide ministers for the colonies in the hope of strengthening the presence of the Church of England in areas that could not afford or attract ministers for themselves. Reports decrying the disorganised state of the Anglican Church in the colonies and a general sense of religious ignorance and apathy gave impetus to the society, which was strengthened by the support of an increasingly assertive Anglican establishment. George Keith, the society's first missionary, viewed the prominence of Quakerism and dissent as a danger which needed to be corrected and noted that South Carolina had a large percentage of dissenters.[14] In order to combat the growth of religious sectarianism and promote the established Church, the SPG quickly became active proponents of Anglican worship in the colonies, including South Carolina. Along with the export of ministers and books, an assertive Anglicanism facilitated the importation of ideology and its attendant views of politics: ministers often became very involved in colonial disputes about the Church. The first SPG missionary to South Carolina, Samuel Thomas, arrived in 1702. Soon officiating with the approval of Governor Nathaniel Johnson in the parish of St James, Goose Creek, Thomas would quickly draw down upon himself the ire of Johnson's political opponents.

English politicians also played prominent roles in spreading a transatlantic High Church ideology through influence and appointments. One of the more vocal leaders of the High Church Tory party movement to discourage dissent and strengthen the established Church was John, Lord Granville. An influential English politician, Granville was also palatine of the South Carolina

[12]   John Flaningan, 'The occasional conformity controversy: ideology and party politics, 1697-1711', JBS xvii (1977), 38-62.

[13]   Hayton, Ruling Ireland, 186-208; Connolly, Religion, law, and power, 163-4.

[14]   George Keith, A journal of travels from New-Hampshire to Caratuck, on the continent of North-America, London 1706.

proprietors and a political ally of Daniel Finch, earl of Nottingham, a leader of the Tory party and one of the most vocal high Tories in England.[15] As palatine Granville served as a vital connection between the party politics of Britain and of South Carolina. He possessed an enormous amount of influence over appointments in the colony and had been responsible for appointing Johnson, a Jacobite, as governor in 1702.[16] This was not Johnson's first appointment. He had begun his political career as an MP under Charles II whom he had supported during the Exclusion Crisis. Appointed governor of the Leeward Islands by James II&VII, in the uncertain period surrounding the revolution in 1688 and the invasion of William of Orange he continued to support James. There were even accusations then that Johnson planned to hand the islands over to the French as a means of supporting James II&VII's claims. After resigning as governor of the Leeward Islands because of his fervent belief in the Anglican doctrines of passive obedience and non-resistance, Johnson moved to South Carolina and soon set his mind on becoming governor there. In the early 1690s the proprietors wrote to the current governor Phillip Ludwell instructing him to keep an eye on Johnson despite the fact that it was unlikely that he would gain another post under William.[17] Johnson's distinguished Tory pedigree was accompanied by a level of notoriety.[18]

Johnson's eventual appointment as governor illustrates the political rehabilitation and legitimation of Jacobitism during the reign of Anne. Johnson had remained a lay nonjuror and a Jacobite until after the death of James II&VII, only swearing the required oaths in 1702 as a prerequisite to becoming governor of Carolina.[19] As a High Church Tory and Jacobite, he shared many of the same political ideas and goals as his patron Lord Granville. Granville, for his part no doubt very aware of Johnson's political leanings and his Jacobite past, probably encouraged him to establish the Church of England in South Carolina as part of a larger attempt to strengthen the Church throughout England's imperial possessions. Tory pressure for establishment was thus now associated not only with a Jacobite-friendly party in England, but also with a Jacobite governor.

Johnson's aim to establish the Church of England in Carolina coincided with a High Church Tory resurgence throughout the British Atlantic. Fearing factionalism, republicanism, atheism, irreligion and the loss of ecclesial dominance, politicians, the bishop of London and members of the SPG pushed

---

[15] For Granville's biography see Hayton, Cruickshanks and Handley, *History of parliament.*

[16] Extract from the Journal of the Assembly of Carolina, 29 June 1702, *CSPC,* item 676.

[17] Lords proprietors of Carolina to Governor Philip Ludwell, 6 Apr. 1693, *CSPC,* 1693, item 269.

[18] 'Copy of John Burrowe's narrative sent to Lord Nottingham by Mr Henley of Bristol', 22 June 1689, *CSPC,* item 206; Joseph Crispe to Colonel Bayer, 10 June 1689, *CSPC,* item 193; Roper, *Conceiving Carolina,* 58–60.

[19] Extract from the Journal of the Assembly of Carolina, 29 June 1702, *CSPC,* item 676.

to establish the Church of England.[20] High Church Tories like Granville and Johnson believed that only a strong presence of the Established Church could hold back the tide of dissent and prevent schism.

The Tory offensive in the colonies began in 1703 when the South Carolina assembly, under the Johnson's leadership, passed an act for the 'effectual suppression of blasphemy and profaneness'.[21] This act, the first passed by Johnson's government, illustrates the imperial awakening of the Church encouraged by a transatlantic Toryism and it also shows the determination of Johnson to make the welfare of the Church of England a priority.[22] The act, in part a response to events in England, provides an early example of the emergence of a transatlantic Church in South Carolina.[23] It was the first step towards a stronger Church presence and the first of many acts aimed at strengthening the Anglican Church in South Carolina.

Not long after, in May 1704, Johnson, with the support, if not actual encouragement and direction of Granville, succeeded in passing Test Acts, followed in November of the same year by an act establishing the Church of England in South Carolina.[24] The Test Act prohibited anyone who did not conform to the Church of England and who refused to receive the sacrament of the Lord's Supper 'according to the rites and usage of the said Church' from serving in the assembly in language designed to mimic the Test Acts and the Occasional Conformity Acts proposed in England in 1702, 1703 and 1704.[25] Proposing such an act assumed the successful passage of occasional conformity acts in England, suggesting knowledge of the English debates and a desire to conform to English law.[26] It also demonstrates the difficulties caused by the time lag created by the vast expanse of the Atlantic Ocean. Critics noticed the assumption underlying the passage of the acts and used pamphlets printed in London to attack the bill because, after the failure of the English parliament to pass acts banning occasional conformity, the South Carolina law did not conform to English law as its authors had anticipated.[27]

---

[20] Francis Le Jau to the Secretary, 30 June, 1707, and Johnston to the bishop of Sarum, 20 Sept. 1708, SPG papers, RHL, ser. A, iii. 142, 97; Fredrick Dalcho, *An historical account of the Protestant Episcopal Church in South Carolina, from the first settlement of the province to the War of the Revolution*, Charleston, SC 1820, 41.

[21] Dalcho, *An historical account*, 41

[22] Nicholas Trott, *The laws of the province of South Carolina*, Charleston 1736, 50.

[23] Dalcho, *An historical account*, 41.

[24] Trott, *Laws of South Carolina*, 105–6.

[25] Dalcho, *An historical account*, 53; Defoe, *Party-tyranny*.

[26] *Copy of an act lately passed in Carolina and sent over to be confirmed here by the Lord Granville*. See also BL, MS Add. 61647, fos 89–92.

[27] Ibid; Defoe, *Party-tyranny; or, An occasional bill in miniature: as now practised in Carolina humbly offered to the consideration of both Houses of Parliament*, London 1705, 15, and *The case of Protestant dissenters in Carolina, shewing how a law to prevent occasional conformity there, has ended in the total subversion of the constitution in Church and State: recommended to the serious consideration of all that are true friends to our present establishment*, London 1706, 28.

A period of intense debate over the role of the Church in the colony followed. Riots, accusations and physical conflict became staples of the local political discourse,[28] together with the outpouring of accusations of sedition, faction, disaffection, nonjuring and Jacobitism. Strangely, these accusations, have been relegated to the bin of absurdities, interpreted as little more than anecdotal examples of an overheated factional rhetoric. However, in reality, they demonstrate the integration of South Carolina's politics into those of Britain. Accusations of Jacobite intrigue aimed at Johnson and his allies unsurprisingly went unheeded by Tory proprietors in Britain. Moreover, Johnson was not the only Jacobite involved in South Carolina's political debates. Indeed, one of his primary detractors was a former nonjuror.[29] The rhetoric and language used in the arguments surrounding the Test and Establishment Acts decisively marks the assimilation of South Carolina into the transatlantic rage of party: the appropriation of party language and accusations of Jacobitism in South Carolina in the first decade of the eighteenth century is an early manifestation of the transatlantic nature of British party politics. The role of the Anglican Church and the proper place in society of those dissenting from the Church were deeply controversial issues in English politics that did more than anything to divide the Whig and Tory parties.[30] The debates surrounding the Occasional Conformity Acts in England were some of the most polarising of the era and contemporaries understood that events in South Carolina were an extension of English politics;[31] they reflected English Whig and Tory party politics. What has been viewed as strong-arm tactics employed by a local faction is more accurately defined as an Atlantic extension of the political crises raging in England.

Responses to the passage of the acts demonstrate the complexity of a British Atlantic political culture. Opponents utilised a number of connections with England to pursue redress and the repeal of the new laws. Furious at the passage of the act, dissenters in Carolina clearly understood the transatlantic context of the debate and sent an agent, John Ashe, to bring their complaints before the proprietors. The grandson of a member of the Long Parliament and the son of a Whig MP active during the Exclusion Crisis, Ashe had an impressive Whig pedigree.[32] Thus South Carolina's controversial church acts stirred up debates in London as well as in Charleston, illustrating the significance of the Atlantic context and tying South Carolina to an incipient public sphere. The Whig interest in Carolina could also boast of allies among the proprietors. John Archdale, a Quaker, former governor of the colony and

[28]   Defoe, *Party-tyranny*, 7.

[29]   Roper, *Conceiving Carolina*, 136; Dalcho, *An historical account*, 82.

[30]   Holmes, *British politics*, 13–81

[31]   Defoe, *Party-tyranny*, and *The case of Protestant dissenters*.

[32]   David McCord Wright, 'Mr. Ash: a footnote in constitutional history', *South Carolina Historical Magazine* lxiii (1962), 227–31.

current proprietor, was a staunch Whig and supported the dissenting interest in the colony.

Unfortunately for the dissenting interest, Ashe died in London before he was able to present their complaints properly. Joseph Boone was sent to replace him and he duly placed a petition before the proprietors. Granville famously responded: 'It [the Test Act] is a prudential act in me, and I will do as I see fit. I see no harm at all in this Bill and I am resolved to pass it.'[33] He was also reported to have said to John Archdale that 'you are of one opinion, and I am of another, and our lives may not be long enough to end the controversy. I am for this bill and this is the party that I will head and Countenance'.[34] This attitude did not bode well for the future prospects of dissent in the colony.

After failing to find redress among the proprietors, Boone sought to bring the issue before parliament. In an anonymous pamphlet 'humbly offer'd' to both houses of Parliament' entitled The case of the Church of England in Carolina, the author employed English party rhetoric, demonising the High Church party in Carolina by tying them to Toryism and Jacobitism.[35] He informed his readers that Governor Johnson, the leader of the High Church faction, had given up his post as governor of the Leeward Islands because of his disaffection to the Revolution, and reminded them that Johnson had 'lived privately as a Non-Juror until the death of King James'.[36] He also noted that by not allowing Protestant dissenters to sit in the assembly, the High Church faction would be able to seize total control because 'there are but very few moderate Churchmen in the province'.[37]

Boone also enlisted the aid of Daniel Defoe to make the case for the dissenters with parliament and English public opinion. Boone's timing was propitious. The Whigs had won important parliamentary victories in England in 1705, based largely on their ability to disparage High Church Tories for their overzealous, anti-dissenter pressure for acts against occasional conformity.[38] Defoe and Boone joined forces in an attempt to have the South Carolina acts repealed but Defoe probably took the leading role, at least in London, due in part to his recent participation in the previous Whig propaganda offensive. He composed two pamphlets in support of Carolina's dissenters, published in 1705 and 1706, attacking the acts and asking parliament to save Carolina from High Church tyranny and to promote the toleration of dissent in the colony. While the desire for toleration may seem benign, the accusatory

[33]   Dalcho, An historical account, 54; Defoe, The case of Protestant dissenters, 39.

[34]   Defoe, Party-tyranny, 27.

[35]   For similarities in England see Sirota, The Christian monitors, 167.

[36]   The case of the Church of England in Carolina, [London, c. 1706], 2.

[37]   Ibid.

[38]   James Richards, Party propaganda under Queen Anne: the general elections of 1702–1713, Athens, GA 1972; Speck, Tory and Whig, 98–109.

language used by Defoe was infused with party rhetoric and was intended to conjure up images of past persecutions and recent party machinations. Defoe described South Carolina's politics in terms of transatlantic party interests. In *Party-tyranny* he argued that the 1704 Act was designed and instigated by an imperial 'faction' led by the Granville and that this faction was bent on imposing a 'high-church-tyranny'.[39] He further argued that the 'designs of the party [i.e. Tories]' behind the tacking and occasional conformity bills was civil and ecclesiastical tyranny and went on to claim that the party in Carolina were 'encouraged from the same expectation'.[40] Defoe defined Whig and Tory party interests according to religion. Using England's emerging public sphere to support a transatlantic Whig and dissenting interest, he reprinted, as an addendum to one of his own pamphlets, a petition authored by John Ashe which insinuated that members of South Carolina's government favourable to the Tory interest were disloyal to the king and participated in secret trade with the French – a particularly egregious breach of trust during the early years of the War of the Spanish Succession.[41] The idea that the Tory party was a party of Jacobites and Francophiles, especially following the passage of an act of indemnity in 1703, allowing former Jacobites to return to Britain, played on existing Whig and dissenting fears of a Catholic, Jacobite threat. Though Defoe – through Ashe – refrained from making specific accusations, Johnson's Jacobite past would have lent credibility to what was being said.[42]

The Whiggish political pamphlets written by Defoe and Boone met a heated Tory response. The proprietors who favoured the Establishment Acts made very clear their fears of unchecked dissent in a printed defence that they presented to the House of Lords in Westminster. This employed High Church rhetoric, claiming that dissenters were attempting to get the 'Government of the Colony into their Hands'. They argued that those 'fixing themselves to no one Communion cannot be denominated of either'; a deliberate echoing of arguments against occasional conformity in England which were designed to stir up English Tory sympathies by reminding them of the motivations underpinning recent debates in England.[43] They were also quick to discredit their opposition by claiming that whatever kindness towards the Church was pretended by Boone, the South Carolina agent, 'tis well known, he designs no

---

[39] Defoe, *The case of Protestant dissenters*, 28, and *Party-tyranny*, 1.

[40] Idem, *Party-tyranny*, 28.

[41] Ibid. 73. For a detailed examination of the significance of trade and exchange during the War of the Spanish Succession see Guy Rowlands, *Dangerous and dishonest men: the international bankers of Louis XIV's France*, Basingstoke 2014, 73–4. See also G. N. Clark, 'War trade and trade war, 1701–1713', *Economic History Review* i (1928), 262–80, esp. p. 271.

[42] Roper, *Conceiving Carolina*, 102.

[43] Anon, *An account of the fair and impartial proceedings of the Lords proprietors, governour and council of the colony of South Carolina, in answer to the untrue suggestions, contained in the petition of Jos. Boon and others, and of a paper intituled, The case of the Church of England in Carolina*, London 1706, 2.

kindness to her; but endeavours to shelter his bad designs under the shew of kindness, for no establishment of the Church or ministry in those parts can be acceptable to him'.[44] Unfortunately, the Tory proprietors, led by Granville, also had to defend Johnson against accusations of Jacobitism.

The debates filtered down into South Carolina society. Dissenting opponents of the acts in South Carolina also utilised extra-parliamentary means to discredit them and garner sympathy for South Carolina's dissenters. In 1705 Archibald Stobo, a Scottish Presbyterian minister in Charleston, wrote to the moderator of a presbytery in Edinburgh, noting that 'the parliament being met in Dec. last, did make an act against the Decenters to the Church of England'. He decried the passage of the act and commented that he hoped 'God in his wise providence shall soe rule the hearts as to make void and null the forsaid act'. He also remarked on the immediate, pernicious consequences of the act, noting that some of his parishioners were conforming to the Church of England for worldly gain and that the act would 'prove of fatal consequence to my indeavors'.[45] Similarly, a number of Presbyterian dissenters in South Carolina petitioned the Moderator of the General Assembly of the Church of Scotland to request help in protesting against the act. The aim was to generate sympathy among Presbyterians in Scotland in order further to inflame a transatlantic dissenting Whig interest against the Church of England and High Church Tories.[46]

The content, timing and ideological ramifications of the debates, reflecting as they did recent debates in parliament, drew the attention of the English House of Lords and even that of the queen. The House of Lords voted the acts unlawful and appointed a committee to address the queen with the intention of using 'the most effectual Methods to deliver the said Province from the arbitrary Oppressions under which it now lies, and to order the Authors thereof to be prosecuted according to Law'.[47] A Whig-dominated committee, appointed to draft the address and desirous of prosecuting the South Carolina proprietors responsible for the act, was held back by the presence of the Tory Simon Harcourt.[48] However, although its efforts to prosecute the authors of the acts were unsuccessful, in June 1706 the queen, on the advice of the House of Lords and the SPG, made null and void Carolina's Test and the Establishment Acts.[49]

The Whig Junto's involvement in the repeal of the acts, following as it did on the heels of the Tories' failure to pass Occasional Conformity Acts

[44] Ibid. 4.

[45] Archibald Stobo to William Carstares, Moderator of the Presbytery of Edinburgh, 10 Sept. 1705, NAS, CH1/2/24/2/3, 224–7.

[46] *LP* xvii. 105.

[47] 'House of Lords Journal Volume 18: 9 March 1706', *Journal of the House of Lords*, XVIII: 1705–1709, <British History Online, http://www.british-history.ac.uk/report.aspx?compid =29452&strquery=carolina>, accessed 13 Mar. 2013.

[48] Brinsfield, *Religion and politics in colonial South Carolina*, 30.

[49] Order of the Queen in Council, 10 June 1706, CSPC, item 366

in England, suggests that this public debate had repercussions reaching far beyond South Carolina's factional disputes. Although one recent account has argued that the passage of the acts had 'little to do with religion', Johnson's past and personal devotion to the Anglican Church, and Granville's support for the act, suggests that this was much more than an attempt to put 'the best interests of the Colony behind metropolitan political interests'.[50] The Atlantic context, which included similar acts, indicates the diffusion of the language and practice of party politics in the reign of Queen Anne.

The repeal of the acts precipitated a new round of debate. Johnson and his allies immediately began to work towards passing a new establishment act which would be acceptable to the queen, the Church and the Whig-dominated House of Lords. They succeeded in passing a new act in November 1706 which did not include Test Acts barring dissenters from office.[51] Dissenters and their Low Church allies, elated by their recent victory, were caught unawares and lashed out, arguing that the new establishment acts, though less oppressive than the previous ones, were destructive to the province and that they were being forced upon the populace by 'profligate men' who were 'pretended to be of the Church of England'.[52] The church party retaliated in kind, playing up Tory fears that the Church was in danger and noting that the Church was likely to be destroyed if the new acts were repealed.[53] Furthermore, it was reported in Britain that the High Church party in Carolina was utilising the Tory slogan of 'the Church in danger'. Abel Boyer, a Whig critic of the High Church party in Britain and Carolina, complained that High Church Tories in Carolina were unscrupulously drawing supporters in to vote for the act by bullying some and by scaring others, warning them about the dangers to the Church from the dissenting party.[54]

One noteworthy aspect of the debates was the role played by Edward Marston. Marston, the Anglican minister of St Philip's, Charleston, reacted strongly against the Establishment Act passed in 1704 because it provided for a lay commission which had the authority to dismiss wayward or negligent ministers. Marston's outspoken resistance to the act resulted in him being the first victim of the commission. Due to his tendency to 'foment continual quarrels', he was brought before the assembly and deprived of his salary.[55] Marston refused to participate in the proceedings, claiming that the assembly had no right to regulate ecclesiastical affairs and that clergymen were responsible only to God.

[50] Roper, *Conceiving Carolina*, 130, 131.
[51] Trott, *Laws of South Carolina*, 129–44.
[52] Robert Stevens to the Society, 21 Feb. 1705/6, SPG papers, RHL, ser. A, ii. CLVIII.
[53] Johnston and Council to the SPG, SPG Journals, Appendix A, 91.
[54] Abel Boyer, *The reign of Queen Anne, digested into annals: year the fifth*, London 1707, appendix x, pp. 93–7. See also 'The deposition of Samuel Eveleigh of Charleston', BL, MS Add. 61647, fo. 112.
[55] Anon, *An account of the fair and impartial proceedings of the Lords proprietors*, 3 n. *.

Marston's strong views concerning the divine right of clergymen should not be surprising in light of the fact that he was a confessed former nonjuror, having refused the oaths on William's accession, only subscribing to them later in William's reign.[56] He openly acknowledged his former nonjuring sympathies in a letter reprinted in Defoe's sympathetic pamphlet. He even went so far as to request that the SPG send other 'quondam nonjurors' with whom he was still acquainted.[57]

Marston's opposition to the establishment of the Church is puzzling for many reasons but primarily because it pitted a clerical nonjuror against a High Church Tory and former Jacobite. These two men should have been natural allies. Indeed, they had been allies. Shortly before Johnson became governor, Marston wrote to the SPG praising Johnson and expressing his hope that he would accept the post of governor because the colony needed a strong supporter of the Church. He also despaired of ever seeing the Church established in the colony and divided into orderly parishes due to the strength of a vocal dissenting opposition.[58] Marston's break with Johnson requires explanation. Marston's resistance to the acts has mistakenly led to the conclusion that the acts represented either a battle between High and Low Church interests in the colony, or factional politics, despite contemporary observations that 'the debates and contests, that are on foot here, are not between High and Low churchmen; but between the dissenters and the Church'.[59] The evidence, including Marston's rejection of the authority of the lay commission, points to a more nuanced battle between various High Church ideologies and a second battle between Tories and a mainly dissenting party which co-opted Marston's discontent.[60] Gideon Johnston noted that the dissenters would never be content until they had brought about the 'downfall of this infant Church', suggesting the existence of parties primarily concerned with religious controversies.[61] Yet Marston is the exception that proves the rule.

It has also been argued that the acts were designed to promote lay control in the Church, but this is only partially accurate.[62] Although some seemingly Low Church attitudes are reflected in some of the provisions of the acts, the lay commission for example, they are there for very specific – and temporary – reasons, such as clerical discipline in the absence of a bishop or commissary, and were promptly removed when the issues were addressed by the proper

---

[56]   For more on the sacerdotalism of nonjurors see Sirota, *The Christian monitors*, 152–4.

[57]   'Letter from Marston to Society', in Defoe, *The case of Protestant dissenters*, 61.

[58]   Edward Marston to Thomas Bray, 2 Feb. 1702/3, SPG papers, RHL, ser. A, i. LX.

[59]   Johnston to Gilbert Burnet, bishop of Sarum, 20 Sept. 1708, SPG papers, RHL, ser. A, iii. 67.

[60]   For the best discussion of nonjuring and High Church Anglicanism see Sirota, *The Christian monitors*, 149–74.

[61]   Johnston to the bishop of Sarum, 20 Sept. 1708, SPG papers, RHL, ser. A, iii. 67.

[62]   Woolverton, *Colonial Anglicanism*, 167.

authorities, but only after they had drawn the ire of Marston.[63] Governor Johnson simply believed that the lack of any proper clerical authority necessitated the temporary establishment of lay commissions.

Marston was clearly displeased with the act but what distressed him the most was that the lay commissions would allow the government to remove him from his position as the minister to Carolina's largest Anglican Church. Marston's temperament and attitude towards dissenters was creating a poor impression of the Church that Johnson was trying to establish in the colony. But it was not purely personal or financial concerns that caused Marston distress. As a 'quondom nonjuror' he advocated a sacerdotalism distinct from state authority, and would aggressively combat any who tried to remove him.

The most surprising feature of Marston's opposition to the acts is the many unlikely allies that he acquired. As a High Churchman and former nonjuror, Marston was no friend of dissenters or their Whig politics. In fact, according to his fellow Anglican minister Samuel Thomas, most of his sermons were invectives aimed at dissenters.[64] Yet, the dissenters were able to convince Marston to put aside his inherent distaste for them and work with them against the act. In retrospect this is not surprising. As Samuel Thomas argued, Marston's arguments against establishment provided much-needed assistance for the dissenters in their efforts to defeat the High Church party, while his own character would damage the entire church party as well (Marston would be accused of Jacobitism and Catholic sympathies). The alliance with Marston would also allow the dissenters in Carolina to claim unity of purpose with Anglicans. They could then claim that aggrieved ministers of the newly established Church (Marston) were supported by the dissenters and that the church party led by Johnson was destroying an established peace. Gideon Johnston noted this and complained to Gilbert Burnet, bishop of Salisbury, that the Dissenters intended to 'gain their point, according to that known maxim, *Divide & Impera*'.[65] His complaint that those Low Church Anglicans who had opposed the Establishment Acts and continued to support Marston were 'half-faced Churchmen, who in reality are Dissenters, and who sometimes come to Church to be able to do us more mischief' clearly echoes High Church concerns regarding the pernicious consequences of occasional conformity.[66] Thomas too noted the strangeness of the Jacobite Marston working with the dissenters and claimed that the dissenters only supported Marston in order to promote 'their interest and increase their numbers'.[67]

---

[63] Anon, *An account of the fair and impartial proceedings of the Lords proprietors*, 2; Governor and Council of South Carolina to the SPG, SPG Journals, appendix A, 91.

[64] Samuel Thomas to the SPG, 17 May 1706, SPG Journals, appendix A, 79

[65] Johnston to the bishop of Sarum, 20 Sept. 1708, SPG papers, RHL, ser. A, iii. 67.

[66] Ibid.

[67] Thomas to the SPG, 17 May, 1706, SPG Journals, appendix A, 79

Marston, either unaware of or indifferent to how he was being used in the dissenting interest in Carolina, saw Defoe reprint copies of his letters to the bishop of London and the proprietors in an English tract intended to achieve the repeal of the acts.[68] His association with his new-found dissenting allies were not at all pleasing to Johnson's government which had used the powers granted by the acts to remove Marston from his position in Charleston. Clearly, Marston was at odds with Johnson and his allies and was not afraid to attack them for anything that he viewed as a weakness. He accused the Anglican minister Samuel Thomas, a close ally of Johnson, of neglecting his mission to the 'Yamose' Indians. He also reputedly compared the government under Johnson to the biblical rebels led by Korah, a notable reference because it ties Marston to a transatlantic High Church Tory and nonjuring culture: the story of Korah was regularly used by the nonjuror Charles Leslie and had previously been used by high Tories to decry rebellion.[69] Marston's reference to Korah is evidence of a sacerdotalism advocated by nonjurors in England and implies that Johnson is the one rebelling against both clerical and state authority. Marston's use of Korah suggested that that the lay commissions set up by Johnson's government under the 1704 Establishment Acts constituted rebellion against the divine right of clergy. It could also be read that Marston believed that by setting up the commission Johnson was attacking the independence of the Church and abandoning God's appointed head of the Church, James II&VII.[70]

It would not be long before Johnson and Thomas retaliated by attacking Marston's motives and character. In a speech given before the assembly Johnson called Marston a Janus who engaged in attacks on the Church 'with her [the church's] hypocryticall pretendors and declared enimies [sic]'.[71] Thomas travelled back to London in 1705 and presented a defence of his actions before the SPG. In his own defence, he provided an unpleasant account of Marston's character. He accused him of continually boasting of his previous stance as a nonjuror. Thomas claimed that 'in the ship in which I came for Carolina', Marston 'comenced very violent quarrels upon that head [the Revolution of 1688]' and that his 'constant applauding King James ... the Jacobites and Papists, and his vile reflections upon King William' made some suspect that he was a Catholic. He added that Marston continued to take all opportunities to

---

[68]   Defoe, *Case of the Protestant dissenters*, 57-64.

[69]   Ibid. 58; Dalcho, *An historical account*, 56. In the biblical story, which can be found at Numbers xvi, Korah led a rebellion against Moses and Aaron, and attempted to institute a new clerical establishment without divine approval. Charles Leslie, *The new association: part II. &c: with farther improvements*, London [1702], 21-2, and *The case of the regale and of the pontificat stated: in a conference concerning the independency of the Church, upon any power on earth, in the exercise of her purely spiritual power and authority*, London 1701, p. vii; Mark Goldie, 'The damning of King Monmouth: pulpit Toryism in the reign of James II', in Harris and Taylor, *The final crisis*, 33-55.

[70]   Marston, however, denied having used such a reference, though why his opponents would accuse him of it remains unclear: Defoe, *Case of the Protestant dissenters*, 56.

[71]   BL, MS Add. 61647, fo. 119.

'cry up the late King James and the Jacobites, whom he generally termed the honest men of England' and went on to say that Marston railed 'scandalously against King William, the Bishops and Parliament then in being'. Moreover he noted that Marston 'joyns with many of his sense in reproaching' the two archetypical Whig clerics: Archbishop Tillotson and Gilbert Burnet. Thomas ended by stating that Marston was 'a violent Jacobite and a great enemy to the Government in Church and State as settled under King William'.[72] This assessment of Marston's character was later confirmed by Gideon Johnston, who claimed as late as 1710 that Marston was disaffected. He accused Marston of having a terrible temper and claimed that he had called his fellow clergymen 'a parcel of schismaticks and Intruders'. According to Johnston, Marston went so far as to condemn all the revolution clergy as rebels, particularly the bishop of London, 'whom he calls a murderer and perjur'd person on the score of the revolution'.[73]

Thomas's accusations not only demonstrate an instinctive political defence, but also shrewd political calculation. By pushing Marston to the fringes of political society and tying him to the nonjurors and Jacobites in England, Thomas was demonstrating his own reasonableness and also the political restraint of his patrons and Tory allies. This was a conscious political manoeuvre which was designed to locate Thomas and Governor Johnson in a more moderate political context, which after the fall of the High Church Tories and the rise of the Whig Junto in 1705 would have been much more politically palatable. Distancing themselves from Jacobitism and High Church Toryism and nonjuring, they deflected accusations and associated their political opponents with those more extreme ideas, effectively positioning themselves as more temperate Tories. The accusations of Johnson and Thomas against Marston were effective: he never regained his position in the church in Charleston. They also contributed to the successful passage of the Church Act of 1706 by shifting the focus away from debates about the act and towards the suspicious character of Marston.

Jacobitism and anti-Jacobitism became staples of the party-political debate. In South Carolina accusations of Jacobitism were not merely a means of discrediting enemies, nor were they simply a favourite accusation of political enemies. It was a very focused and direct use of a term which was understood to carry great weight throughout the British Atlantic, especially in relation to emerging party differences. This is exemplified by the manner in which Samuel Thomas and Gideon Johnston used it against Edward Marston. Although after 1706 party political manoeuvring concerning the Church Acts no longer played such a prominent role in the politics of Carolina, the party divisions stirred up by the debates remained and continued to be affected by British politics.

---

[72]   Thomas to the Society, 17 May 1706.
[73]   Johnston to the Secretary, 5 July 1710, SPG papers, RHL, ser. A, v. 371-430.

This is illustrated by the arrest in 1708 of Thomas Nairne, an ally of Marston and a vocal opponent of Governor Johnson. Arrested on Johnson's order on a charge of high treason, for having allegedly said 'the Prince of Wales was King James' son' and the 'Right Heir to the Crown',[74] Nairne was confined to prison, protesting his innocence. Coming on the heels of the Anglo-Scottish Union, the failed Jacobite invasion of 1708, and the rise of the virulently anti-Jacobite Whig Junto, accusations against Nairne were likely to have been successful. Nairne, a Scot, was possibly unhappy with the Union of 1707 which might explain his seditious expression, yet even support for Marston, a nonjuror and alleged Jacobite, would have been enough to lend credence to the assertion. In fact it is probable that Nairne was guilty of having spoken seditious words.[75] Johnson, himself having been accused of Jacobitism, and knowing the currency of credible accusations of Jacobitism, employed them in order to destroy his political opponent. He also understood the value of having political allies in Britain.

Nairne similarly understood the significance of party politics and the value of securing influential patrons. Through letters from Whig correspondents, Nairne had learned of the 'noble character' and Whig attitudes of Charles Spencer. More important, he also understood that the earl was employed in the Whig ministry as the Secretary of State for the Southern Department and therefore had a great deal of influence in the politics of the colonies and in appointments to them. Nairne wrote to Sunderland hoping that the earl could protect him from the worst abuses of Governor Johnson.[76] In fact, Nairne defended himself by claiming that Governor Johnson was the true Jacobite. Accusing a High Church Tory of Jacobitism would likely not have been especially effective under the administration of Nottingham or the proprietorship of Granville, but Johnson's Tory patron Granville had died in 1707 leaving him exposed to new Whig-leaning proprietors. Also, with Sunderland's appointment as Secretary of State, charges of Jacobitism against a High Church Tory governor who had used his authority to pass a divisive act establishing the Church of England carried a great deal more weight. Thus, it was Johnson's accusation of and arrest of Nairne and the resulting political fallout that would lead to his own political downfall. Johnson's Jacobite past and his High Church Tory politics did not endear him to the new administration led by the Whig Junto in England, and Nairne's accusations gave it reason enough to remove Johnson from his post. This is significant because it further demonstrates the transatlantic nature of British party politics: the conflict over establishment reflected both the diffusion of English party-political rhetoric and also the complex

---

[74]   Nairne to [Sunderland], 28 July 1709, CSPC, item 662.

[75]   J. D. Alsop, 'Thomas Nairne and the "Boston Gazette no. 216" of 1707', *Southern Studies* xxii (1983), 209–11.

[76]   Nairne to [Sunderland], 28 July 1709, CSPC, item 662.

interactions between local political conflicts and a larger dynamic British Atlantic political culture.

Despite Johnson's removal as governor in 1709 and the Whig supremacy in Westminster, the acts passed in 1706 establishing the Anglican Church in South Carolina remained in force. Indeed, the establishment of the Church led to a substantial increase in attendance at Anglican churches over the next twenty-five years:[77] dissenting ministers continued to complain that parishioners were going over to the Church of England.[78] Moreover, conflict between dissenters and the established Church continued, often mirroring conflicts in Britain. For instance, in 1710 two 'restless and factious' Scottish Presbyterian ministers called the Church of England a 'scandalous church' and wrote a covenant requiring their parishioners never to attend an Anglican Church, a reflection of the religious tensions simmering in Britain.[79]

The successful establishment of the Anglican Church in South Carolina, the continued support of the British-based SPG, and transatlantic denominational conflict fostered a High Church culture in the colony which was further encouraged by the electoral successes of the Tory party in 1710. During the ten years following the passage of Carolina's church acts in 1706, a number of the missionaries sent to the colony to serve in newly established parishes tended to sympathise with the High Church Tory party and were swept up in the High Church zeal which predominated during the reign of Anne. This in turn fuelled party identification. For instance, Gideon Johnston complained that dissenters labelled him a 'High Flyer".[80]

As they increasingly embraced features of a High Church political culture, clergymen also participated in elements of Toryism and Tory political culture which often looked suspiciously like Jacobitism. A number of them were accused of disaffection and Jacobitism during the heyday of party rivalry. In 1716, after news of the Jacobite rebellion had reached Carolina, a group of Anglican clergymen and people in Charleston were noted 'drinking the health of the duke of Ormonde'. Their Low Church critic, Ebeneezer Taylor confronted them, telling them that 'Ormonde was a traitor and a rebel against King George', though this did little more than alienate him from his fellow clergymen, who he claimed did not like him because they could not 'discourse so freely of some things and drink some healths with such freedom and pleasure' in his presence.[81]

Yet suspicions of Jacobitism were not directed only at clergymen. For instance, in 1715 Alexander Skene, a leading vestryman of St Andrew's parish

[77] Thomas J. Little, 'The origins of southern evangelicalism: revivalism in South Carolina, 1700–1740', *Church History* lv (2006), 768–808, esp. pp. 778–9.

[78] James Sqyre to the ` General Assembly, 1715, NAS, CH1/2/35, 189–94.

[79] Johnston to the Secretary, 1710, SPG papers, RHL, ser. A, v. 371–430; Le Jau to the SPG, 1707, ser. A, iii. 254–8.

[80] Johnston to the Secretary, 27 Jan. 1711, SPG papers, RHL, ser. A, vi. 151–205.

[81] Taylor to the bishop of London, 18 Apr. 1716, ibid. xi. 163–205.

in South Carolina, worked to get rid of a Low Church minister who, he felt, was not performing the rites of the church with enough reverence. Skene, a Scottish Episcopalian who had served as Secretary in Barbados, was associated with the nascent church party there and was removed from his post by the Whig Governor, Robert Lowther, in 1713.[82] He was later reinstated until the Tory proscription resulted in his being again turned out of his position after the accession of George I. In 1715 he relocated to South Carolina and within a year was a leading vestryman in his new parish where he sought to oust the Low Church Ebenezer Taylor. Skene's dismissal following the proscription, his Tory politics and his Scottish Episcopalian background, suggest Jacobite sympathies, a notion eagerly seized upon by his clerical antagonist. Taylor's background also provides evidence that party conflicts and religious controversies were Atlantic in scope. Taylor had immigrated to the colony as a Presbyterian minister from England but had been persuaded to conform to the Church of England by Gideon Johnston.[83] He none the less remained a Low Church Anglican. This caused friction between Taylor and his High Church parishioners led by Skene. The vestry and parishioners sent a formal complaint to the bishop of London in 1716 requesting that Taylor be discharged for reasons including 'Not administering the Holy Sacraments on Christmas Day, or reading psalms on that day', and placing the pulpit in front of the altar, both actions being evidence of very Low Church attitudes. Taylor responded by complaining that one of his antagonistic parishioners was a 'villain Torrey'.[84] Even Johnston, who had been friendly with Taylor, confessed that the minister had a Presbyterian style of preaching which would have been unacceptable to a High Church audience.[85]

Taylor retaliated with accusations of Jacobitism. In a letter to the bishop of London, he argued that' 'I little thought that he [Skene] who pretends to more learning, to better breeding, and to be a better church of England man, but as far as I can perceive, his is one of the worst sort; I mean a mighty friend to the pretender and a Jacobite.'[86] He continued, arguing that the reason that Skene, who in his mind had nefariously influenced others in the parish, was set against him was so that 'the Parish may have a better minister' who would no doubt be a 'greater Jacobite and a more jolly companion'.[87] He also complained that 'Mr. Skene has done and will do a great deal of harm in my parish with respect to King George and the pretender's interests' and that 'he is making King George as few and the Pretender as many friends as he can'.[88] In

[82] Governor Robert Lowther to the CTP, 20 Dec. 1711, *CSPC*, item 228.

[83] Johnston to the Secretary, 27 Jan. 1716, SPG papers, RHL, ser. A, xi. 106–17.

[84] Parishioners of St Andrew's parish to the SPG, 11 Feb. 1716, SPG papers, RHL, ser. B, iv. 84, 85.

[85] Johnston to the Secretary, 27 Jan. 1716, SPG papers, RHL, ser. A, xi. 106–17

[86] Taylor to the bishop of London, 18 Apr. 1716, ibid. xi. 163–205.

[87] Ibid.

[88] Ibid.

such accusations, both those of the vestry and Taylor, there is an unmistakable mixture of party affiliation and religious belief, which naturally reflected views regarding the Protestant succession. The High Church vestry was dissatisfied with Taylor's Low Church approach to ministry. But Taylor understood the vestry's complaints, rooted in High Church beliefs and influenced by Skene, as little more than poorly-veiled Jacobitism. Taylor's accusations may seem farfetched. However, William Guy, the minister whom the vestry was hoping to bring in to replace Taylor, had twice been accused of Jacobitism and had even been brought before the governor of the colony to answer charges of drinking healths 'under the name of Job', a curious equation of the suffering servant with the exiled Stuarts.[89]

A High Church Tory and Jacobite culture persisted into the 1720s. The daughter of the nonjuror Thomas Brett, herself an ardent lay nonjuror, moved to South Carolina and was 'mighty pleased with the people she is amongst'.[90] Despite complaining that the majority of the population were Whigs, she commented to her father in 1723 that 'the hearts of the people are as we could wish, for they are loyal to the last degree and the governour fired seventeen guns on his majesty's [James III & VIII] birthday and the gentlemen over their punch and the ladies over their tea table equally drank to his majesty's long life and prosperous reign'. She also noted that 'the minister here [Alexander Garden] is a very honest man ... a Scotsman' who had 'promised us all the assistance he can give us'.[91]

Manifestations of Whig and Tory party divisions were the primary cause of the debates surrounding the passage of the act establishing the Anglican Church in South Carolina in the early eighteenth century. The appointment of a High Church Tory governor by a partisan Tory proprietor during the rage of party indicates a concerted effort to promote High Church Toryism throughout the British Atlantic. The establishment acts and the subsequent political debates both clearly replicated events in England and Ireland, suggesting a colonial political culture well attuned to British politics. The Tory push in South Carolina fostered transatlantic partisan interests in the colony, which in turn encouraged South Carolinians, Englishmen and Scots to participate in a transatlantic exchange of ideas facilitated by Britain's emerging transatlantic public sphere. The emerging party divisions and the increasing participation in an emerging Atlantic public sphere during a time of intense party strife dominated by the Stuart threat necessarily sparked accusations of Jacobitism. These were not without foundation, yet the characters involved and the utility

---

[89] Thomas Hasell to the SPG, 20 Sept. 1717, ibid. xii. 83–5. For examples of the use of Job in Jacobite propaganda or material culture see Guthrie, *Material culture of the Jacobites*, 46.
[90] Brett to Campbell, 12 Sept. 1724, NAS, CH12/15/109, 172–6.
[91] Ibid.

of the accusations reflect the changing realities and rehabilitation of Jacobitism in the early eighteenth century.

Although party rivalries in South Carolina's legislature cooled after the debates surrounding the passage of the establishment acts, religious disputes continued to inspire party affiliation. The establishment of the Church of England in the colony and the High Church Tory ascendancy in Britain from 1710 to 1714 nurtured the development of a High Church Tory interest in South Carolina, which in turn fostered elements of a Jacobite political culture, although just how prevalent Jacobite sympathies really were in South Carolina remains an unsolved problem.

5

'An Echo to That on the Other Side': Jacobitism and anti-Jacobitism in the Mid-Atlantic colonies, c. 1710–1717

In 1710 Robert Hunter sailed for New York City to take up the post of governor of the British colonies of New York and New Jersey. Hunter had hopes of an easy time, pursuing the interests of Queen Anne, but vicious transatlantic party rivalries were alive and well in the colonies and not isolated to Westminster and Grub Street. The early years of Hunter's tenure (1710-19) were a time of increasing dynastic uncertainty and witnessed a series of seismic political changes including the death of Queen Anne, the Hanoverian succession and the Jacobite rebellion of 1715. That Hunter successfully survived the political morass of the two colonies, each with its own unique political issues made all the more uncertain by the vagaries of an adolescent imperial structure influenced by the rage of party, is a tribute to his political acumen. An examination of the period surrounding Hunter's government, however, provides more than a biographical tribute to a single man; it captures elements of Whig and Tory British party conflicts, religious controversies and the integration of an Atlantic public sphere. Hunter's period in office is a fascinating example of the increasingly transatlantic nature of party politics, communications and the currency of Jacobitism and anti-Jacobitism in the British Atlantic World in the contentious final years of Queen Anne.

Accusations of Jacobitism featured prominently in the political and religious controversies engulfing the mid-Atlantic in the early eighteenth century. A thorough examination of Jacobitism and anti-Jacobitism provide compelling evidence that the transatlantic nature of Britain's rage of party contributed to the anglicisation of the mid-Atlantic. Accusations of loyalty to the Stuarts, nonjuring or outright Jacobitism were an integral part of transatlantic political, religious and print debate. Such accusations reflect more than petty expressions of local antipathy. Accusations and expressions of Jacobitism in the mid-Atlantic not only point towards the significance and currency of Jacobitism and anti-Jacobitism in the British Atlantic, they also demonstrate the integration of the colonial region into a British Atlantic political culture.

Religious controversies facilitated the extension of Britain's rage of party into the mid-Atlantic colonies. Governor Hunter's troubled relationship with High Church Tories in New York and New Jersey provides a perfect illustration of the complexity of imperial politics and the prevalence of shared ideologies.

Hunter's worried interactions with High Church Tories in New York and New Jersey demonstrate the changing nature of Jacobitism and, therefore, the evolving transatlantic understanding of the problematic relationship of Jacobitism and the rage of party throughout the British Atlantic world. While some scholars have mentioned Hunter's defence of 'Revolution Principles', his opposition to the 'Jacobite party', or have noticed the accusations of Jacobitism made against his opponents, no one has yet satisfactorily explained the purpose, implications or effectiveness of such accusations.[1] Assuming that they were simply political mudslinging underestimates Hunter's antagonism towards an aggressive High Tory Anglicanism in a period when the religious beliefs and politics of High Church Tories were intricately interwoven with a Jacobite political culture.

Like South Carolina, both New York and New Jersey had a long history of violent factional strife. In 1689, amidst uncertainties regarding the success of William of Orange's recent invasion of England, and the problematically slow receipt of news, Jacob Leisler seized the government of New York from Francis Nicholson, the lieutenant-governor. Leisler attributed his actions to a desire to support the Protestant William and Mary and to save the colony from popery and tyranny, but his subsequent decisions as acting governor and persecution of those who disagreed with him created turmoil. His subsequent downfall and eventual execution created violent divisions throughout the region.[2] As successive governors rose and fell in accord with party politics in Britain, so too the power of the various parties or factions stirred up by Leisler and encouraged by the governors waxed and waned. The various political disputes have generally been understood in terms of local faction,[3] but after 1702 they were subsumed into a transatlantic political culture.[4]

An emergent regional High Church interest, supported by the High Church Tory party in Britain, played a vital role in shaping political language and disputes, and accusations of Jacobitism highlight the development of transatlantic Whig and Tory party interests. Historians noting accusations of Jacobitism

[1]   Webb, *Marlborough's America*, 261; Mary Lou Lustig, *Robert Hunter, 1666–1734: a New York Augustan statesman*, Syracuse 1983, 129–30; Alison G. Olson, 'Governor Robert Hunter and the Anglican Church in New York', in Anne Whiteman, J. S. Bromley and P. G. M. Dickson (eds), *Statesmen, scholars, and merchants: essays in eighteenth-century history presented to Dame Lucy Sutherland*, Oxford 1973, 44–64, esp. pp. 59–60.

[2]   Lovejoy, *The Glorious Revolution in America*; Patricia Bonomi, *A factious people: politics and society in colonial New York*, New York 1971; David William Voorhees, 'The "fervent zeale" of Jacob Leisler', *WMQ* li (1994), 447–72, and '"To assert our right"', 5–27.

[3]   Brendan McConville, *These daring disturbers of the public peace: the struggle for property and power in early New Jersey*, Ithaca, NY 1999; Bonomi, *A factious people*.

[4]   Runcie, 'The problem of Anglo-American politics', 191–217; Patricia Bonomi, *The Lord Cornbury scandal: the politics of reputation in British America*, Chapel Hill 1998; Webb, *Marlborough's America*, 291–329.

and the presence of nonjuring clergymen have not adequately addressed their implications.[5] Hunter's tenure as governor of the two mid-Atlantic colonies was largely shaped by ecclesiastical concerns, but scholars have explained the inter-section of religious and political controversies as an accident of circumstance or argued that a politicised established Church was a political club to be wielded by colonial governors interested in creating a court party.[6] It is imperative, however, to examine the Church of England and High Churchmen within the context of the transatlantic rage of party if their instrumental role in shaping the political culture of the mid-Atlantic in the last years of the reign of Queen Anne is to be understood.

The Church of England did not enjoy a very auspicious start in the mid-Atlantic colonies: it was not established in either New York or New Jersey. Most of the population of West Jersey and Pennsylvania was Quaker, and ethnic diversity in New York encouraged a diversity of religious beliefs.[7] The Church was only able to ensure the support of a minority of the population and was often unable to supply ministers for all of its parishes. For example, in the early part of the 1690s there was often only one Anglican minister in New Jersey and he had been dismissed from his post as chaplain in New York due to suspected Jacobite sympathies.[8]

There was, however, a growing Anglican presence in the mid-Atlantic in the late seventeenth century. Governor Benjamin Fletcher (1692–8), a Tory appointee, encouraged the fledgling Church by supporting the establishment of Trinity Church in New York City and pushing through a Ministry Act in 1693, which provided for Protestant ministers in four counties. An ambiguity in the act made it possible for Fletcher and subsequent Tory governors to interpret it as having established the Church in the four counties.[9] The Church of England grew slowly in large part due to the structure of the Church which inhibited growth in the absence of a resident bishop. However, the influence of the Church in New York far outweighed its numerical significance.

English party politics soon brought the period of official government support for the Church under Fletcher to an abrupt end. After the Whigs came to power following the discovery of a Jacobite plot against William III

[5]   George Morgan Hills, *A history of the Church in Burlington, New Jersey: comprising the facts and incidents of nearly two-hundred years, from original, contemporaneous sources*, Trenton, NJ 1885; Edgare Pennington, *Apostle of New Jersey: John Talbot, 1645–1727*, Philadelphia 1938; Woolverton, *Colonial Anglicanism.*

[6]   John E. Pomfret, *Colonial New Jersey: a history*, New York 1973, 123–38; Olson, 'Governor Robert Hunter and the Anglican Church', 44–64.

[7]   Landsman, 'Roots, routes, and rootedness', and *Crossroads of empire: the middle colonies in British North America*, Baltimore 2010; Joyce Goodfried, *Before the melting pot: society and culture in colonial New York City, 1664–1730*, Princeton 1992.

[8]   Nelson R. Burr, *The Anglican Church in New Jersey*, Philadelphia 1954, 14.

[9]   Thomas E. Carney, 'A tradition to live by: New York religious history, 1624–1740', *New York History* lxxxv (2004), 301–30.

in London in 1696, they replaced many Tory appointees, Fletcher included. Fletcher's replacement was Richard Coote, Lord Bellomont, a Whig appointee. While serving as governor from 1698 to 1701, Bellomont allied himself with Fletcher's former opponents and acted against what the Church in New York considered its interests by promoting the interests of dissent and attacking William Vesey, the minister of Trinity Church. Refusing to surrender recently acquired privileges, Vesey used his pulpit as a means of galvanising opposition, exemplifying the politicisation of the Church. Before Vesey could bring about Bellomont's removal, the governor died.

It was not until the early eighteenth century that the Church of England began to rise to prominence within the colonies. The accession of Queen Anne had lasting imperial consequences. Anne's support for the Church of England was made manifest in the appointment of the High Church Tory Edward Hyde, Lord Cornbury, as the first person to serve as governor of both New York and the new royal colony of New Jersey simultaneously. As the queen's cousin and a zealous promoter of High Church interests, he was warmly welcomed by members of the Church of England in the colonies that he governed. He also received a great deal of support from, and was a member of, the SPG. During Cornbury's administration (1702–9), the Church enjoyed strong official support and a period of rapid growth which was encouraged by the missionaries sent to New York, New Jersey and Pennsylvania by the SPG. In fact, Cornbury welcomed the first SPG missionary, George Keith, a Quaker turned Anglican. During Cornbury's administration the missionary work of Keith and his assistant John Talbot (later the nonjuring bishop) and the prospect of incoming ministers encouraged fledgling congregations to build new churches. At least six were built, or refurbished, in the region.[10] In addition to ministers and churches, Cornbury pushed through policies favourable to the Anglican interest including forcing an Anglican minister on a largely dissenting church in the town of Jamaica on Long Island.

The rapid growth of the Church was also due to the work and beliefs of the clergymen sent to the region. The years 1702–10 witnessed the battle over occasional conformity in Westminster, Ireland and South Carolina, and also the Union of Scotland and England which further threatened an already beleaguered Anglican Church in Scotland by furthering the entrenchment of Presbyterianism. Many of the clergymen sent to the mid-Atlantic were Scots Episcopalians unable to secure work in Scotland who were ordained into the Church of England and sent out as missionaries. During a period fraught with religious controversies, it is little wonder that clergymen in the mid-Atlantic found encouragement in the writings of Charles Leslie and other churchmen whose attacks on Quakers and moderate churchmen resonated in a region dominated by Quakers and other dissenters. John Talbot often complimented Leslie's works in letters to friends and requested that some of his publications

[10]   Burr, *The Anglican Church in New Jersey*, 489–526.

be sent to him so that they might be used as resources for the conversion of Quakers.[11]

Religious controversies also engaged laymen. In 1705 the almanackist Daniel Leeds, one of Talbot's parishioners, and a former Quaker converted by George Keith, penned and published a tract which excoriated Quakers and mocked George Fox. Leeds echoed Leslie, arguing that the Quaker principle of the inner light was the same as the beliefs of 'Heathen deists'. Leeds praised Leslie as the author of the anti-Quaker tract *The snake in the grass*,[12] and also used his almanacs as an evangelistic tool, including in them politically-charged Anglican holidays celebrated by the Church and important Anglican political anniversaries such as 29 May (Restoration Day) and 30 January (execution of Charles I).[13] With congregations placed in the midst of so many dissenters during a period rife with religious controversies, it is little wonder that parishioners heeded the calls of the clergymen to come to the defence of a Church deemed to be in danger.

As tensions rose, moderation on the part of some clergymen was often in short supply. Talbot received many letters from the SPG counselling him to moderate his temper and his zeal against the Quakers. In fact, in one letter, the Secretary of the SPG voiced his concern that Talbot had called the toleration of dissent 'Amersterdamnable'.[14] Talbot's comment came perilously close to sedition by questioning and attacking revolution principles; it almost resulted in his dismissal from the society. But Talbot's views were not out of place during this period. The prevalence of High Church attitudes among the SPG in Britain meant that his potentially seditious comments remained unpunished. It was not the Society's generous spirit that allowed him to remain in their service but, according to one critic, 'Providence' and the abundance of those full of a 'warm spirit' in Britain which prompted the Society to let him remain.[15]

Cornbury's encouragement for the Church of England throughout his time as governor rallied its members and clergy, and as a corollary this Tory-affiliated church party served as his primary support throughout his administration. This set a precedent: opposition to his policies was opposition to and oppression of the Church. His support for the Church so endeared him to certain circles that many missionaries, ministers and laymen remained loyal to him even after his removal from office in 1708 by the Whig ministry. The churchwardens and vestry of Burlington later lamented, 'How happy were our churches under the administration of the Earl of Clarendon [Cornbury]

11   Talbot to Keith, 14 Feb. 1707, SPG papers, RHL, ser. A, vii. 173.

12   Daniel Leeds, *The great mistery of Fox-Craft discovered and the Quaker plainness & sincerity demonstrated*, New York 1705, 7, 14.

13   Idem, *The American almanac, 1705*.

14   Secretary to Talbot, 25 Feb 1710, SPG papers, LPL, xii. 239, 251

15   Ibid

... to whom we never applied in vain for anything that might promote its interest.'[16]

The unification of New York and New Jersey under a single crown-appointed governor served also to direct the interests of the Church towards a single executive, though specific acts and policies regarding the Church in each colony remained different. One notable example of the growing cooperation and shared interests of the clergy in the region was the regular meeting of conventions of the clergy, usually called by the governor. Clergymen from Pennsylvania, New Jersey, New York and New England all attended at different times and discussed various issues, including the state of the Church and the need for a resident bishop. They also used the conventions to support one another by setting up rotations to serve congregations without settled ministers. There were at least eight different conventions of clergymen between the years 1702 and 1713.[17] Such cooperation fostered a unity of purpose among the clergy and their parishioners.

Not everyone was fond of Cornbury or his administration. His opponents despised his policies and his manner of governing and increasingly employed party political language to bring about his removal. Consequently, transatlantic party interests, cultivated since the Revolution of 1688 were strengthened during Cornbury's administration as the interests of the Church in the colonies of New York and New Jersey were increasingly aligned with the High Church Tory party in Britain and the diverse dissenting and Low Church interest grew ever closer to the Whig party. After Cornbury's removal and return to England, he remained a vital point of contact for the region's High Church party, which also appealed to the SPG and the bishop of London. As a counterpart to this, Whig governors and their supporters developed a variety of Whig contacts. Slander, complaints and accusations, therefore, were most effectively employed in terms shaped by prevailing party politics, and this would prove especially true during Hunter's administration.

When Governor Hunter arrived in New York in 1710, he entered a political battleground defined in large part by the transatlantic nature of the rage of party. Unfortunately for Hunter, the Whig ministry in Westminster was brought down by a Tory backlash following the mismanagement of the Sacheverell affair in 1710. A resurgent Tory party in Britain did not bode well for a new governor who owed his appointment to the patronage of John Churchill, 1st duke of Marlborough, and the previous Whig ministry. Hunter was placed in a very difficult situation, as the period of intense party conflict in both Church and State did not allow for prevarication. Like his patron, his political inclinations were moderate, and in general he supported the Whig party of his friend John

---

[16]   Churchwardens and Vestry of the church of St Mary's, Burlington, 25 Mar. 1714, SPG papers, RHL, ser. A, ix. 92; Burr, *The Anglican Church in New Jersey*, 282–5.

[17]   Thomas Halliday to the Secretary, 23 Aug. 1714, ibid. 153–5, Burr, *The Anglican Church in New Jersey*, 282–5.

Dalrymple, 2nd earl of Stair. Although Hunter was himself a member of the Church of England and of the SPG, he was a Low Church Anglican Whig who had converted in 1707 from Scottish Presbyterianism in order to accept the post of lieutenant-governor of Virginia.[18] A conversion of convenience made him deeply suspect in the eyes of those with High Church sympathies, and he was seen as little better than an occasional conformist. His zeal for the Church was certainly in doubt.

Despite his early attempts to avoid conflict with the High Church party, Hunter outraged sensibilities by asking the SPG to moderate its missionaries' fervour. He noted that the church party treated him as though he 'declared for fanaticks against the church' and he complained to the Secretary of the Society that the Church of England was 'not without her fanaticks', a description unlikely to endear him to High Churchmen.[19] Hunter's first major misstep occured in 1711 when the SPG missionary to Jamaica, Long Island, William Urquhart died. The SPG in London promptly appointed Thomas Poyer to replace him. Before Poyer could assume his new post, however, the dissenting majority in the town forcibly took control of the church building and the largely dissenting or Low Church vestry denied Poyer his salary. Poyer appealed to Hunter and the SPG, but although the SPG was sympathetic to Poyer's plight, Hunter was not willing to alienate a large number of dissenters in order to support one Anglican missionary. Nor was he enthusiastic about pushing the interests of the Anglican Church outside of what he considered the bounds of New York law. Instead, he attempted to remain neutral, either not understanding or not caring that neutrality was next to impossible during the rage of party. Rather than arbitrarily using his executive power, he encouraged Poyer to bring the case to court. Poyer, however, distrusted the justices, who were dissenters appointed by Hunter, and doubted that he would win a court case. He did not wish to set an unwanted precedent regarding the legal position of ministers in relation to the vestries.[20] Hunter's decided lack of support for a displaced Anglican minister strained his relationship with the High Church party. Even the bishop of London commented on Hunter's 'false step in the beginning'.[21] Poyer's appeal to the SPG proved more successful; the SPG appealed to the queen, who took Poyer's part.[22] This episode demonstrated to the High Church party that they, not Hunter, had the backing of the SPG. More important, the SPG and the Church had the queen on their side; her

---

[18] Lustig, *Robert Hunter*, 40; Carney, 'A tradition to live by', 301–30 at p. 325.

[19] Hunter to the SPG, 21 Mar. 1710, SPG papers, RHL, ser. C, box 1, item 7.

[20] Thomas Poyer to Hunter, 30 Jan, 1711/12, in *Documents relative to the colonial history of the state of New-York procured in Holland, England, and France by John Romeyn Brodhead*, ed. F. B. O'Callaghan, Albany, NY 1853, v. 327; 'Address from the clergy of New York to his excellency Robert Hunter', v. 325

[21] Bishop of London to the SPG, 5 June 1713, SPG papers, RHL, ser. C, box 14, item 35.

[22] 'Address from the clergy of New York to his excellency Robert Hunter', v. 325

support, and that of the SPG, was instrumental in strengthening the interests of the High Church party in the colonies.

While Poyer's predicament was unfolding in New York, members of the Church in New Jersey were occupied in their own struggles against Hunter. In 1711 the Assembly, the majority of whom were Quakers, tried to push through a bill allowing Quakers to make an affirmation instead of swearing an oath in order to serve on juries. Churchmen in the province, including Daniel Coxe and Daniel Leeds, claimed that allowing Quakers to serve without an oath would endanger the colony. They feared that if given too much power in government the Quakers would be 'empowered by a law to destroy our religion, lives, libertys, reputations and estates at their pleasure'.[23] (Although the Quakers were able to secure a majority in the Assembly through election, they were often unable to secure the passage of acts favourable to their party because the governor's council, controlled by High Churchmen previously appointed by Cornbury, were opposed to them.) Hunter's most prominent opponents on the council – including Daniel Coxe, Hugh Huddy and William Hall – were all parishioners of Talbot's church in Burlington. These men refused to allow the bill, and their obstinate opposition forced Hunter to seek their removal. The High Church party resented Hunter's attempts to reshape the council. The six men Hunter replaced were all active churchmen and many served as church-wardens and vestrymen in various Anglican parishes. Their removal from the council, taking place so soon after Poyer's problems in New York stoked fears amongst High Churchmen who believed that Hunter was intentionally trying to replace churchmen with dissenters or churchmen of weaker convictions in order to cripple the power and influence of the Church.

The Poyer case, which remained unresolved as late as 1714, strengthened High Church opposition to Hunter. It also increased High Church suspicion of Hunter's religious sympathies. In a representation against Hunter written in 1712, *The state of the case of the Church in New York and New Jersey*, Jacob Henderson, a SPG missionary who officiated in Pennsylvania and New Jersey, argued that far from being a misstep, the actions against Poyer were actively countenanced by Hunter who had promoted dissenters to positions of influence, such as the New Jersey Council.[24] Henderson argued that Hunter's actions were malicious and purposeful, and also had consequences for the region as a whole. Henderson understood that the state of the Church was legally different in each colony, but he believed that it was in danger throughout the region because of the governor's role as executive of both colonies. But, according to Henderson, it was not only Hunter who was to blame. Henderson also described Lewis Morris, one of Hunter's most prominent supporters in both New York and New Jersey as 'a professed churchman' who 'calls the

[23]   'Address of the Minister, Churchwardens and Vestry of the Church of St Mary's in Burlington to the queen', 30 July 1711, *CSPC*, item 58i.
[24]   Jacob Henderson, 'The state of the case of the Church in New York and New Jersey', *New York documents*, v. 334–5

service of the Church of England pageantry'.[25] By questioning the sincerity of Morris's support for the Church, Henderson was equating him with moderate 'false brethren' who were the bogeymen of High Church sermons in Britain.

Fears for the future of the Church of England were widespread and some New York clergy, though not all as suspicious of Hunter's motives as Henderson, petitioned on Poyer's behalf. Their address expressed their fear that the same ill-treatment might set a precedent and encourage further attacks on the Established Church.[26] The problems encountered by Poyer and the New Jersey councillors led High Churchmen increasingly to view dissenters as 'enemies' of the Church of England with Hunter at their head.[27] Several ministers wrote to the High Church champion Francis Nicholson complaining that 'Presbyterian violence has been countenanced against the church.' They deliberately attacked the dissenters and they also equated Hunter's Presbyterian background with questionable sympathies.[28] Poyer's predicament and the precarious position of the New Jersey councillors demonstrated the need to develop transatlantic political interests and, more important, to acquire a governor who strongly supported the Church.

Hunter was no political novice, and understood that he was in a difficult situation. Any move which would encourage clerical opposition was not in his best interests politically, especially because the clergy and Church had the backing of the SPG and the ear of the queen. It was also unlikely that an unfriendly Tory administration would take much heed of Hunter's explanations. Hunter vented his frustrations on the Council of Trade and Plantations, arguing in 1713 'that if clandestine representations ... should gaine creditt and countenance at home, the Governour whoever he be, must have a very uneasy time of it, who knowing nothing of his accusation or accusers and liveing remote from his equall and just judges, suffers in his reputation and perhaps in his fortunes without a remedy'.[29] But explaining his difficulties to an unfriendly ministry would not solve his problems nor make his opponents less aggressive. As a result, Hunter began to employ the same 'clandestine' methods in the hope that he might discredit his opponents.

After 1710 the lines between High Church Toryism and a Jacobite political culture became increasingly blurred in Britain, Ireland and the colonies. This was very much the case in New York and New Jersey. Hunter wrote to the SPG informing them that some of their ministers were articulating nonjuring principles. He explained that Henderson and Talbot, two of his main clerical opponents, both omitted prayers for 'victory over Her Majesties enemies' when preaching at Talbot's church. Although Talbot's parishioners claimed that they

25   Ibid. v. 355
26   'Address of the clergy to Hunter', ibid. v. 325
27   Poyer to the Secretary, 10 June 1714, SPG papers, RHL, ser. A, ix. 122.
28   Several ministers to General Nicholson, 11 May 1714, ibid. 208.
29   Hunter to the CTP, 14 Mar. 1713, CSPC, item 293.

were unhappy when Henderson omitted the prayer, they allowed it from Talbot because while they were 'long acquainted with Mr. Talbot's exemplary life they were willing to bear with his scruples'.[30] He also wrote to a friend complaining that certain clergymen were 'disturbing the peace in Jersey'.[31] Hunter hoped that by demonstrating the questionable principles of certain SPG ministers to the Society, he could undermine the SPG's support for the High Church party in the colonies. Unfortunately for Hunter, the Tory ascendancy in Britain rendered his accusations unsuccessful at the time, although they did lay the foundation for future success.

Hunter had misled himself into thinking that High Church opposition was restricted to individual clergymen. Although Hunter's initial complaints were directed against individuals, he quickly realised that opposition was more widely spread. He had not fully realised that there was a coalition of clergymen and laymen determined to oppose any perceived attacks on the Church of England. He admitted as much when he complained in 1712 that he had 'flattered' himself that he 'had gained the good will and affection of the clergy in those parts'.[32] He also complained to the bishop of London that 'the best guarded conduct is not superior to the malice of designing men'.[33]

Hunter and his Low Church and dissenting allies realised that High Church interests were rapidly consolidating into an opposition party under the leadership of William Vesey. Vesey's role is significant because both he and his father had been accused of Jacobitism in the 1690s. Vesey was said to have voiced his disaffection by referring to King William as a 'Dutch King' or saying 'their King won't live always'. His father was sentenced to stand in the pillory 'for uttering desperate words against His Majesty'.[34] A couple of decades on, in 1712, Hunter's close associate Lewis Morris noted that 'Mr. Vesey begins to set up a party', and in a letter to the bishop of London, Hunter accused some of the clergy of 'faction' and 'blind zeal'.[35] As Hunter and his allies increasingly viewed their opponents as a unified church party, they also associated them with a larger transatlantic High Church political culture.

Opposition to Hunter's policies was becoming ever more hostile as Hunter's actions continued to reinforce fears that the Church was in danger. After Hunter secured the removal of the High Church members from the New Jersey council in 1712, the assembly and the newly constituted council passed an act allowing Quakers to affirm rather than take an oath. Quakers were also permitted to serve on juries. In a region where Quakers and dissenters were the

[30]   Governor Hunter to the Secretary, 11 Feb. 1711, *New York documents*, v. 316.

[31]   Governor Hunter to Popple, 11 May 1713, *CSPC*, item 338.

[32]   Hunter to the bishop of London, 1 Mar. 1712, *New York documents*, v. 310.

[33]   Ibid.

[34]   Minutes of the Council of New York, 27 Apr. 1702, *CSPC*, item 387; Governor the earl of Bellomont to the CTP, 22 July 1702, *CSPC*, item 675.

[35]   Colonel Lewis Morris to John Chamberlayne, 20 Feb. 1711/12, and Hunter to the bishop of London, 1 Mar. 1712, *New York documents*, v. 318, 310.

majority, this act terrified those High Church Anglicans who had previously held positions of authority for they viewed Hunter's policies as creating a Whig oligarchy which would undermine the precarious position of the Anglican Church in the colony. Members of the High Church party believed that the act would 'defeat all those good designs ... and ruin our infant church'.[36] In a letter to the queen complaining about Hunter's handling of the desecration of Vesey's Trinity Church in New York, which was broken into and vandalised in early 1714, the churchwardens and vestry in Burlington, New Jersey, requested that as 'God's image and immediate representative' she would support the Church against the dangers posed if 'Quakers are made rulers and, guardians of the Church'.[37] Hunter refused to view the new act as a danger to the Church, but rather saw the zeal of the churchmen as dangerous. He complained to the SPG of the 'disorders' caused by some of the missionaries and was dismayed by the fact that if 'we but interpose with some advice we are enemies to the church'.[38] Hunter remained astonished by his opponents' deep animosity despite the ideological differences regarding the position of the Church in the colonies.

Hunter's relationship with the High Church party continued to deteriorate throughout the final years of Anne's reign. Relations were so strained that even the most random of events could cause conflict. His reaction to the desecration of Trinity Church which in addition to destruction and theft, involved vandals covering Vesey's clerical robes in 'ordure' or as Vesey delicately put it, they were 'beskirted and bedaub'd with what I must not name!', did not help.[39] Churchmen throughout the region were furious at the affront and demanded that Hunter find and punish those responsible. Hunter did not act quickly enough for their tastes and some began to suspect that not only was he unsympathetic, but that he was involved.[40]

In response, Hunter exploited an emerging colonial print culture to embarrass and harass his opponents. He wrote a satirical play, probably printed in 1716, as a means of disparaging his detractors. Throughout the play Hunter demonstrated a keen awareness of transatlantic political realities. He mocked the notion that the Anglican Church was in any danger and implied that the desecration of Trinity Church was done by churchmen intentionally so that

---

[36] Churchwardens and vestry of St Mary's, Burlington, 25 Mar. 1714, SPG papers, RHL, ser. A, ix. 92.

[37] Churchwardens and vestry of St Mary's, Burlington, to the queen [c. 1714], ibid. ix. 199–202.

[38] Hunter to the Secretary, 10 May 1714, ibid. ix. 105–6.

[39] 'To the honourable gentlemen of her majesty's council for the Province of New York', 14 Feb. 1714, ibid. ix. 191. For similar examples of such actions see Susan Juster, 'Heretics, blasphemers, and sabbath breakers: the prosecution of religious crime in early America', in Beneke and Grenda, The first prejudice, 123–42

[40] Lustig, Robert Hunter, 116.

they might have an excuse to cry out 'the Church in danger'.[41] Although Hunter may have overstated his case, he was absolutely correct in his assumptions that the Trinity Church incident would further inflame belief that the Church was in danger. This was true not just in New York. That the churchwardens and vestry of Burlington wrote to the queen about the affront to Trinity Church, demonstrated the strong unity of purpose among the High Church party.[42]

Already beleaguered by the twin threats of local opponents and the imperial Tory ascendancy, Hunter suffered major political setback in 1712 when Francis Nicholson was appointed by the Tory ministry in London to supervise and inspect certain aspects of the imperial administration and the compliance of governors in the colonies.[43] This commission, combined with his role as governor of Nova Scotia, provided Nicholson with an inordinate amount of influence and power and represented the Tory attempt to exert greater control over the empire. Indeed, both the High Church party and Hunter saw Nicholson's position as an affront to Hunter's authority. The church party understood this slight to be a blessing, noting in an address to the Queen the 'extraordinary mark of your Majesty's affections in ... authorising his excellency Gen. Francis Nicholson to inspect into and represent the affairs of Church and State here'.[44] The High Church party began to work closely with Nicholson in the hope that he might replace Hunter as governor of New York and New Jersey.

Nicholson's appointment was a direct threat to Whig appointees in the colonies. In fact the years between 1713 and 1714 looked like the beginnings of a purge of Whig appointees and their replacement by Tory supporters. Samuel Vetch, the governor of Nova Scotia and son-in-law of Robert Livingston, an ally of Hunter in New York, had been removed from his post to make way for Nicholson. Both Vetch and Hunter, on poor terms with the Tory ministry, distrusted Nicholson's intentions and believed that he intended to report any failings to the ministry. Vetch's proximity to and interaction with Nicholson in Boston allowed him to see and report aspects of Nicholson's character and behaviour to Livingston and Hunter. He wrote to Livingston, 'I doubt not you know that G.[eneral] N.[icholson] is no friend to your governor and will do all that he can to expose him and his management' and suggested that Livingston send 'what you think proper to communicate to your governor'.[45] He also claimed that Nicholson was a 'violent enemy of Govr. Hunter's and

[41] Hunter, *Androboros*, 9–11.

[42] Churchwardens and vestry of St Mary's, Burlington, to the queen, [c. 1714], SPG papers, RHL, ser. A, ix. 199–202

[43] Copy of His Majesty's commission to Colonel Francis Nicholson, 14 Oct. 1712, *CSPC*, item 97.

[44] Churchwardens and vestry of Trinity Church to the queen, 11 May 1714, SPG papers, RHL, ser. A, ix. 181–5.

[45] Vetch to Livingston, 25 Jan. 1714, and Margaret Vetch to Livingston, 3 May 1714, Livingston papers, microfilm, reel 3.

will endeavor to separate you from his interest'.[46] This news, communicated to Hunter by Livingston, undoubtedly increased Hunter's misgivings.

Nicholson was not acting alone. The High Church interest in the mid-Atlantic, represented by Vesey and Talbot, wrote to him detailing their sufferings at the hands of Hunter's government. Vesey and Talbot were confident that with Nicholson's influence, they could outmanoeuvre Hunter and secure his removal, after which Nicholson would take his place. Working together, Talbot, Vesey and Nicholson agreed that Vesey would sail for England and present the complaints of the High Church party to the Board of Trade and the SPG. Hunter suspected that his opponents were conspiring against him and knew that Vesey had gone to 'cry out Fire, and Church at all hazards'. and was later able to prove it after intercepting some letters sent by Talbot which outlined his hopes that Nicholson would replace Hunter.[47]

Before the High Church party and its agent Vesey were able to secure Hunter's removal, the vagaries of British party politics would destroy their hopes. On 1 August 1714 Queen Anne died and was succeeded by George I. Hunter received the news and immediately recognised his good fortune. On 18 October he proclaimed the king in New York and noticed, amidst the 'universal transport', some 'awkward half-huzzahs', suggestive of Tory or Jacobite discontent.[48]

In order to secure his position and discredit his opponents, Hunter was able to make use of an extensive network of high-ranking correspondents, including John Dalrymple, James Graham and Joseph Addison. On the same day that he proclaimed the new king, he wrote to Dalrymple, explaining that Nicholson's appointments under the Tory administration had encouraged 'two or three of the clergy, and those profest Jacobites to flye in my face' and explained that he would take 'noe provocation or any notice of their seditious conduct, lest they should occasion to crye the Church here as they had done elsewhere'. Hunter not only vilified his enemies but asked Dalrymple to mention him to Lord Sunderland, Lord Somers, or any other Whig ministers who he knew would likely rise to positions of prominence with the Hanoverian succession.[49] He also sought help from Montrose, a Scottish Whig who was a strong supporter of the Hanoverian succession.[50] Similarly, he wrote to Joseph Addison (recently appointed the secretary of the regents prior to the arrival of George I) of the joy that 'the friendship and esteem I have ever had for you' gave him but more importantly of the 'delightful prospect your [Addison'a] promotion gave me of

---

46 Vetch to Livingston, 27 Jan. 1714, ibid.

47 Hunter to Popple, 9 Nov. 1715, *CSPC*, item 663; Hunter to the CTP, 13 Aug. 1715, *CSPC*, item 569.

48 Hunter to Popple, 18 Oct. 1714, *CSPC*, item 68.

49 Hunter to Dalrymple 18 Oct. 1714, *CSPC*, item 645ii.

50 Hunter to Montrose, 20 Dec. 1714, NAS, GD220/5/1895.

honest as well as able men being taken into the administration'.[51] Moreover, he now understood that heated party divisions had divided former friends, commenting to Addison that 'your old acquaintance of the Tale of a Tub [Swift] who it seems had power with the ruined faction was not pleased to interpose in my favour'.[52]

Hunter's correspondence with his friends and patrons was not simply an attempt to vilify his opponents in the minds of Whig politicians in Westminster. As his complaints demonstrate, like many of his Whig contemporaries, he perceived an underlying Jacobite conspiracy in the larger workings of transatlantic Tory politics. As early as November 1714, one month after the news of George I's accession, Hunter wrote that 'all things are quite and easey since H.M. accession to ye crown' and he orchestrated loyal responses from officials in New York including an address to the king reflecting on the 'fatal consequences which must have attended the success of a Pretender'.[53] The alliance of Nicholson, Vesey and Talbot with the Tories in Britain at a time when many high-profile Tories were advocating a Stuart Restoration was politically damaging in immediate terms, but it also implicated them in a larger alleged conspiracy. Talbot's nonjuring sympathies lent immediate credence to Hunter's theory that there was a larger Tory/Jacobite scheme afoot. This is further illustrated by an address from the Grand Jury of New York, probably drafted by Hunter's ally Lewis Morris, and sent to Hunter in 1715. In it the Grand Jury proclaimed that

> We are in no fears of a Pretender from abroad, whilst a truely Protestant King acting by advice of a truely Protestant Ministry guides the helm, and as a deliverance particular to this Province, we think ourselves rescued from a mischiefe contrived with that craft and subtilty by which he who presides over all evil usually directs his Agents. For however false those complaints were, which were carry'd home against yr. Excellency, yet so were they timed that with reason we fear'd the event. But Heaven interposed, and those who digged the pit, we hope, are themselves fallen therein.[54]

The reference to a 'truely Protestant Ministry' is not simply an innocent statement of praise. It is an attack on the previous Tory ministry in Britain which had entertained the complaints sent by Hunter's antagonists and had often sided with the High Church party in New York and New Jersey and, as such, it directly connects complaints against the governor to larger transatlantic

---

[51] BL, MS Egerton 1971, fo. 15

[52] Ibid.

[53] Hunter to the CTP, 8 Nov. 1714, and Address of the Justices of the Peace, sheriff, and grand jurors of the city and county of New York at quarter sessions to the king, 2 Nov. 1714, CSPC, items 83, 83i.

[54] Address from the grand jury of New York to Hunter, 29 Sept. 1715, CSPC, item 629vii.

fears of the equivocal relationship between High Church Tories and a Jacobite political culture.

The accession of George I and the appointment of a Whig ministry initially set Hunter's mind at ease concerning his future as governor and it also allowed him to make use of an emerging regional print culture to disparage his political antagonists and celebrate the Protestant monarchy. His satirical play *Andorboros*, written and printed following the death of Anne, celebrated the demise of the Tory party.[55] He also oversaw the printing of his speeches to the New York General Assembly extolling the accession of George I. In 1715 Hunter claimed that he had 'waited with some impatience for this meeting' where the assembly might express 'the joy of their Hearts for this happy and Peaceable accession to the Crown'. He also condemned those who were responsible for bringing 'all that is Dear, Religious or Civil' into the 'utmost Danger'.[56]

Hunter understood how precarious his position had been with an unfriendly ministry at home. He had worried greatly, prior to news of the Hanoverian succession, about Vesey's trip to London to lay complaints before the Board of Trade and SPG. With the news of the Hanoverian succession he was confident that it would yield few results. In August 1715 he wrote happily that 'the plot, in all other of its parts soe well concerted happen'd to be deficient in ye point of time and season'.[57] The timely intervention of fate simultaneously secured Hunter's position and dashed the hopes of his High Church opponents. He now rightly assumed that his government was safe from the plots of Vesey, Talbot and Nicholson and their Tory allies in Westminster.

The associations of the High Church opposition with Bolingbroke, the exiled former secretary of state, Nicholson and the Tory party, in addition to the nonjuring sympathies of some of the most vocal clergymen in the colonies, connected them to a larger High Church political culture intimately associated with Jacobitism, and Hunter was quick to make the most of these associations. In April 1715 he wrote to a friend explaining that Talbot 'has incorporated the Jacobites in ye Jerseys in the name of a Church in order to sanctify his sedition and insolence to the Government'. He stated in the same letter that the 'noisy fool Coxes [Daniel Coxe], has betrayed the publick service so avowedly that I verily believ'd he had orders from home to do so'.[58] Hunter's primary opponents in New Jersey were all influential members of Talbot's church and he outlined the connections between Talbot's nonjuring and the political opposition that he encountered. But as the accusation against Coxe illustrates, Hunter was also clearly locating the politics of the mid-Atlantic within a larger

---

[55]   Hunter, *Androboros*.

[56]   [Robert Hunter], *His excellencys speech to the General Assembly of New York*, New York 1715, 1

[57]   Hunter to the CTP, 13 Aug. 1715, CSPC, item 569

[58]   Hunter to Popple, 9 Apr. 1715, CSPC, item 337.

imperial framework and understood the High Church opposition that he encountered to be no different from that in Britain.

Hunter's accusations of Jacobitism against Talbot and his congregation reached London by June 1715 while Vesey was still in the city after unsuccessfully voicing his complaints. The Council of Trade and Plantations wrote to the bishop of London informing him that some of the missionaries were being accused of Jacobitism.[59] Hunter assumed that his accusations would temper the zeal of his opponents but he did not realise that the High Church party in the mid-Atlantic still possessed a few allies in Britain. After receiving notice of the complaints, the bishop of London responded to the accusations against Talbot by appointing Vesey his commissary with orders to investigate the charges against Talbot and his congregation.

Hunter was indignant when he discovered that Vesey had been given authority over the clergy in the region as well as the task of investigating the charges against Talbot. His disgust was made all the more explicit when Vesey 'enter'd New York in triumph like his friend Sacheverel'.[60] He sarcastically wrote 'I hope his Lordpp has also constituted Talbott his Commissary for the Jerseys.'[61] He knew that Vesey's appointment was a result of the 'Bishop's spleen' which he had hoped was 'long ago forgot' but knowing the reason did not make Vesey's appointment sit any more easily.[62] Hunter now sought to undermine the authority of the new commissary by accusing him of being a 'sower Jacobite' and he complained to the Council of Trade and Plantations that 'Since there is a happy issue put to ye confusion at home, it is to little purpose to propagate what was by the meanes of that man rais'd here, which cannot be his Lordps [the bishop of London] intention tho' it may have that effect.'[63]

Hunter's insinuations and outright accusations had resulted in frustratingly little change in his circumstances despite the collapse of the Tory ministry in Britain. Although the new Whig ministry was more favourable to him than the previous one had been, his enemies in the colonies continued to exasperate him. Vesey was now a commissary appointed to inquire into the other accusations, and Talbot and Vesey continued to conspire with Nicholson, holding fast to their hopes of replacing Hunter. Members of Talbot's church wrote to the SPG to defend themselves and their parson against charges that they considered 'intirely false'.[64] Jeremiah Basse, one of their number, defended himself and his fellow parishioners by arguing that he could not 'see any

[59] Commissioners to the bishop of London, 24 June 1715, SPG papers, RHL, ser. A, x. 170.

[60] Hunter to Popple, 9 Nov. 1715, *CSPC*, item 663

[61] Hunter to Popple, 10 Oct. 1715, *CSPC*, item 645.

[62] Hunter to Popple, 9 Nov. 1715, *CSPC*, item 663.

[63] Ibid; Hunter to the CTP, 13 Aug. 1715, *CSPC*, item 569.

[64] Jeremiah Basse to the SPG, 6 Oct. 1715, SPG papers, RHL, ser. A, xi. 257–60.

ground for so base a scandal unless it be our early and constant zeal for the church against the prevailing heresy of Quakerism'.[65] The churchwardens and vestry of Talbot's church defended themselves and Talbot by explaining that in the twelve years that they had listened to Talbot they had never heard him say anything that 'might tend towards encouraging sedition'.[66] In the absence of any direct proof of involvement in a conspiracy, their denial of Jacobitism was a strong enough defence against Hunter's complaints, which could be explained away as fanciful rhetoric.

In September 1715 events in Scotland dramatically altered Hunter's circumstances. When John Erskine, earl of Mar, raised the standard of James Stuart, the Old Pretender, at Braemar, there were no longer simply fears of a conspiracy, there was a large-scale open rebellion. Although it was quickly crushed, the rebellion amplified transatlantic fears of the Pretender and accusations of Jacobitism gained greater currency.

In April 1716, after receiving news of the Pretender's defeat and flight, Hunter addressed the New Jersey assembly entreating them to do their duty to the king. It is remarkable how Hunter framed his explanation of their duty, equating duty with obedience and arguing that obedience was all the more necessary at 'a time when that unreasonable and damnable spirit of fraction [faction] at home cloathed with a pretended danger to the church has created a real danger to the state and has disturbed the government of the best prince that ever filled the throne'. He continued by explaining to the assembly that the new King George had 'well nigh confounded all the devices and Hellish endeavours of his restless and rebellious subjects'.[67] His speech was both a celebration of George's victory and a direct attack on those in the region who had been crying out 'the Church in danger'. In Hunter's mind this had simply been a Tory means of masking Jacobitism and sedition. He equated sedition against the colonial government with sedition against the crown. In his mind, colonial sedition was no different from sedition in Britain and was therefore Jacobitism. After years of frustration, this connection between the cries of 'the Church in danger' and sedition was exactly what Hunter needed to destroy his High Church political opponents.

In a similar speech to the Assembly of New York, printed in June 1716, Hunter expounded on similar themes, claiming that the 1715–16 Jacobite rebellion had been a 'desperate attempt' supported by 'unnatural subjects'.[68] He intended this celebration of the Hanoverian succession and the defeat of the Jacobites to further marginalise his Tory or Jacobite opponents by associating them with the party responsible for the uncertainty regarding the succession

[65]   Ibid.

[66]   Vestry of the Church of Burlington to the SPG [1715], ibid. xi. 300.

[67]   Hunter's speech to the assembly, NJA xiv. 8.

[68]   [Robert Hunter], His excellency's speech to the general assembly of his majesty's colony of New York, New York 1716, 1.

in 1714 and, ultimately, the Jacobite rebellion. When he stated that George I 'has not a province where fewer look a squint on his rightful title and righteous cause; for I think, not one has ventured to speak', he was not stating a fact, he was seeking to link himself and the colony that he governed to the ascendant Whig ministry and celebrate the transatlantic defeat of the Tory party.[69]

Soon after receiving news of the defeat of the Jacobites, Hunter sent word to the Board of Trade that Vesey had 'acknowledged his errors and promised to behave better in the future'.[70] It appears as though the rebellion in Scotland had spooked Vesey who understood that High Church opposition to Hunter had just become very dangerous. In contrast, Talbot and his parishioners refused to submit and the 'furious zeal of Talbot' continued to inflame 'the lower rank of people' in New Jersey.[71] Hunter attributed the trouble caused by Coxe and Talbot to their High Church sympathies and argued that their continuing disturbances were only possible because Quakers were not allowed to serve on juries, itself a result of their crying out 'the Church in danger'. He argued that 'the Quakers, who are the only friends of the present establishment in the country where he lives (thanks to the Rev. Mr. Talbot) ... are not capable by the laws of serving on Petty Juries in criminal cases'. Therefore it was proving difficult to galvanise a dissenting opposition to help stamp out High Church sedition.[72]

Not long afterwards Hunter and the Council in New Jersey stumbled upon a means of attacking their High Church opponents. In May 1716 they discovered that Talbot, 'a presbiter or pretended presbiter of the Church of England had not then taken the oaths', and argued that a 'spirit of division and faction industriously raised ... has endangered the publick peace'. They further argued that Talbot's 'leaving out petitions and prayers in the liturgy as he did not like or approve' had turned his congregation against the civil authority and encouraged them to fly in the face of lawful authority and concluded that Talbot was 'one of the chief stirrers up and promoters and encouragers of that seditious and dangerous humour'. Accordingly, they sent the sheriff of the county to force Talbot to subscribe to the oaths of abjuration and gave instructions that, if he refused, he was to immediately 'forbear to exercise his ministerial function of preaching'.[73] Later that month, Hunter and the council also accused Daniel Coxe and ten others of being 'disaffected to his majesties person and government and confederating and conspiring against the same' and ordered their arrest.[74]

Rather than taking the oaths, Talbot fled, with Coxe, Hunter's primary opponent in the New Jersey assembly, to the neighbouring colony of

---

[69] Ibid.
[70] Hunter to the CTP, 30 Apr. 1716, CSPC, item 133.
[71] Ibid.
[72] Ibid.
[73] Council of New Jersey, 21 May 1716, NJA xiv. 16–17.
[74] Council of New Jersey, 25 May, 2 June 1716, NJA xiv. 25, 29–32.

Pennsylvania,. Flight indicated guilt and Hunter understood the importance of this victory. He was also aware that the recent rebellion and High Church Tory association with Jacobitism had strengthened his position. He demonstrated a keen understanding of the situation in a letter to William Popple, noting that Talbot and Coxe would go over and apply to the House of Commons in Westminster since they 'cannot apply with the king, the ministers, the lords. Ha Ha Ha'.[75] Moreover, fleeing to Pennsylvania did not save Talbot from further trouble. The governor of Pennsylvania wrote to the SPG that Talbot was disaffected and refused to subscribe to the oath of allegiance to King George and 'the other usual oaths'. He also accused him of 'speaking disrespectfully of the House of Hanover and not praying for the King'.[76]

Early in the following year, Talbot decided to make his peace with Hunter. He brought forward information about a 'hellish contrivance' and informed Hunter that some in his party were plotting to pull or burn down a Quaker meeting house and Quaker dwelling houses in New Jersey. Details of the plot are a bit thin primarily because it never came to fruition. It was intended to have taken place at some point in 1716 and Hunter believed that it was supposed to coincide with the meeting of the Assembly. He claimed that only 'the hand of Providence' saved the Assembly from meeting in Burlington at that time.[77] According to George Willocks, Talbot claimed that he was able to convince his party not to follow through with the plan even though they promised him that if he were arrested, they would tear down the jail to help him escape.[78] According to Hunter, Talbot seemed 'very penitent' and 'squeamish' about the plot and Willocks stated that after Talbot informed them of the plot he was determined to avoid politics.[79]

This plot to burn down the Quaker meeting house illustrates a continuing High Church antipathy towards Hunter and the Quakers in the region. Furthermore, and perhaps most important, it is very similar to anti-Whig and anti-Hanoverian protest in Britain. The riots and protests which occurred in Britain were directed at dissenters and Whigs, and during many of them dissenting meeting houses were torn down and destroyed.[80] Hunter was convinced that this plot was tied to a transatlantic High Church Toryism which, in 1716, was often indistinguishable from crypto-Jacobitism. He had often accused Talbot and Vesey of Jacobitism and nonjuring and he had accused Coxe and others in the party of disaffection, but now he was willing to accuse him of acting out of sympathy with the Pretender. After receiving

[75]   Hunter to Popple, 8 June 1716, CSPC, item 195.

[76]   Colonel Charles Gookin to the Secretary, 7 Jan. 1716/17, SPG papers, RHL, ser. A, xii. 185.

[77]   Hunter to the Lords of Trade and Plantations, 13 Feb 1717, NJA iv. 273–6.

[78]   Ibid.; 'Deposition of George Willocks, relating to the conversations had with the Rev. John Talbot', NJA iv. 301–3.

[79]   Ibid.

[80]   Monod, Jacobitism, 185–94.

knowledge of the planned attack, Hunter wrote to his agent that he had evidence that Coxe had spoken 'long before the Pretender's landing, that he was at the head of 50,000 men in Scotland' implying that Coxe was well informed as to the Pretender's movements. He also accused him of stating that 'the Whig lords will never be quiet till twenty of their heads are struck off' and sarcastically noted that he carried a 'testimonial of his great moderation and affection to the Protestant Succession, signed by some who are just as moderate and as well affected'.[81] Although the riot and tumult envisioned by the plot never occurred, the plotting itself was enough for Hunter; he now had further evidence of sedition fuelled by Jacobitism.

By the following year Hunter was firmly in control of both the New York and New Jersey assemblies and the influence of the regional High Church party was essentially neutralised. Many of Hunter's High Church opponents had submitted and asked for a pardon, especially after the High Church plot in New Jersey had been revealed.[82] Talbot and Vesey's leadership of a High Church party was at an end. Vesey, after having been indicted for disturbing the public peace, had wisely submitted following the '15 knowing that continued opposition was increasingly dangerous.[83] Talbot was subdued only after the threat of arrest and the possibility of riots and assault. By the beginning of 1717 Hunter could write to his friends in Britain that 'the Jerseys which about a year ago was the most tumultuous, is at present one of the most quiet and best satisfied of his Majestys provinces'.[84] Moreover, he was able to use his friendly relationship with Joseph Addison and a vibrant British print culture to further denigrate his opponents. At Hunter's request, Addison presented an address of the Grand Jurors of New York to the king in person. Later printed in London's *Daily Courant*, it observed that

> This whole province is heartily and sincerely well affected to your government, and that if there be any of a different opinion amongst us, they are so insignificant and contemptible as to their fortunes and understandings that is will never be in their power to give your Majesty's well affected subjects the least uneasiness.[85]

Hunter's battle and eventual victory over the High Church party in the mid-Atlantic colonies illustrates the significance of the rage of party, religious controversies and Jacobitism in the early eighteenth-century transatlantic British political culture. It demonstrates in a number of ways the transatlantic nature of many of the political and religious divisions in Britain and by doing so it illustrates the significance of Jacobitism and the currency of

---

[81]   Hunter to Ambrose Phillips, 27 July 1717, NJA iv. 323-4.
[82]   Hunter to Popple, 24 May 1717, NJA iv. 297-300.
[83]   Webb, *Marlborough's America*, 325.
[84]   Hunter to the Lords of Trade and Plantations, 13 Feb. 1717, NJA iv. 273-4.
[85]   *Daily Courant*, 28 Sept. 1717, 4974.

anti-Jacobitism in the British Atlantic world. Hunter did not see himself simply as a governor of a colony or as participating in the local factional politics of individual colonies. He was an active participant in a much wider struggle with High Church Toryism, nonjuring and Jacobitism. In the middle of 1717 he explained that

> The Militia is in very good order ever since Mr. Cox and his associates were turned out of it, it was not indeed safe in their hands who had for the last years of H.M. reign rung the peal of the Churches danger, under the auspicious influence of the nonjuring Mr. Talbot, lowder than ever it had been rung in England, and indeed their whole conduct was but an *echo to that on the other side*.[86]

Hunter clearly saw the defeat of the High Church party in the mid-Atlantic colonies as a victory in the larger transatlantic battle against a conspicuously seditious element in High Church Toryism. His regional political battle was not simply a colonial conflict; it was an important part of a larger British conflict against the Pretender and his numerous supporters.

Accusations of Jacobitism were, in this instance, more than petty personal attacks. The political culture of the mid-Atlantic was firmly rooted in a British Atlantic world. The divisive, factional politics of the mid-Atlantic, though in many respects local, cannot be understood without an understanding of the growth of a transatlantic High Church party rooted in a resurgent High Church ideology which prospered under the Tories during the reign of Anne. After 1710 this party increasingly developed transatlantic ties with High Church Tories in Britain. As a result, they participated in elements of a High Church Toryism which, after 1710, looked suspiciously like Jacobitism.

Disputes over the role of the Established Church and dissent in the mid-Atlantic contributed to the extension of Britain's rage of party into the mid-Atlantic. These debates were driven by disagreements between the Whig governor Robert Hunter and opposing High Church Tory interests, interests rightly associated with nonjuring and Jacobitism. The informal alliances of the High Church party in the mid-Atlantic colonies with High Church Tories in Britain fairly or unfairly associated them with a suspected Tory/Jacobite conspiracy, realised in the rising of 1715–16, which resulted in the political defeat of the High Church interests in the mid-Atlantic by the end of 1716. Just as the Hanoverian accession, the Tory proscription and the Jacobite rebellion in 1715 dashed the immediate hopes of both the Tories and Jacobites in Britain, so the consequences of these events reverberated across the Atlantic ending the hopes of the High Church interest in New York and New Jersey.

---

[86] Hunter to Phillips, 27 July 1717, *CSPC*, item 674. Emphasis mine.

6

'Now the Mask is Taken Off': Jacobitism and anti-Jacobitism in Colonial New England, 1702–1727

Jacobitism and New England make seemingly strange historiographical bedfellows, though this need not be the case. A handful of recent works have addressed the curious relationship between the two, noting the frequency of accusations of Jacobitism in New England in the early eighteenth century. although generally arguing that the accusations were a reaction to an 'imagined' threat or simply 'rhetorical hysteria'.[1] Jacobitism provided a foil and played 'an essential role in constructing the Protestant interest's identity'.[2] Such studies, while noting important elements of a transatlantic dialogue and demonstrating support for the Protestant succession, posit the absence of real Jacobites or Jacobitism in New England. By doing so, they isolate New England from elements of British political culture, implicitly articulating a belief that Jacobitism was a movement or culture that could not survive an Atlantic crossing.

This chapter argues that Jacobitism and anti-Jacobitism were fundamental elements in religious controversies and in the transatlantic political culture of colonial New England from 1702 to 1727. This in turn further suggests the lasting significance of Britain's 'rage of party' throughout the British Atlantic world. In many respects, the controversies concerning Jacobitism in New England best reflect the changing nature of Jacobitism and anti-Jacobitism in the British Atlantic World. In New England, as in England and Scotland, Jacobitism was a vital element in overlapping local and transatlantic political cultures. The integration of New England into the larger British political world, a process encouraged by imperial wars, controversies involving the Church of England, and the intensification of Atlantic communications, created an environment in which Jacobite sympathies or antipathy towards Jacobitism could be expressed in a colonial context.

Accusations of Jacobitism levelled by Congregationalists at their political or religious enemies are indicative of the changing face of Jacobitism throughout the British Atlantic: from a French Catholic threat to a British nonjuring or High Church Toryism. Nevertheless, it was not solely fears of Jacobitism which

---

[1]   Kidd, *The Protestant interest*, i16; Clark, *The language of liberty*, 255.

[2]   Kidd, *The Protestant interest*, 116–17.

illustrate the significance of Jacobitism in colonial New England. Expressions of Toryism or High Church Anglicanism 'shade equivocally' into Jacobitism, and thus provide reminders that Britain's pan-Atlantic political culture was dynamic and multi-faceted.[3] Thus, the eruption of crypto-Jacobite debates about passive obedience in New England arguably exemplify expressions of an evolving transatlantic British political culture shaped by struggles between Whigs and a conspicuously Jacobite-friendly Tory party.

A number of compelling recent works have demonstrated the integration of the New England colonies into a British imperial political culture. Both Owen Stanwood and Thomas Kidd have argued that a shared Protestantism brought the colonies into imperial conflicts and strengthened the Anglo-American bond after the 1688-9 revolutions. Following William's accession, colonial participation in imperial wars with France, the Nine Years Wars (1689-7) and Queen Anne's War (1702-13) helped to bridge the cultural divide created by vastly different religious establishments.[4] Others have insisted that British monarchical political culture was instrumental in creating a focal point for a common social system.[5] Moreover, scholarship on colonial newspapers, print culture and the role of taverns and coffee houses indicate the means by which colonists connected to British political culture.[6] The dissemination of news through newspapers allowed for increased awareness of and participation in debates arising from metropolitan concerns. Similarly, extensive work on the religiosity of New England suggests the likely significance of the association of Jacobitism with High Church Anglicanism, especially in light of the increasing cosmopolitanism of colonial leaders.[7]

The 'anglicisation' of New England has, understandably, primarily been viewed through the lens of a largely Whiggish British political culture, thus minimising the transatlantic significance of the 'rage of party'.[8] This can be attributed to a lack of understanding of Jacobitism. Historians of New England have analysed Jacobitism within a Whiggish framework. Older studies

[3]   Clark, *English society*, 143

[4]   Stanwood, *The empire reformed*, and 'The Protestant moment', 481–508; Kidd, *The Protestant interest*; Johnson, *Adjustment to empire*; B. Tucker, 'The reinvention of New England, 1691–1770', *New England Quarterly* lix (1986), 315–40.

[5]   McConville, *The king's three faces*; R. Bushman, *King and people in provincial Massachusetts*, Chapel Hill, NC 1985.

[6]   Conroy, *In public houses*; Clark, *The public prints*; Steele, *English Atlantic*; Hunter, 'Transatlantic news', 63–82; Heyd, *Reading newspapers*; Shields, *Civil tongues and polite letters*, and *Oracles of empire*.

[7]   P. Miller, *The New England mind: from colony to province*, Cambridge, MA 1953; M. J. Crawford, *Seasons of grace: colonial New England's revival tradition in its British context*, Oxford 1991; Kidd, *The Protestant interest*; S. Foster, *The long argument: English Puritanism and the shaping of New England culture, 1570–1700*, Chapel Hill, NC 1991; L. R. Jannuzzi, '"And let all the people say amen": priests, presbyters, and the Arminian uprising in Massachusetts, 1717–1724', *Historical Journal of Massachusetts* xxvii (1999), 1–27.

[8]   Murrin, 'Anglicising an American colony; Breen, 'An empire of goods', 467–99.

viewing the expansion of Anglicanism as an imperial conspiracy treat accusations of Jacobitism as little more than Congregationalist slander in response to Anglican aggression, an impulse replicated in recent studies.[9] Though true to a degree, this examines only one aspect of a complex, divided political culture. Although accusations and controversies regarding Jacobitism appear in numerous Boston pamphlets and newspapers, especially between the years 1716 and 1727, scholarly understanding of the meaning and significance of these references in an Atlantic context remains underdeveloped. Studies of John Checkley and Timothy Cutler, prominent recipients of accusations of Jacobitism, have illustrated the importance of religious controversies, which were likely impacted by a transatlantic cultural understanding of Jacobitism, without examining the accusations.[10] Thus, despite the concurrent liveliness of Jacobite scholarship and Atlantic history, Jacobitism, now recognised as a fundamental element in British political culture, has received marginal attention in an Atlantic context.[11]

Any understanding of the significance of Jacobitism in New England hinges on definition. In its broadest sense, Jacobitism entails support for James VII&II and his heirs. This support need not be active rebellion; rather, it need only be sympathy or an expression of support. Articulations of Jacobitism in the New England colonies are examples of the expression of a complex British subculture in a remote British province. This was inextricably linked to High Church Anglicanism, the Tory party and nonjuring. Thus, accusations of Jacobitism in New England, while illustrating the perceptions of the largely Whiggish puritan culture, simultaneously hint at the existence of a local High Church Anglican Tory political culture closely bound to Jacobitism.

The rise of a native High Church interest, which in England and Scotland was often indistinguishable from Jacobitism, brought elements of a cultural Jacobitism to Boston's doorstep. Certainly, not all High Churchmen were Jacobites, but as the Sacheverell trial amply illustrated, Jacobitism was easily masked by doctrines espoused by High Church Tories. This is not to suggest that a handful of Boston Jacobites or Jacobite sympathisers posed any significant threat to the government. Rather, it suggests that even New England was susceptible to the waxing and waning of Tory and Jacobite sympathies within a dynamic, transatlantic political culture. Integrated into a British Atlantic community through newspapers, imperial conflicts and ecclesiastical politics, the people of Boston and New England were exposed to more than an 'imagined' threat as they participated in controversies associated with Jacobitism that spanned the Atlantic.

[9] Bridenbaugh, *Mitre and sceptre*, p. xiii, 74; Kidd, *The Protestant interest*, 115–35.

[10] T. C. Reeves, 'John Checkley and the emergence of the Episcopal Church in New England', *Historical Magazine of the Protestant Episcopal Church* xxxiv (1965), 349–60.

[11] Pincus, 'Rethinking mercantilism', 3–34.

In order to demonstrate the significance of Jacobitism in New England, this chapter first examines the impact of an emerging transatlantic communications network on perceptions of Jacobitism in New England during the reign of Anne. In Britain, Anne's reign witnessed the rise of party politics rooted in religious differences, and colonists were drawn into this. Party conflicts were inseparable from religious divisions, and news of party strife was communicated to colonists through an incipient transatlantic public sphere. Secondly this chapter explores the consequences of the growth of the Anglican Church in New England in relation to expressions of Jacobitism and anti-Jacobitism, looking specifically at the print debates stirred up by John Checkley, an outspoken High Church Anglican Tory and Jacobite. The relation of events in New England has tended towards a dichotomisation between Congregationalists and Anglicans. Though this has some value, it does not fully express the complexity underlying party divisions. As the Checkley case illustrates, the Church of England was riven by factions which were inseparable from Whig and Tory party divisions linked closely to questions about the Protestant succession. As such, the print controversies initiated by Checkley provide a compelling example of the integration of New England into a transatlantic British political culture.

In the early years of the eighteenth century New Englanders were increasingly transfixed by news of the threats posed to Britain by Jacobitism. As early as 1702 participants in the 5 November Pope's day processions were burning effigies of both the pope and the Stuart Pretender.[12] Although fears of Catholicism were rife, the relationship between Jacobitism and religious beliefs, including High Church Anglicanism, Scottish Episcopalianism and nonjuring, was a particular issue. The acquisition of information was facilitated by a maturing local print culture and an increasingly reliable transatlantic communications network.[13] Through imported and local newspapers, private correspondence and pamphlets, the population of New England was drawn into a British Atlantic world. Consequently, they were also drawn into British party controversies. The availability of British and local news, which both shaped and reflected a dynamic transatlantic political culture, encouraged the local populace to appropriate and employ the language of Britain's rage of party.[14]

Interest in news about Jacobites and their suspected counterparts, nonjurors and High Church Tories, was driven partly by antipathy to the growth of what Jeremy Gregory has shown was a popular and indigenous Anglicanism in New England. This developed rapidly after the grant of a new charter in 1692 with the support of the SPG.[15] The steady increase of Anglicanism involved colonial

---

[12] McConville, *The king's three faces*, 58.

[13] Steele, *English Atlantic*; Clark, *Public prints*; Hunter, 'Transatlantic news', 63–82.

[14] Clark, *Public prints*; Hunter, 'Transatlantic news', 63–82; Heyd, *Reading newspapers*, 1–27.

[15] J. Gregory, 'Refashioning Puritan New England: the Church of England in British North America, c. 1680–1770', *Transactions of the Royal Historical Society* xx (2010), 85–112.

analogues of the High Church party. This posed problems for converts to Anglicanism in New England because the ideology of Jacobitism was rooted in the beliefs of nonjurors and was associated with the resurgent High Church in England and nonjurant Episcopalianism in Scotland. Moreover, High Church Tories in Britain became increasingly sympathetic towards Jacobitism during the final years of Anne's reign. This is clearly illustrated by High Church Tory support for the High Church Anglican cleric Henry Sacheverell following his impeachment by the Whig ministry in 1709 for preaching and printing a sermon which celebrated the doctrines of passive obedience and non-resistance.[16] His sermon was viewed as an attack on the Revolution settlement of 1689 and a tacit reminder that the Stuarts were the rightful heirs to the kingdom. Although not all High Church Tories were Jacobites, the conflation of Toryism and High Church Anglicanism, epitomised by Sacheverell, brought about by fears that the Church of England was in danger from dissent and an unsupportive monarch, drew many High Church Anglicans ever closer to supporting the exiled Stuarts as the succession of the Lutheran Hanovers approached.

Thus, articles in Boston's newspapers regarding religious controversies shaped local views of Jacobitism. For instance, Congregationalists were disturbed by Anne's encouragement of Scottish Episcopalians whom they rightly understood to be Jacobite.[17] Many in New England saw parallels between the Congregational establishment in New England and the Presbyterian establishment in Scotland.[18] This affected the manner in which they contextualised Jacobitism. For example, following proposals for the toleration of Episcopalian worship in Scotland in 1703, the *Boston News-Letter* reprinted an article from a London newspaper arguing that 'Jacobites and Papists' were pursuing religious liberty for Episcopalians in Scotland so as to foster divisions in the country.[19] The New England Puritan divine Cotton Mather remarked in 1704 in a letter to an acquaintance that 'another storm is begun; God knows how it will terminate. The Prince of Wales has a strong party in Scotland; the highlands and the High Church are for him … and mischief is hatching there; there is breeding a whirlwind out of the North'.[20] Reports about an attempted Jacobite landing on the east coast of Scotland in 1708 filtered into Boston causing further worry about Jacobitism. The *Boston News-Letter* kept the New England populace apprised of the increasing dangers of the growing strength of the Episcopalians in Scotland and the attempts of the Jacobites. The paper also

---

[16] See chapter 2 n. 32 above.

[17] Bowie, *Scottish public opinion*, 36–9; Lenman, 'The Scottish Episcopal clergy', 36–48.

[18] Colin Kidd, 'Religious realignment between the restoration and the union', in John Robertson (ed.), *A union for empire: political thought and the union of 1707*, Cambridge 1995, 145–68.

[19] *BNL*, 24 Apr. 1704. For a discussion of the Scottish debates in 1703 see Bowie, *Scottish public opinion*, 36–9.

[20] Cotton Mather to Wigglesworth, 17 Apr. 1704, *Selected letters of Cotton Mather*, 68.

published numerous Scottish Presbyterian addresses of loyalty to Queen Anne following the failed rebellion of 1708.[21] This bolstered a sense of fraternity among Puritan New Englanders and their Scottish Presbyterian brethren but it also reminded them of the recurring threat posed by the Jacobites and informed their understandings of Jacobitism.

The threat of a local assertive Anglicanism became all the more pronounced as High Church Anglicanism continued to prosper in Britain in the later years of Anne's reign. Events in Britain continued to impact attitudes in Boston. Frantic reports of the riots and the pulling down of dissenting meeting houses in England during the trial of Henry Sacheverell, were printed in the *News-Letter* in 1710. These reports laid the blame for the commotion and destruction at the feet of the nonjurors.[22] When High Church Tories in Britain, encouraged by popular unrest caused by the trial, won a substantial parliamentary victory and established a Tory ministry in 1710-14, Congregationalist concerns about Tory hegemony were fanned by the news that a majority Tory parliament had passed the Toleration Act of 1712, forcing the toleration of Episcopalian worship in Scotland contrary to articles in the Act of Union of 1707. These developments led Cotton Mather to express his fears that the Church of England was 'disturbing and distracting the church of Christ' and that 'it is likely to be a dreadful time not only in Gr. Britain, but here also'.[23]

Cotton Mather received valuable information from his Scottish Presbyterian correspondent, the minister Robert Wodrow of Eastwood parish near Glasgow. In his correspondence with Wodrow, Mather actively sought information about the condition of religion in Scotland, especially after Wodrow's comment in 1713 that religious unrest was such that 'the flame is rising so high' that 'the bush is like to be consumed'.[24] Wodrow regretfully informed Mather that the toleration of Episcopalian worship 'encouraged the French and Jacobite interest' in Scotland.[25] He also warned that only the disbursement of money from London maintained peace with the numerous disaffected clans.[26] Mather's response revealed his view that New England was experiencing the same advances of the 'daughter of Babylon [episcopacy] that was encroaching upon Scotland'.[27] Wodrow replied to Mather's eschatological concerns by arguing that the loss of Scottish sovereignty in the

[21] *BNL*, 7 June 1708, no. 216; 14 June 1708, no. 217; 29 Nov 1708, no. 241.

[22] *BNL*, 29 May 1710, no. 319.

[23] *The diary of Cotton Mather D.D., F.R.S., 1712*, ed. William Manierre, Charlottesville, VA 1964, 14-15, 26.

[24] Robert Wodrow to Cotton Mather, 23 Jan. 1713, in *The correspondence of the Rev. Robert Wodrow, minister of Eastwood, and author of the History of the sufferings of the Church of Scotland*, ed. T. McRie, Edinburgh 1842, i. 388.

[25] Ibid. i. 390.

[26] Wodrow to Cotton Mather, 15 Dec. 1713, ibid. i. 534

[27] Cotton Mather to Wodrow, 21 Aug 1713, ibid. i. 530.

Union of 1707 had been 'wisely ordered' by God for the 'carrying on his own designs at present by our Popish and disaffected party' which might 'prepare matters for the bringing in of the Pretender among us' in order to discipline the Scottish Kirk. Indeed, he observed, 'matters seem [to be] ripening very fast for an attempt of this nature', a comment likely to promote unease in New England.[28] In 1714 the *Boston News-Letter* reprinted a letter from the General Assembly of the Church of Scotland to the queen which argued that the toleration was leading to the spread of episcopal worship and reminded the queen that Episcopalians in Scotland were disaffected to the Protestant succession.[29]

Similarly, the Low Church advocate and dean of Peterborough, White Kennett, corresponded with the latitudinarian Benjamin Colman, a prominent Presbyterian minister in Boston, on the implications of the Sacheverell affair. Kennett noted that 'the spirit of Dissention and faction, nay, infatuation has raged horribly' and that 'under this delirious Cant, the poor souls were prepared to cry out *The Church, The Church*', and to 'idolize a seditious, not to say ignorant Doctor [Sacheverell]'. According to Kennett the nonjurors and High Churchmen were smoothing the way for the return of 'a Popish Pretender'.[30] This was all taking place under the cover of nonjuring arguments concerning 'divine and hereditary rights', 'Sacerdotal absolution', and also 'the invalidity of Baptism out of episcopal communion'.[31]

Despite their personal antipathy and past disagreements, both Colman and Mather recognised the danger not of popery but Jacobitism, as suggested by the doctrine and behaviours of High Church Anglicans, nonjurant Anglicans and Scottish Episcopalians. Nor was it only fears of a distant Jacobite threat that haunted Massachusetts. The potential existence of colonial Jacobitism did not escape the notice of some in the region. Governor Hunter of New York and New Jersey was in conflict with what he understood to be a 'Jacobite' party led by High Church clergymen eager to 'cry out Fire, and Church at all hazards' during the later years of Anne's reign.[32] Cotton Mather's correspondence reveals his knowledge of this High Church party and his understanding that he had to be circumspect in his correspondence with Hunter because it would be a 'disadvantage to Gov. Hunter' and enrage the governor's Jacobite opponents if they knew that he was corresponding with someone of Mather's 'well-known circumstances'.[33] Mather also remarked upon a 'Jacobite' High Church party in Pennsylvania, stating in 1718 that 'the better people, at Pennsylvania fly to

[28] Wodrow to Cotton Mather, 15 Dec 1713, ibid. 534.
[29] *BNL*, 27 Dec 1714, no. 558.
[30] White Kennett to Colman, in Ebeneezer Turell, *The life and character of the Reverend Benjamin Colman, D.D.: late pastor of a church in Boston, New England*, Boston 1749, 131.
[31] Ibid.
[32] Hunter to Popple, 9 Nov 1715, CSPC xxviii (1714-15), item 663.
[33] Cotton Mather to Hunter [c. 1714], *Selected letters of Cotton Mather*, 147.

me, that I would serve them' by combating 'great mischiefs from the Jacobite party among them'.[34]

Correspondence and newspaper reports demonstrate awareness in New England of a High Church threat, alleged as 'Jacobite', in England, Scotland and nearby colonies. They also demonstrate the increasingly instrumental position afforded to Jacobitism within British political culture. The growing sense that Scottish Episcopalians, Anglicans, Tories and Jacobites were inseparable, and were to be found in the colonies, heightened the fears of many Congregationalists concerning the ever-present danger of Jacobitism. Wodrow regularly remarked upon the growth and spread of popery and Jacobitism in Scotland and stated in 1714 that 'things are very near a crisis, and the Lord must appear, otherwise we and all the Reformed Churches will be swallowed up'.[35] Mather suggested that the population of New England was 'not without our share in the fears which arise from the condition to which it [the 1713 peace of Utrecht] has restored and advanced the grand enemies of our holy religion', and he complained that 'attempts to propagate the Church of England in these colonies are often renewed by a sort of people, whose characters you are no stranger to'. Mather would not have hesitated to second Wodrow's assertion that the enemies included the 'Episcopal Jacobite clergy'.[36] In fact, he forwarded such information along to a correspondent.[37] Mather did not differentiate between Scottish Episcopalians and the Church of England. In his mind, they were all Jacobites. The potential danger of tolerating Anglicans in New England was made abundantly clear when word reached Mather early in 1716 that the 'tolerated prelatical party' in Scotland had 'joined Mar in rebellion'.[38]

In 1714 Anne's failing health prompted questions about the succession and any uncertainty regarding the future security of the Hanoverian succession was laid at the feet of High Church Anglican Tories and Scottish Episcopalians. In these circumstances, the association between Jacobitism and High Church Tories in England and their Scottish coreligionists became so pronounced that Jacobitism was perceived as the very real, and very dangerous, consequence of an assertive High Church Anglicanism, supported by the Stuart queen. The rise of a Jacobite threat in the reign of Anne had been significant enough for Mather to remark that 1 August 1714, the day of Queen Anne's death and George I's accession, had triggered 'a greater revolution than November 26 years ago'.[39] When open Jacobite rebellion soon followed George I's accession,

---

34   *Diary of Cotton Mather*, New York 1957, ii. 526.

35   Wodrow to Cotton Mather, 22 May 1714, *Wodrow correspondence*, i, 560.

36   Cotton Mather to Wodrow, 17 Mar. 1714, and Wodrow to Cotton Mather, 11 Dec 1714, ibid. i. 626, 629.

37   *Diary of Cotton Mather*, ii. 173.

38   Wodrow to Cotton Mather, Feb. 1716, *Wodrow correspondence*, ii. 154.

39   Cotton Mather to Timothy Woodbridge, 20 Jan 1715, *Selected letters of Cotton Mather*, 168.

Mather and others in New England would have recognised these rebellions as the simply physical manifestation of an existing sympathy.

News of the Jacobite rebellions, which broke out in September 1715, reached Boston in October.[40] Wildly inaccurate reports trickled in slowly, feeding fears and uncertainties. Numerous High Church Anglicans, Tories and Scottish Episcopalians participated in the rebellion, which reinforced in the minds of many in New England the problematic relationship between these groups and Jacobitism. In January 1716 the *News-Letter* reported George I's speech to parliament of October 1715, which blamed High Church Anglicanism for 'endeavouring to persuade my people that the Church of England is in danger under my government'. This, he stated, had been 'the main artifice imployed in carrying out this wicked and traitorous design'.[41] This strengthened the notion that High Church Anglicans like Sacheverell were responsible for the rebellion, a sentiment that can also be found in thanksgiving sermons preached in New England in response to news of the defeat of the rebellion in 1716.[42] New England commentators also blamed the Tories. Benjamin Colman invoked traditional tropes of Catholic Jacobitism in portraying the failure of the rebellion as a providential defeat of popery and tyranny, equating it with the Gunpowder Plot, the Spanish Armada and other Protestant victories.[43] But Colman was more concerned by those Tory counsellors who neglected their 'Royal Oath' and 'cover'd treacheries and perfidy' in the 'last scene of the late reign'.[44] Colman linked the Tories and Jacobites together by arguing that the rebellions began with 'a stupid faction mindless of God's wonders' which led to 'murmuring first and mutiny and then rising in arms against God and his anointed'.[45]

Leading Tories, including Ormonde, Mar and Bolingbroke were implicated in the Jacobite rebellion, and numerous broasides and pamphlets detailing this were reprinted in Boston.[46] In January 1716 the *News-Letter* informed its audience that these and numerous other prominent Tories had been involved in Jacobite plotting,[47] It also reminded its readers that

> The rebels are come to a greater height of insolence than could be expected; but when we consider the principal instruments of that rebellion, and compare their

---

[40]   *BNL*, 31 Oct. 1715, no. 602.

[41]   *BNL*, 2 Jan 1715, no. 612.

[42]   Increase Mather, *Two discourses shewing, I: That the Lords ears are open to the prayers of the righteous; II: The dignity & duty of aged servants of the Lord*, Boston 1716, 44; Benjamin Colman, *A sermon preach'd at Boston in New-England on Thursday the 23d. of August. 1716: being the day of publick thanksgiving, for the suppression of the latevile and traiterous rebellion in Great Britain*, Boston, MA 1716.

[43]   Colman, *A sermon preach'd at Boston*, 13–15.

[44]   Ibid. 10, 14.

[45]   Ibid. 26.

[46]   *Instructions by the citizens of London; Abstract of the French king's will.*

[47]   *BNL*, 2 Jan 1715, no. 612.

present management with their carriage during the time of the late ministry, we may see what they all along aimed at. A toleration obtained to who were known to be enemies to the Protestant Succession and all pains taken to encourage Jacobitism, tho not avowedly, but *now the mask is taken off*.[48]

The idea that Jacobitism could be masked under the guise of High Church zeal reflects the blurred boundaries between High Church zeal and disaffection to George I. The notion of masking Jacobitism was reinforced by the reprinting of an address of the Lord Mayor and commissioners of London to the king which claimed that 'As the Mask of Faction is taken off ... We see *Non-Resisting Rebels, Passive-Obedience Rioters, Abjuring Jacobites* and *Frenchify'd Englishmen*.'[49] Increase Mather further expounded upon the idea of hidden Jacobitism when he tied together information from Wodrow's letters with news published in the local paper. In 1716 he published a sermon arguing that it was unbridled arrogance for an 'ungrateful generation' not to be 'thankful to God, for so great a favour of heaven, to a sinful nation' for having been rescued from 'treacherous ministers' of state and a 'wicked sort of men who assume and arrogate to themselves the name of the church, but are enemies to the true church of Christ'.[50] High Church Tory participation in the Sacheverell riots of 1710, which saw the destruction of the 'houses in which the Lord's servants used to worship him', and the rebellion of 1715 solidified in the mind of the New England Congregationalists the inseparable ties between High Church Anglicanism, Tories and Jacobitism. This fed further the anxieties harboured by Congregationalists about the potential consequences of a successful Jacobite rebellion and the successful encroachment of Anglicanism.[51] Ultimately, in the mind of Mather and other anxious Congregationalists, Jacobite success would end with a High Church Anglican ascendancy which would precipitate the destruction of dissenting meeting houses and the dismantling of the Independent establishment.

After the rebellion in 1715 reports and letters further confirmed the suspicion that Anglicans and Scottish Episcopalians were thoroughly disaffected as far as the Hanoverian dynasty was concerned. As a consequence, the Church of England in the New England colonies, which was now associated with disaffection to George I, became the target of vitriolic Congregationalist animosity. If a Jacobite rebellion was understood to be the ultimate physical manifestation of principles propagated by the Church of England, then Congregationalism must be protected at all costs from the advance of Anglicanism in New England. Ministers believed that falling away from Congregationalism to the Church of England would lead to disaffection, murmuring and ultimately to

48   *BNL*, 30 Jan 1716, no. 615. Original emphasis.
49   *To the king's most excellent majesty, the humble address of the Lord Mayor of London, and the rest of your majesty's commissioners of lieutenancy for your city of London*, Boston 1715.
50   Increase Mather, *Two discourses*, 44.
51   Ibid.

rebellion. There is little doubt that Cotton Mather agreed with Wodrow, that the Tories, Anglicans and Scots Episcopalians were 'builders of Babylon'.[52]

The association of Anglicans with Jacobitism was compared with the devoted loyalty to the Protestant succession of the Congregationalists in New England. In 1717 Ebenezer Pemberton, minister of Boston's Old South Church, argued that 'there is not one minister or single person known in their [the Congregationalist] communion but what are full of duty, zeal and affection to the succession of the crown in the illustrious Protestant house of Hanover'.[53] With his published sermon, Pemberton sought to bolster existing notions of loyalty to George I among his co-religionists and also to remind readers that this affectionate loyalty was not true of all communions. Benjamin Colman lamented the spirit of 'parties and factions' and informed his audience that 'The venerable name of religion and the Church is made a sham-pretence for the worst of villanies', and included in his list of 'villanies' perjury, disloyalty, rebellion and treason against the king. He also explicitly decried the fact that members of the Church of England participated in the late rebellion despite having taken oaths of abjuration.[54]

Sermons, like those of Pemberton and Colman, published after the 1715 rebellion, demonstrated a common and growing assumption that disaffection was not only prevalent, but firmly rooted in both the Church of England and the Scottish Episcopal Church. Congregationalists in New England were increasingly fearful of and had little time for, as Wodrow named them, the 'high-flyers' who were 'papists at heart' and a 'reproach upon the reformation'.[55] New England Congregationalists continued to associate Jacobitism with the Catholic beliefs of the exiled Stuarts and this would remain an important aspect of anti-Jacobite rhetoric; but Catholicism was no longer the primary trope associated with Jacobitism. Congregationalists in New England were also increasingly aware of the connections between the Church of England, the Scottish Episcopal Church and Toryism and the ways in which the Union of 1707 had facilitated these connections.[56] Anti-Jacobite rhetoric became more sophisticated and the Congregationalists began to target in their attacks all aspects of transatlantic Jacobite political culture.

In the first few years following the rebellion, reports continued to reach Boston detailing the activities of the Stuarts and their adherents, reminding those in New England that the Jacobite threat had not passed. Wodrow

---

[52] Wodrow to Cotton Mather, 11 Dec. 1714, *Wodrow correspondence*, i. 628.

[53] E. Pemberton, *A brief account of the state of the province of the Massachusetts-Bay in New-England, civil and ecclesiastical*, Boston 1717.

[54] Benjamin Colman, *A brief enquiry into the reasons why the people of God have been wont to bring into their penitential confessions, the sins of their fathers and ancestors, in times long since past*, Boston 1716, 29-31.

[55] Wodrow to Cotton Mather, 18 Feb. 1716, *Wodrow correspondence*, ii. 153.

[56] Raffe, 'Presbyterians and Episcopalians', 570-98; Hayton, 'Traces of party politics, 74-99.

informed the Mathers that the clemency of the government following the defeat of the rebels in 1716 only served to encourage the 'restless enemies' who were seeking to 'raise new disturbances'.[57] The continued restlessness of the Jacobites was further acknowledged when newspapers in Boston reported the failure of the attempted invasion of 1719. Congregational ministers disseminated news in sermons and were sure to remind their parishioners of their providential deliverance from Jacobite aggression. They reminded their auditors that in addition to Mar's open rebellion of 1715, they had been saved in 1715 from Tory statesmen who first had attempted to invite in the 'Old Pretender' in order to bypass the Hanoverian succession.[58] Ministers also made sure to inform their audiences that such scheming was still taking place. In a 1719 sermon that he himself identified as 'whiggish', Cotton Mather preached against 'new plotters', including those who objected to subscribing to the oaths of abjuration which rejected the Stuarts' right to the throne. Mather made no distinction between potential Jacobites and nonjurors at home and those abroad and made nonjurancy the primary means by which Jacobitism could be identified.[59]

After 1715 the Church of England in New England experienced steady growth, so much so that in 1722 the congregation of King's Chapel had grown so large that it became necessary to build a second Anglican church in Boston. Though the number of churches and communicants remained comparatively small, and Anglicans were a numerical minority, the influence of the Church of England was becoming more pronounced. The SPG was supporting a growing number of Anglican ministers in the region. By 1725, one Anglican minister in Boston stated that 'this great town [Boston] swarms with them [churchmen]' and noted that local Anglicans were pursuing two of the four Assembly seats in Boston.[60] Many of the parishioners of King's Chapel were prominent members of society. They included Thomas Selby, the owner and proprietor of The Crown Coffee House, the most popular coffee house in the city, and James Franklin, a local printer. Numerous merchant captains were also members.[61] The Church of England also catered to merchants and sailors from Britain. Benjamin Colman complained about the disconcerting fact that 'gentlemen of Scotland, that

[57] Wodrow to Cotton Mather, 8 July 1717; 22 Aug. 1716, *Wodrow correspondence*, ii. 282, 208.

[58] Cotton Mather, An *history of seasonable interpositions: especially relating to the twice memorable fifth of November*, Boston 1719, 21–7.

[59] For the reference to whiggish see Cotton Mather to John Winthrop, 19 Jan 1719, *Selected letters of Cotton Mather*, 300; Cotton Mather, An *history of seasonable interpositions*, 21–3.

[60] Timothy Cutler to Zachary Grey, 2 Apr. 1725, in John Nichols, *Illustrations of the literary history of the eighteenth century consisting of authentic memoirs and original letters of eminent persons*, London 1818, iv. 269.

[61] H. W. Foote, *Annals of Kings Chapel: from the Puritan age of New England to the present day*, Boston, 1882, 239–65.

are not inhabitants here go off strangely to the Church of England'. He also noticed that 'the gay houses of entertainment, Custom-house officers, etc., are mostly of the Church of England here'.[62] The rapid growth and prominence of the Church of England allowed for the emergence of a High Church Anglican culture. There are numerous references, both from Anglicans and Congregationalists in the years 1720-4 to highflyers and the High Church or Jacobite party in Boston.[63] One local Low Church critic maintained that defection from the Protestant interest could be ascribed to 'Scotch Highlanders and other strangers, who flocking over into this country in great numbers have fomented divisions and propagated their seditious principles'. Such comments demonstrated the pervasive sense that transatlantic connections were fostering disaffection in New England.[64]

Nothing better illustrates the significance of the emergence and controversy surrounding a New England High Church culture than the debates stirred up by John Checkley, a native of Boston and a High Church Anglican Tory layman. Checkley was educated at Oxford sometime between 1700 and 1710, a period of intense religious controversy, and returned to Boston sometime before 1713 where he opened a bookshop.[65] He also happened to be a fearless advocate of the Church of England. Having witnessed the debates surrounding the Church of England in the first decade of the eighteenth century and aware that the High Church was experiencing a resurgence in response to the Bangorian controversy, in 1719 Checkley underwrote the publication and sale of a reprint of Charles Leslie's attack against deists, *The religion of Jesus Christ the only true religion* (1697).[66] Appended to the work was a letter of Ignatius of Antioch, an Early Church Father, which argued for the necessity of episcopal government in the Church.[67] Checkley, tapping into a long, distinguished line of Anglican martyrology including Charles I, Sacheverell and later Francis Atterbury, viewed himself as a Bostonian Sacheverell and intentionally provoked his opponents in the hope of galvanising a High Church response.[68] Checkley's publication of the work of a notorious nonjuror on the heels of the failed Jacobite conspiracy

[62] Colman to Wodrow 27 June 1725, in 'Some unpublished letters of Benjamin Colman, 1717-1725', ed. Neil Caplan, *Proceedings of the Massachusetts Historical Society* lxxvii (1965), 101-43, quotation at p. 137.

[63] Colman to Wodrow, 26 May 1724, ibid. 134; Mr [?] Mossom to the bishop of London, 17 Dec, 1724, *FP* iv. 142.

[64] Henry Harris to the bishop of London, 22 June 1724, ibid. iv. 117-21.

[65] Edmund Slafter, *John Checkley; or, The evolution of religious tolerance in Massachusetts Bay*, Boston 1897.

[66] For the Bangorian controversy see Andrew Starkie, *The Church of England and the Bangorian controversy, 1716-1721*, Woodbridge 2007.

[67] Charles Leslie, *The religion of Jesus Christ the only true religion; or, A short and easie method with the deists*, Boston 1719.

[68] For a discussion of Anglican martyrology see Knights, 'Introduction: the view from 1710', 1-15.

of 1719 rekindled local fears of Jacobitism. Charles Leslie was one of the most notorious nonjuring polemicists and an unrepentant supporter of the exiled Stuarts. An assertive High Church Anglicanism rooted in the works of Leslie was fraught with implications and many in New England responded quickly.

In December of that year, the General Assembly of Massachusetts, in response to the Jacobite conspiracy in 1719 and Checkley's publication, enacted a law giving authority to justices of the peace to tender the oaths of allegiance and abjuration to anyone suspected of disaffection to George I. Two justices of the peace requested that Checkley take the required oaths. He refused. He was then forced to appear in court where he publicly refused to take the oaths and was fined six pounds. He was also required to put up £100 in sureties, which, despite his open disaffection, some of his fellow Anglicans helped him to raise.[69] It is necessary to note that nonjuring was deemed Jacobitism by default. By refusing the oaths, Checkley was tacitly acknowledging the exiled Stuarts' right to the throne. The fact that he received assistance from fellow Anglicans suggests that they were not entirely repulsed by his overt disaffection.

Checkley's nonjuring is not at all surprising given his extreme High Church opinions. His numerous correspondents included prominent High Churchmen and nonjurors in England, such as Zachary Grey and Robert Moss, the dean of Ely.[70] In a letter of 30 January 1720, Checkley wrote that he planned to close up his shop so that he might better remember the death of the 'royal martyr' Charles I. He also connected New England Congregationalists to the English Civil War when he complained that 'there are too, too many who defend the horrid Regicides and glory in their being of their King-killing, hellish principles'.[71] His refusal to swear the oaths of abjuration and allegiance was a principled stand rooted in the nonjuring understanding of the doctrines and culture of the Church of England. By refusing the oaths he was conforming to the Congregationalist caricature of a seditious High Church Tory, but he was a firm believer in High Church Anglicanism and would continue to advocate its doctrines in New England.

Checkley's publication of Leslie's work was the first shot in a vigorous pamphlet war that encapsulates the nature of Jacobitism in New England. Following his initial publication, Checkley anonymously published a tract titled *Choice dialogues between a godly minister and an honest countryman* which ridiculed predestination, a key doctrine of New England Congregationalists.[72] Although there was nothing inherently Jacobite in what Checkley wrote, his work intentionally mimicked the dialogues found in Charles Leslie's newspaper, *Rehearsal*. His opponents noticed the similarities and explicitly complained that 'Lesley's rehearsals and other works falling into this man's hands, they work'd

[69]   Slafter, *John Checkley*, i. 39.
[70]   Ibid. ii. 158–82.
[71]   John Checkley to John Read, 30 Jan, 1720, ibid. ii. 173–4.
[72]   Checkley, *Choice dialogues*.

so powerfully upon his distempered brain that he was very impatient till he had communicated his discoveries to the rest of mankind'.[73]

The most notable response to Checkley's *Dialogues* came from Thomas Walter, a Congregational minister in Roxbury and nephew of Cotton Mather. In 1720 he anonymously published *A choice dialogue between John Faustus a conjurer, and Jack Tory his friend* under the pseudonym 'Christopher Whigg'.[74] This tract shows that the debate launched by Checkley was firmly rooted in terms defined by British political culture. In his response, Walter politicises important aspects of Checkley's theological argument. Even within his title, he unambiguously lampoons the Tory party. The character 'Jack Tory' cleverly brings Jack, shorthand for both Jacobite and John, and Tory together and associates him with Faustus, the alchemist who sold his soul to the devil.[75] That he signed his preface as 'Christopher Whigg'[76] – Christopher meaning Christ-bearer, conjoined to Whigg – leaves no doubt as to which political party God favours. The distinction between the Tory and the Whig is given even greater weight by accusations made in the preface. Walter informed his readers that Charles Leslie, the 'reverend and labourious' original author of Checkley's dialogues, was a 'Jacobite clergyman, who, I dare vouch has served the Pretender ten years, where he has served the flock of Christ one'.[77] This reminded the audience that Checkley's tract was not simply a dialogue on predestination; a work parroting the Jacobite Leslie also carried serious political undertones.

Walter drew the connections for his readers between Checkley's work, the politics of High Church Toryism and Jacobitism in one devastating attack. He also demonstrated a keen understanding of the politics of religion when he makes sport of the Tory propensity to cry out 'the Church in danger'.[78] But the end of Walter's piece leaves his audience little doubt as to the implications of Checkley's work. His Jack Tory character exclaims that

> The next touch shall be a vindication of Jacobus Tertius et Octavus, together with the adjustment of the monarchies of Europe, a Resurrection of the King of Sweden, and a formal invitation of the Czar of Muscovy, to make a visit to the British Dominions; and essay to put the King of Spain upon his Legs again, and either Rout or Drown the Dutch. These are great and noble Subjects much upon my heart.[79]

---

[73] Harris to the bishop of London, 22 June 1724, *FP* iv. 117–21; Thomas Walter, *A choice dialogue between John Faustus a conjurer, and Jack Tory his friend*, Boston 1720.

[74] Walter, *A choice dialogue*, 21.

[75] For examples of the use of Jack for Jacobites see *CSPC* xvi, no. 760; Monod, *Jacobitism*, 226, 228; and Holmes, *British politics*, 17–18.

[76] Walter, *A choice dialogue*, p. xxi.

[77] Ibid. pp. ii–iii

[78] Ibid. 22.

[79] Ibid. 30

Walter does not limit his character to propagating foreign support for the Jacobites. He also aims to 'invite Lesly over to New-England; and send out an hue-in-cry after Marr, Oxford, Ormond and Bolingbroke, and we'll set the World to Rights'.[80] In Walter's mind, Jacobitism was not a distant or perceived threat. The politics of Toryism and Jacobitism, both inextricably linked to Anglicanism, threatened New England as well as Great Britain.

Although Walter's vitriol in 1720 was primarily directed at Checkley, it is likely that he was also responding to the existence of Jacobitism in neighbouring colonies and the continuing growth of a native High Church party in the city. Jacobitism was certainly extant in Pennsylvania and in 1721 the Boston News-Letter reported that two men in Philadelphia had recently been pilloried for denying the king's right to the throne and calling him a usurper and had likely been encouraged by a 'senseless high flying' Church of England minister.[81] Furthermore, within three years, Richard Welton, the notorious English nonjuror, was officiating in Philadelphia's Anglican Church after having been appointed by the vestry, suggesting that Jacobitism was not restricted to the two men prosecuted. This news further reinforced the notion that high flying Anglican doctrines bred disaffection.

The importance of the growing confidence of an Anglican party in Boston is seen in a controversy over inoculation for smallpox that erupted in 1721, a year when Boston was ravaged by the disease. As early as 1714 Cotton Mather had read in the Royal Society's transactions an article discussing the merits of inoculation, so when smallpox broke out in the city he advocated inoculation even though it was untested. This potentially dangerous procedure met fervent opposition from some local physicians including William Douglass, the only university educated physician practising in Boston. On the other side, leading supporters of inoculation included prominent Congregational ministers like Benjamin Colman, and another local physician, Zabdiel Boylston.[82]

Public objections to inoculation were voiced primarily by a group of Anglicans in Boston. Lacking an outlet for their views, they decided to publish a newspaper with the help of a local printer, James Franklin. The New England Courant, born out of the inoculation controversy, became the 'voice of Anglicanism' in Boston.[83] Certainly, the nonjuring Checkley and many of his fellow Anglicans at King's Chapel were heavily involved in writing many of the paper's controversial pieces which lampooned the Congregationalist majority.[84] Leading members of the Congregational clergy understood the

---

[80] Ibid.

[81] BNL, 10 Apr. 1721, no. 891. For the reference to the minister see Wendal, 'Jacobitism crushed', 59.

[82] For two different interpretations of the inoculation controversy see Miller, The New England mind, 347-58, and M. Minardi, 'The Boston inoculation controversy of 1721-1722: an incident in the history of race', WMQ lxi (2004), 47-76.

[83] Sloan, 'The New England Courant', 108-14.

[84] Ibid.; Clark, Public prints, 127-30.

implications of the emergence of the paper and complained that it was the mouthpiece of a 'hell-fire club'. Checkley's involvement also resulted in charges that the club was led by a nonjuror; a fact with transatlantic repercussions.

In Britain debates about inoculation had also become political. [85] This news began to filter into Boston, where local newspapers were reporting that London's presses 'begin to grow warm with the dispute about inoculation'. The newspapers also noted that the 'High Church' party in England was against inoculation, arguing

> as soon as the children of the Royal Family, and some of our chief Ministers pass'd thro' this operation, the High Church began to open with loud clamours & fierce wrath against it. Mr. Massey, one of that party, led the van; and to make his Sermon the more conspicuous preach'd it in Dr. Sacheverel's Desk at St. Andrew Holborn.

Thus, in Britain it became a 'party controversy among us'.[86] The fact that a 'highflying party' was contesting inoculation in Boston therefore gains greater significance when the politicised smallpox debate is linked to larger trans-atlantic events as it was by Benjamin Colman who asserted that 'the High Church I find rave at it [inoculation] in London as they did here. I suppose because the princess [princess of Wales] passed well thro' it'.[87] The transatlantic context also provided a basis for Cotton Mather's belief that the opposition to smallpox inoculation in Boston was led by a 'jacobite or highflying party counting themselves bound in duty to their party to decry it'.[88] Colman and Mather connected the High Church, Checkley and his party in Boston to a High Church party in Britain thoroughly tainted with Jacobitism. By doing so, even the smallpox controversy became enveloped in debates concerning Jacobitism. Colman and the rest were participating in an actively evolving trans-atlantic political culture dominated by a continuing Jacobite threat.

New England rarely lacked for controversy, and shortly after the debates on inoculation subsided, the region was again aghast at the spectre of an emergent High Church. In September 1722, amidst the continued controversy surrounding Checkley's publications and the recent appearance of the *New England Courant*, Timothy Cutler, Rector of Yale College, two Yale tutors, and four neigh-bouring ministers renounced their adherence to Congregationalism and declared themselves for the Anglican Church. Their conversion, which spoke to the belief that episcopal ordination was necessary and that its absence invalidated a minis-ter's work, sent shockwaves through New England for it implied that the entire Congregational establishment in New England was invalid. This was a position

85   Parrish, 'A party contagion', 41–58.

86   *NEC*, 5 Nov 1722, no 66.

87   Colman to Wodrow, 23 Nov 1722, 'Some unpublished letters of Benjamin Colman', 101–43 at p. 127.

88   Cotton Mather to James Jurin, 21 May 1723, *Selected letters of Cotton Mather*, 361.

increasingly associated with Jacobitism.[89] The *News-Letter* and the *Courant* were quick to report the event and letters came pouring in denouncing Cutler and his associates. The *News-Letter* reported Cutler's claim that there was no salvation outside of the Church of England, echoing Checkley.[90] Cutler's statements were a major affront to Congregational sensibilities, but more importantly the idea of the invalidity of dissenting ordination was traditionally an important nonjuring position. James Wetmore, Samuel Johnson and Daniel Brown, three of the ministers who declared themselves with Cutler, penned a brief vindication of Cutler for the Anglican-inclined *New England Courant*. In it they argued that they were being treated as though to 'have declared in favour of the Church of England, had been as bad as to have declared for Popery or something worse'.[91] Three of the converts sailed to England to receive episcopal ordination in November carrying with them letters of introduction to the Revd Edmund Massey, the High Church demagogue.[92] They were later joined in England by John Checkley who remained their regular companion.[93] Perhaps even more damning in the eyes of their opponents, before they left for England they were entertained in Bristol, New England (now in Rhode Island), at the house of a Colonel Mackintosh, a Scottish Jacobite from a Jacobite family.[94] Their timing could not have been worse.

In September news began to filter into Boston informing the population of the discovery in Britain of another major Jacobite conspiracy. Francis Atterbury, Anglican bishop of Rochester, was suspected of plotting to restore the exiled Stuart monarch, James III&VIII, the Old Pretender. Over the next few months newspapers in Boston continued to provide further information about Jacobite plotting in Britain. Early in 1723 the *News-Letter* and the *New England Courant* each published a speech by King George regarding the recent discovery of a plot against his crown detailing the 'dangerous conspiracy' in favour of a 'Popish Pretender'.[95] Within weeks, further details arrived and newspapers were reporting that the main actor in the conspiracy was none other than Atterbury.[96] News that a High Church Anglican bishop was at the centre of the conspiracy did not surprise those in New England who had long associated High Church Tories with Jacobitism. In fact, many relished the information. The fact that a bishop of the Church of England who had sworn the oath abjuring the exiled Stuarts could still conspire for their restoration confirmed in the minds of New England Congregationalists that not even jurant Anglicans could be

[89] Sirota, *The Christian monitors*, 180.
[90] *BNL*, 15 Oct 1722, no. 976.
[91] *NEC*, 5 Nov, 1722, no. 66.
[92] *Post Boy*, 19 Jan 1723. For Massey see further TNA, SP 35, xxxiii, fos 1–3, and Parrish, 'A party contagion', 41–58.
[93] Beardsley, *Life and correspondence of Samuel Johnson*, 23.
[94] Ibid. 23; TNA, SP35, xxvi, fo. 33b.
[95] *NEC*, 11 Feb, 1723, no. 80; *BNL*, 14 Jan 1723, no. 989.
[96] *NEC*, 25 Feb, 1723, no. 82.

fully trusted. This blatant reminder that members of the Church of England, as well as nonjurors and papists, were plotting a Stuart restoration resonated with a populace shaken by the recent conversions. In 1723 the *News-Letter* reprinted a satirical letter, originally printed in London's *Flying Post*, authored by a 'Father Francis' and written to James III on behalf of 'all the papists, and perjured Protestants in Great Britain, in behalf of themselves and those of their brethren'. The author asserted that 'by principle and inclination we are so firmly attach'd to your highness' and proudly boasted that 'we have, 'tis true, many of us, frequently, and in a solemn manner Abjured you and all your Rights or Pretensions to these Dominions'.[97] Furthermore, in 1722 the anonymous British tract, *A letter to the clergy of the Church of England*, was reprinted in Boston. This pamphlet defended the government's arrest of Atterbury and called on preachers to condemn the recent conspiracy arguing that silence 'was almost to Rebel against not only the State but our Religion too'. It also included a section written explicitly for clergymen who hoped for a Stuart restoration, reminding readers that Jacobitism was rampant even within the established Church.[98]

It did not take long for some in New England to notice a connection between Checkley's publications, the conversions at Yale and the recent conspiracy against the crown. A poem printed in the *New England Courant* made this connection abundantly clear.[99] In it the author writes

> but if the Mother Church, her new sons now lurch,
> and of them be very shy,
> Lest they to the High Church fly,
> and to the Pretender make a free surrender:
> Pray you turn no more,
> Lest at the last you turn so far and fast
> as to court the Whore.[100]

He continues:

> But perhaps in the Tower he [Cutler] may find
> Great Gentlemen that to him be very kind:
> To see such New-England sons, how will they rejoice
> If on the Block the Ax hath not spoil'd their voice
> But our Male-Contents another step very high,
> They may to the Pretender and the High Church fly.[101]

---

97   *BNL*, 16 May 1723, no. 1007.

98   Anon., *A letter to the clergy of the Church of England: on occasion of the commitment of the right reverend the lord bishop of Rochester to the Tower of London*, London, repr. Boston 1722. 13.

99   This poem is exceedingly interesting because it represents a popular understanding of the situation. Furthermore it allows a brief glimpse of the role of the newspapers as the *Courant* clearly mocks the poem and does not subscribe to the author's opinion.

100   *NEC*, 11 Mar. 1723, no. 84.

101   Ibid.

High profile conversions during a period of Jacobite conspiracy had brought the Jacobite threat home to Boston. But the author of the poem was not only interested in connecting Cutler and the others to the Atterbury plot; he also linked the conversions at Yale to Checkley's early publications. The author encouraged his audience to 'pray to God the dividing devil for to restrain, and not to send his servant Cheklie into New Haven again'.[102] Checkley's outspoken advocacy of High Church principles, as well as his nonjuring, lent credence to the notion that his nefarious and seditious influence was responsible for the conversions. A later pamphlet, referring either to Cutler or Checkley, complained about those who were 'debauching' the 'unthinking youth'.[103] The large number of malicious reports being spread regarding the disaffection of the Yale converts forced Samuel Myles, the Rector of King's Chapel in Boston, to write to the bishop of London 'to take away suspicion of their being disaffected to the government'.[104]

Also in 1723 'a lover of the present happy constitution' printed in Boston a pamphlet celebrating the Hanoverians titled *Gloria Britannorum*. In it the anonymous author explicitly argues against the High Church Tory or Jacobite belief that the Church was in danger, stating that 'great Brunswick' saved 'church and laws'. Moreover, he attacks Jacobites and the equivocal relationship between Jacobitism and High Church Toryism, writing

> Religious Truths in Purity shall shine,
> Tho' Rome in bloody league with *High-Church* join,

Further on, the poet wrote

> How did the palace ring with Joy!
> Sad Omen to the Rival Boy [James III],
> And all the Tory crew,
> Tho' forc'd some of 'em to proclaim
> Great Brunswick's Title and his Name,
> And swear Allegiance too.
>
> The self same Faction that before
> Had south th' Impostor to Restore,
> And overturn the State;
> Now perjur'd and the publick Scorn,
> Yet serv'd his Triumph to adorn, Such was the Will of Fate.[105]

Amidst the bad press of an untimely Jacobite conspiracy and voluminous accusations that his works promoted Jacobitism, Checkley remained undeterred. He

---

[102] Ibid.
[103] Anon., *The madness of the Jacobite party*, p. i.
[104] Samuel Myles to the bishop of London, 1 Nov, 1722, *FP* iv. 81.
[105] Ibid. iv. 26.

relished his participation in a larger High Church or Jacobite political culture and viewed controversy as the most effective way to gain converts. In 1723 he published and sold a new edition of Charles Leslie's *Short and easie method with the deists*.[106] This occasioned various responses both in print and in law including prosecution for seditious libel for which he faced trial in 1724. Even more significant was Checkley's anonymous publication in 1723 of an attack on the Congregational churches, *A modest proof of the order and government of the Church as settled by Christ and his Apostles*, originally published in London in 1705.[107] This publication, which directly attacked the legitimacy of Presbyterian ordination, was in some measure a response to events at Yale. The audacity of the work, advertised by Checkley over the two weeks from 27 May to 10 June, can hardly be overstated.[108] Not only did Checkley advertise it during a significant period of the Jacobite calendar, which included Restoration day (May 29) and, more specifically, the birthday of the pretender James III (June 10), but within five pages of it he was trumpeting the Jacobite-tinged virtues of passive obedience and non-resistance.[109] The fact that Checkley advertised this publication on such important days in the Jacobite calendar strongly suggests the tenor of his political sympathies as advertising often reflected a symbiotic relationship between authors, printers and audience. Since he was the most vocal proponent of the Church of England in Boston, his politics reflected on the whole of his denomination.

Checkley's Jacobite foray was met with a barrage of biting replies directed against him and his fellow Anglicans. Newspapers continued to play a vital role in the debate. For example the *New England Courant*, which by 1723 was an open forum for differing views, printed a letter and an article reminding its readers of the recent plot against the crown and Atterbury's recent imprisonment and banishment.[110] Also, two weeks after Checkley's publication was advertised, the *Courant* printed an anonymous letter written by 'a true lover of Passive Obedience and Non Resistance' which attacked Checkley's explanation of the doctrines. This letter sought to explain that the doctrines had been wrongly practised by their 'pretended patrons', the High Churchmen and nonjurors. It reminded the Boston populace that nonjuring and High Church supporters of these doctrines had plagued the nation with 'plots and conspiracies' and sarcastically asserted that 'pure Passive Obedience' had so influenced its adherents that 'after they had taken the Oaths to the Powers in being' they took up arms against the government in 1715. The author continued that 'if I should attempt

[106]   Charles Leslie, *A short and easie method with the deists*, eighth ed, London 1723.

[107]   [John Checkley], *A modest proof of the order and government of the Church as settled by Christ and his Apostles*, Boston 1723.

[108]   For the advertisements see *NEC*, 27 May 1723, no. 95; 3 June 1723, no. 96; 10 June 1723, no 97.

[109]   Checkley, *A modest proof*, 5. On the significance of advertisements see Parrish, 'A party contagion', 53–4.

[110]   *NEC*, 17 June 1723, no. 98.

to speak of the carriage of such persons in the present reign, time would fail me to enumerate the many Rebellions, Plots, and Conspiracies which have been hatch'd, carried on and supported by those who have been the greatest sticklers for these doctrines'. He also complained that the 'nation at this time feels the fatal effects of the passive obedience and non-resistance which consist only in pretences'.[111] In fact, the hypocrisy inherent in propounding these doctrines while conspiring against the crown continued to plague Anglican proponents of the doctrines as the Atterbury plot had so recently demonstrated. In response to local events, the *Boston News-Letter* printed one of Cato's letters, originally written in England by John Trenchard and Thomas Gordon, two staunch Whigs. After complaining that 'there having lately been great endeavours used by a sort of people (formerly unknown to this and other provinces of New England) to debauch the minds of unheeding youth, as to their religion' the paper observed that it thought it wise to publish 'two of the celebrated British CATO's lucubrations' lampooning the High Church party and their nonjuring allies.[112]

Alongside the newspapers, clerical opponents of Checkley continued to attack him through pamphlets and sermons. Thomas Walter, the minister who had written the devastatingly satirical reply to Checkley's dialogues, responded in 1724 to Checkley's more recent works by stating, 'let us make the onset, and try if we can't beat out the little pert Jacobite, from his fancied secure retreat and oblige him to make a surrender of his false apostolical episcopacy'.[113] However, Walter's response was far more informed than this accusation might suggest. Walter understood that arguments in favour of episcopacy were a bastion of High Church and nonjuring doctrine. He accused Checkley of promoting a union with the Gallican Church in France, which was supported by nonjurors as a means of legitimating a Stuart restoration. For support, he quoted Benjamin Hoadly, the Low Church bishop of Bangor, loathed by advocates of the High Church, and sure to be inimical to Checkley.[114]

Walter was not the only minister to respond to Checkley. Edward Wigglesworth, the president of Harvard, penned a reply to Checkley entitled *Sober remarks* which castigated his promotion of passive obedience and non-resistance if they were, as he suspected, intended to undermine the Protestant succession in the House of Hanover. Wigglesworth argued that these were essentially code words for the Jacobite interest and that the majority of members of the Church of England would agree with him, 'unless Occasional Perjury is much more practiced by some sorts of persons than ever Occasional

---

[111] *NEC*, 24 June 1723, no. 99

[112] *BNL*, 12 Mar. 1724, no. 1050.

[113] Thomas Walter, *An essay upon that paradox, infallibility may sometimes mistake; or, A reply to a discourse concerning episcopacy, said in a late pamphlet to be beyond the possibility of a reply. to which is prefixed, some remarks upon said pamphlet, entituled A discourse shewing, who is a true pastor of the Church of Christ: as also remarks upon St Ignatius's Epistle to the Trallians*, Boston 1724, 12.

[114] Ibid. 64. For the High Church support for Gallicanism see Every, *High Church party*, 70.

Conformity was by others'.[115] Wigglesworth clearly believed, and reminded his audience, that not even Anglicans willing to take the oaths should be fully trusted.

The strongest attack on Checkley, anonymously published in 1724, was entitled *The madness of the Jacobite party*.[116] According to the author, the publication was timely because 'faction runs high in our nation and so many restless sprits would conspire its ruin'. In his view, the concurrent timing of the Atterbury plot, the Yale conversions and Checkley's publications was no accident. The author saw clearly the dangers and stated that the reason for publication was to combat

> some among ourselves, who, (being zealous sticklers for Hereditary Right, have entertained too pompous ideas of imperial greatness) are labouring by all possible means to corrupt and debauch the minds of Men (and of our own unthinking youth especially) by infusing into them the most absurd notions of Government and loyalty, as well as of religion.[117]

He makes no distinction between Jacobites at home in New England and those in Great Britain. Moreover, he appealed not just to those already inclined towards his point of view, but also reminded his Anglican opponents of the inevitable consequences of their doctrines. They might naively suppose that they are protecting or fighting for the established Church, but if a 'popish Pretender' is put on the throne, 'episcopal see's [sic] will soon be filled with Romish Bishops' and the Anglican Church would suffer most of all.[118] The author's appeal is in some respects a clarion call to all Protestants to unite against the Stuarts, but he also sent out a rallying cry to the Congregationalists arguing

> you, who have been all along Traduced and Cursed, as men of Anti-Monarchical principles, levellers, enemies to kings, and Kingly government, by your malicious adversaries; you I say, may boldly challenge them to 'oblige you with the names of Presbyterian ministers ... Presbyterian soldiers, or mobs that appeared or acted in any of the late horrid rebellions!'[119]

Of course, these responses did not deter Checkley from issuing a strong retort. During 1724, prior to being tried for seditious libel, he authored and published a reply to his numerous detractors, printing and distributing over 500 copies in

---

115   Edward Wigglesworth, *Sober remarks on a book lately re-printed at Boston, entituled, A modest proof of the order and government settled by Christ and his Apostles in the Church: in a letter to a friend*, 2nd edn, Boston 1724, 17.

116   Anon, *The madness of the Jacobite party*.

117   Ibid. p. i.

118   Ibid. 6.

119   Ibid. 11–12.

Narraganset County alone.[120] Knowing that he had pricked a nerve, he praised his own influence and argued that his opponents 'offer themselves evidences of its not being so contemptible a piece as they would represent it; since with all the efforts of intemperate malice, they fly from every quarter to hiss and spit their venom on it'.[121] Checkley primarily argued for the necessity of episcopacy but, in comments interspersed throughout, he could not help but belittle his opponents. He responded to his detractors with common High Church accusations including 'enthusiasm' and that 'schism and sedition are near a-kin'. Checkley noted that 'presbytery was hardly any where ever established, but on the ruins of Kings or Kingdoms', and reminded his readers of the chaos of the English Civil Wars, arguing that one of his detractors was possessed with one of the 'Furies of Forty One'.[122]

Checkley's latest publication would not remain unanswered long. Jonathan Dickinson, who had replied to A modest proof, made another attempt to humble Checkley and expose the Jacobitism which he believed was inherent in his arguments.[123] In his Remarks upon the postscript to the defence, Dickinson again reminded his readers of the seditious principles linked to Checkley's party. He asserted that Checkley is of the 'High–Church party' and informed his audience that 'we have a Tory to deal with'. But if his readers were still unsure of what this implied, he was quick to inform them of the dangers represented by fervent High Church beliefs. He questioned whether it was wrong to 'call the doctrines of Passive Obedience and Non Resistance, (as proposed in the Modest Proof, without any limitations) Jacobite principles? Be pleased Sir, to read the trial of your late Brother Dr. Sacheveril'.[124] This connected Checkley directly to Sacheverell, once again associated the High Church with closet Jacobitism and reminded the audience of the transatlantic nature of the threat. Furthermore, Dickinson asserted that 'all the rebellions and seditions that have been raised' during the reign of King George had 'their rise from that doctrine as unlimitedly proposed in the Modest Proof'.[125]

Checkley was not the only Anglican promoting crypto-Jacobite ideas in New England. An Anglican minister in New Haven, Connecticut, complained to the bishop of London that 'it is certain that the nonjurors have sent over two Bishops into America [Richard Welton and John Talbot]' and noted that 'one of them has travelled through the country... to promote their cause'. He also expressed concern that 'my well meaning people otherwise well enough affected will be in great danger of being imposed on and led aside' and was

---

[120] John Checkley, A defence of a book lately re-printed at Boston, entituled A modest proof of the order and government settled by Christ and his Apostles in the Church, Boston 1724; Checkley to Zachary Grey, 21 June, 1725, Nichols, Illustrations, iv. 271-4.

[121] Checkley, A defence, 53.

[122] Ibid. 4, 40.

[123] J. Dickinson, Remarks upon the postscript to the defence, Boston 1724.

[124] Ibid. 4.

[125] Ibid.

'sensible that their [the nonjuring bishops] powers of persuasion are very considerable'.[126] Similarly, the Yale convert Timothy Cutler, rector of Christ's Church in Boston, made light of criticism offered by an occasional auditor of his, who complained that he should 'preach more on true conversion ... and not so much on Passive Obedience and Non-Resistance' and noted that he should pray in the 'little prayer before the sermon for King George and the Royal Family'.[127] Moreover, Cotton Mather maintained that Cutler and his congregation had little to distinguish them beyond baseness, impiety and 'Jacobitism'.[128] Though Cutler dismissed the complaints, passive obedience and non-resistance were increasingly associated with Jacobitism, especially after the Jacobite rebellion of 1715.[129] Despite charges of disaffection and the expression of High Church views, Checkley and Cutler continued to receive support from the vestries and churchwardens of the two Anglican churches in Boston suggesting, at the very least, support for High Church doctrines. As in England, a failure to rebuke smacked of a thinly veiled disaffection.[130] Furthermore, the vestry of King's Chapel, allies of Checkley, censured Henry Harris the Low Church assistant rector of King's Chapel, who after seeing some of Checkley's publications 'thought it his duty to animadvert in a sermon upon tenets of such a pernicious tendency'.[131] This led Harris to complain that the 'Jacobite party' was 'enraged' against him, while David Mossom, a supporter of Harris and the Anglican minister of a neighbouring town complained about the 'flaming zeal' of Checkley and the 'party which abets him'.[132]

In March 1724, amidst the extended exchange of caustic pamphlets, the Massachusetts government brought charges against Checkley for publishing a seditious work filled with 'insinuations against his Majesty's rightful and lawful authority'.[133] One of Checkley's critics gleefully wrote that the lieutenant-governor, William Dummer, by prosecuting Checkley, had 'employed his authority and influence' in protecting the Church against 'open enemies and pretended friends, from nonjurors and Jacobites'.[134] The accusations of sedition referred specifically to his selling in 1723 of Leslie's *A short and easie method*. In May of the same year, before he was brought to trial, Checkley decided to take the necessary oaths of abjuration and allegiance, which he

[126]   Joseph Browne to the bishop of London, 15 Mar. 1725, FP i. 210–11; Broxap, *The later nonjurors*, 88.

[127]   Timothy Cutler to Grey, 7 May 1726, Nichols, *Illustrations*, iv. 279.

[128]   *Diary of Cotton Mather*, ii. 804.

[129]   Susannah Abbott, 'Clerical responses to the Jacobite rebellion in 1715', *Historical Research* lxxvi (2003), 332–46.

[130]   Ibid, 335–6.

[131]   Harris to the bishop of London, 22 June 1724, FP iv. 117–21

[132]   Ibid; David Mossom to the bishop of London, 17 Dec 1724, FP iv. 142.

[133]   Slafter, *John Checkley*, i. 56.

[134]   Harris to the bishop of London, 22 June 1724, FP iv. 117–21.

had refused five years earlier.[135] Even fellow Anglicans suspected that he had taken the oaths in order to avoid the 'impending penalties' and not out of any new-found loyalties.[136] In July 1724 Checkley went on trial for the publication which was accused of questioning the right of George I to the throne. He was found guilty but was allowed to appeal and appeared before the Superior Court in November. This court found him guilty of libel but innocent of sedition and he was fined fifty pounds and forced to put up £100 in sureties.[137] Throughout the debates and despite his nonjuring, Checkley was supported once again by many of his fellow Anglicans, who assisted him by acting as legal counsel and helping him pay his fines and sureties.

Checkley's controversial works had stirred up such division in the colony both among Congregationalists and Low Church Anglicans in Boston that the bishop of London was forced to involve himself in order to settle the dispute. Both Benjamin Colman and Henry Harris, the assistant rector at King's Chapel, had written to contacts in Britain complaining of Checkley's aggressive attempts at proselytising. Colman wrote to the staunchly latitudinarian White Kennet, while Harris wrote directly to the bishop of London informing him that Checkley had actively promoted belief in the invalidity of dissenters' baptism which had been a nonjuring position during the reign of Anne.[138] The Whig bishops were especially sensitive to complaints of this nature following the High Church disturbances caused by the Atterbury plot and trial. The bishop of London addressed the complaints and wrote to Samuel Myles, the rector of King's Chapel, that he would consider any missionary propagating the argument of invalid dissenting baptism to be an 'enemy of the Church of England and the Protestant succession' and would 'deal with him accordingly'.[139] The prosecution of Checkley and the letter from the bishop of London effectively put an end to the controversies propagated by the High Church interest in New England. Perhaps more importantly, as Mather remarked, 'our *Cutlers* High Principles, were strangely going down the wind in the Ch: of E. and growing out of fashion'.[140] For many more years, the High Church party continued to strive for pre-eminence in the affairs of King's Chapel, but apart from a few minor instances, Jacobite scares had largely subsided.

The twenty-five years following the accession of Anne witnessed the growth of a remarkable interest in Jacobitism in New England. The on-going Jacobite threat in Britain was an integral aspect of a transatlantic political culture and,

[135] Slafter, *John Checkley*, i. 58.
[136] Harris to bishop of London, 22 June 1724, FP iv. 117–21.
[137] Slafter, *John Checkley*, i. 74.
[138] Harris to the bishop of London, 22 June 1724, FP iv. 117–21.
[139] Bishop of London to Myles, 21 Sept. 1724, FP iv. 132.
[140] *Diary of Cotton Mather*, ii. 806.

consequently, it affected the manner in which the people of New England responded to local expressions of a transatlantic Jacobitism. Although the immediate danger posed by an assertive High Church Anglicanism in New England was not the eruption of a local Jacobite rebellion, fears that the steady growth of a High Church party in the Church of England might eventually result in widespread disaffection towards the Hanoverian dynasty and a failure to uphold the Protestant succession in lieu of a Stuart restoration, reminiscent of the ambivalence of many Anglicans in England towards the succession, were widespread. In Boston, the battle against the encroachment of a High Church Anglican ideology was, in part, a battle against a transatlantic Jacobitism.

Newspapers, pamphlets, sermons and letters illustrate the subtle evolution of the religious and political ideas held by New England Congregationalists. Their responses to the Jacobite threat were self-consciously British, Whiggish and transatlantic. Yet they were responding to an indigenous High Church Toryism, which in Britain often served as a mask for Jacobitism. Thus, the debates also demonstrate that Whig fears were rooted both in local realities and an informed understanding of the transatlantic scope of Jacobitism. The rise of a High Church Anglicanism in New England may not seem a credible Jacobite threat in the same manner as the rebellions of 1715 and 1745, but for Congregationalists the presence and espousal of crypto-Jacobite principles in New England associated with a High Church Tory party masked the first step towards disaffection to the Protestant succession.

In addition to demonstrating the significance of Jacobitism in New England, religious debates clearly echo elements of Britain's 'rage of party', and consequently hint at the likely importance of both themes in an increasingly cohesive political culture spanning the British Atlantic world. Moreover, the debates are an important reminder that the integration of New England into a larger transatlantic political culture was a complex, multi-faceted process which necessarily included Tory imports, even in the predominantly Whig bastion of New England. Religious and party discourses thus speak of a dynamic Atlantic world in the early eighteenth century and provide further evidence of the anglicisation of political cultures in Britain's Atlantic colonies.

Conclusion

What then is to be made of Jacobitism in the British Atlantic world? Several important conclusions emerge from this study though two remain preeminent. First and foremost Jacobitism and anti-Jacobitism were important aspects of the British Atlantic world for over thirty years following the Revolution of 1688. Moreover, Jacobitism did not simply consist of a series of romantic rebellions or plots against the British government: Jacobitism persisted as an integral element of British political culture and religious controversies in England, Scotland, Ireland and the colonies from 1688 to the death of George I in 1727. Anti-Jacobitism developed in parallel. This then was a period fraught with religious controversies and party-driven political tensions which reverberated not just through England, Scotland and Ireland but also in the numerous British Atlantic colonies. It should no longer be possible to ignore Jacobites in the colonies as some sort of cultural or political aberration. Although it is true that Jacobites were not actively plotting colonial rebellions or participating in transatlantic conspiracies to restore the exiled Stuarts, Jacobitism – and therefore anti-Jacobitism – was part and parcel of a transatlantic British culture because it was an enduring feature of British political and religious discourse throughout the first half of the eighteenth century.

The prevalence of Jacobitism and anti-Jacobitism in the British Atlantic colonies points towards a second conclusion: the vibrancy of political and religious exchanges in the British Atlantic world. Political and religious controversies were diffused throughout a pan-Atlantic public sphere, which, in turn, facilitated the anglicisation of the British Atlantic world. As the complexity and cultural depth of Britain's Atlantic colonies becomes increasingly evident, it is necessary to broaden our understanding of Britain. In recent years, historians of colonial America have made admirable advances by conceiving of the colonies as part of an Atlantic world and incorporating scholarship examining the British Isles in order to revise traditional Whig narratives. British historians – though much fewer in number – have also benefitted from taking an Atlantic turn and envisioning the colonies as an integral part of early modern Britain.[1] This book builds upon this established tradition in order to encourage British historians to think in more expansive geographical terms, and imperial and colonial historians to more actively embrace and engage with the diversity evident in historical scholarship examining the British Isles.

---

[1]   See, for example, Abigail Swingen, *Competing visions of empire: labor, slavery, and the origins of the British Atlantic empire*, New Haven 2015.

Over the past forty years, studies of Jacobitism have reshaped our under-standings of late Stuart Britain. The prevalence and persistence of Jacobite sympathies throughout British society illustrates a severe ideological divide. This manifested itself in the partisan politics of the rage of party and religious disputes, both of which contributed to an increasingly vibrant Atlantic public sphere. Jacobitism was an enduring subculture, popular as well as elite, present in Scotland, England Ireland and the colonies. It was ultimately rooted in disaffection with the Revolution settlement, and centred on High Church and nonjuring ideas of divine right, passive obedience, non-resistance and hereditary succession. Jacobitism penetrated all levels of society, creating a population hungry for the partisan prints made available within an emerging public sphere.

British party politics were inherently connected to Jacobitism and anti-Jacobitism. Jacobite political culture in England was often indistinguishable from that of High Church Tories. Seditious words, riots and the celebrations of Henry Sacheverell in England were all inflected with a mixture of High Church Toryism and Jacobitism, a pattern also observable in Britain's colonies. Moreover, when Queen Anne passed an act of indemnity in 1703 allowing former disaffected exiles the opportunity to return to British political life, those returning were almost exclusively Tories. This contributed to the creation of a Jacobite wing of the Tory party, further influencing the equivocal relationship between Tories and Jacobites. Thus, for example, in 1714, due in large part to the intransigence of Jacobite Tories, Harley's moderation was eschewed in favour of Bolingbroke's single party government, arguably as a means of securing the return of 'James III&VIII'. Perhaps more important, the Jacobite wing of the Tory party created a legitimate perception throughout the British Atlantic that the Tory party was far too friendly with a disaffected minority and therefore inseparable from Jacobitism, or at the very least, inseparable from a Jacobite political culture. This in turn contributed to the development of anti-Jacobite – and often pro-Hanoverian – political attitudes tied to the Whig party.[2]

The rage of party was a defining feature of British politics in the early eight-eenth century. Even those outside London proper – Scots, Irish and colonists – began to conceive of issues, and participate, within the larger context of Whig and Tory politics. The appointment of officials in Ireland and the colonies was, in large part, a party affair. Just as this facilitated the integration of Irish and British politics, so it stimulated the integration of British colonists into what became a transatlantic rage of party. Thus Tory opponents of Whig governors cultivated alliances among High Church Tories in Britain, creating fears among Whigs of a transatlantic Jacobitism. These fears were further reinforced by the lacklustre response of the 1710–14 Tory ministry to complaints of Jacobitism in the colonies and its appointment of former Jacobites to posts of importance

---

[2]   Smith, *Georgian monarchy.*

there – once again, echoing events in Ireland. A Jacobite-friendly Tory party does not mean that all High Church Tories in the colonies were likewise disaffected, but nor were Whig fears of Tory Jacobites a mere chimera. They were rooted in the reality of transatlantic party politics which were in turn inherently coloured by both fears and hopes of a Jacobite restoration.

Religious controversies and party political divisions were often inseparable. Many of the most prominent political fissures in England and Scotland were caused by a heady blend of politics and religion. Debates about occasional conformity in England and the toleration of Episcopalian worship in Scotland were inseparable from Whig and Tory party politics, and religious controversies were part and parcel of a contested political culture: High Church Anglicans were essentially the clerical wing of the Tory party. The politics of religion was a major source of controversy reflecting on the succession. Religious controversies were transmitted to the colonies by zealous Anglican ministers and parishioners, who though in the colonies continued to participate in transatlantic debates. Moreover, because religious controversies were often inseparable from politics, they were inherently linked to Jacobitism. The attempt to impose a Test Act in South Carolina was instigated by the High Church Tory Jacobite Nathaniel Johnson, while religious controversies in the mid-Atlantic were inflamed by John Talbot, a High Church clergyman who would later accept ordination as a nonjuring bishop. Similarly, religious controversies in New England were coloured in fundamental ways by understandings of Jacobitism.

Religious controversies were often rooted in or influenced by questions about the royal succession and the legitimacy of the Revolution settlement. The Revolution of 1688 fractured the English and Scottish Churches, creating deep and lasting clerical and societal divisions. The accession of William and Mary drove a small but influential group of English clergy and laymen into the arms of the exiled Stuarts. An even more profound rupture occurred in Scotland, creating a pool of men and women disaffected to the new monarchs and unwilling to swear oaths of allegiance. Nonjurors were inherently Jacobite, whether they openly canvassed Stuart restoration or not. They provided and trumpeted the intellectual foundations for Jacobitism, including hereditary right, passive obedience and non-resistance, ideas which persisted among High Churchmen throughout the eighteenth century. Thus the existence of nonjuring bishops in the colonies, deliberately sent out sent by nonjurors in England, suggests the transatlantic impact of the nonjuring movement and the diffusion of religious controversies.

Colonists, like their Scottish and Irish counterparts, were further integrated into British party politics and religious controversies *via* the emergence of a vibrant transatlantic public sphere. They were kept apprised of the relationship between Jacobitism and political and religious controversies through the importation and reprinting of British newspapers and pamphlets. Furthermore, the maturation of indigenous print cultures in a number of colonies encouraged colonists to participate in these controversies as provincial Britons. The introduction of a contested political calendar by the Tory almanacker Daniel Leeds serves as a notable example. Nor was the transmission of ideas achieved solely through the diffusion of print. The migration of Jacobites and their subsequent settlement in local communities provided British colonists with immediate and visible reminders that the Jacobite threat was not merely imagined or distant but real and local. It also suggests an audience literate in elements of a Jacobite subculture. Seditious words, nonjuring, expressions of High Church Toryism and expressions of anti-Jacobitism therefore need to be understood in terms of a a transatlantic political and religious culture, and not simply as isolated colonial examples of a British phenomenon.

Thus, when political and religious debates about occasional conformity and passive obedience erupted in South Carolina and New England respectively, or controversies between a Whig governor and an emergent High Church Anglican party in the mid-Atlantic colonies resulted in accusations of disaffection or Toryism, Jacobitism or anti-Jacobitism became prominent features of the religious and political discourse. Colonists were not responding to a distant, British threat. They were reacting to what they understood to be evidence of a transatlantic Jacobitism and they did so using the familiar, pan-Atlantic language of anti-Jacobitism. When these events and accusations are viewed and understood within the context of a British Atlantic world which manifested a transatlantic Jacobite political culture inextricably linked to High Church Toryism, the fears and accusations become far more significant.

Although expressions of Jacobitism in the colonies in the thirty-nine years following the Revolution of 1688 were often analogous to their counterparts in Britain, it would be a mistake to assume that its survival or otherwise followed the same pattern. Variations in the actual practice of politics in many colonies when compared to Westminster made this so. The party-driven political appointments of colonial officials which had done so much to encourage colonial participation in Whig and Tory party politics effectively ended after the Tory proscription in 1715. This, in turn, discouraged the continued growth of a Tory interest in many colonies. Though the Tory party persisted as a viable political movement in Britain, and retained its close association with Jacobitism, its inability to secure power in Westminster led to a Whig dominance in colonial appointments for the next forty-five years. Though Tories continued to exert influence in a pan-Atlantic political culture at least until 1724, especially in the guise of High Church Anglicanism, the effects of the Atterbury plot and the resulting collapse of the Tory party were especially profound in the colonies. Following the exposure of the plot and the Tory defeat in the elections of 1722, decreasing fears of Jacobite plots and Tory victories led to a corresponding decrease in the heat of party conflicts. The decisive failure of the Atterbury plot effectively sealed the fate of the Tory party and the Jacobites in Britain for another generation. This resulted in decades of Whig hegemony in the colonies, effectually rendering Toryism in the colonies (in contrast to Britain) relatively impotent after 1727.

This, of course had a profound effect on political culture. Following both the collapse of the Tory party and the eclipse of a Jacobite political culture, an anti-Jacobite and pro-Hanoverian political culture came to the fore. Britons throughout the British Atlantic world demonstrated an increasingly Whiggish – and therefore antagonistic – understanding of the Jacobite threat. As the significance of the Jacobite threat declined, anti-Jacobitism gradually assumed a very different character to that of the late seventeenth and early eighteenth centuries. No longer was it as strongly anti-Tory or anti-High Church; it once again became virulently anti-Catholic, and, as time progressed, anti-Scottish.[3]

This was by no means a predictable nor an obvious outcome. It was the product of thirty years of contest and conflict. Anglicisation was a fraught process without a predetermined outcome. This book reinforces existing arguments positing the anglicisation of Britain's colonies in the eighteenth century by arguing that Jacobitism and anti-Jacobitism demonstrate the integrative influence of Britain's rage of party. Anglicisation was, however, complex and was the consequence not of an English Atlantic alone, but of an increasingly British Atlantic. It was a result of interactions between the various entities that comprised the British Atlantic world – Ireland, Scotland, England and the individual colonies.

This book has tackled a frustratingly complex phenomena within an expansive geographical framework. It offers a useful Atlantic dimension to Jacobite studies; at the same time arguments proposing the monarchical, increasingly anglicised character of the British colonies in the early eighteenth century add a dimension to the history of colonial America. For those interested in the broad fields of eighteenth-century British and Atlantic history, it provides a wider Atlantic context to recent work on the Glorious Revolution and post-Revolutionary politics, religious culture and the public sphere. If it has encouraged conversation between the often disparate fields of eighteenth-century British history, Atlantic history, Jacobite studies and the history of colonial America, it will have served its purpose.

---

[3]   McConville, *The king's three faces*, 264–6; Hawkins, 'Imperial '45', 24–47; Plank, *Rebellion and savagery*, 77–100.

Bibliography

Unpublished primary sources

Edinburgh, National Archives of Scotland
Church papers: CH1/2/24/2/3; CH1/2/35
Episcopal Chest papers: CH12/15/109: CH12/12/209
Miscellaneous Ecclesiastical papers: CH8/196
Papers of the Graham family, dukes of Montrose papers: GD220/5/253;
  GD220/5/330; GD220/5/455; GD220/5/577; GD220/6/1754;
  GD220/5/1895; GD220/5/1910
Other: GD298/379

Kew, The National Archives
SP 35

London, British Library
MSS Add. 36125, 61647
MS Egerton 1971

London, Lambeth Palace Library
Fulham papers colonial (microfilm)
SPG papers (microfilm)

Oxford, Rhodes House Library
SPG archive: American material, 1635–1812 (microfilm)

USA
Baltimore, Maryland Historical Society
MS 2001, Lloyd papers, 1658–1910, Tilghman-Lloyd collections (microfilm)

Boston, Massachusetts Historical Society,
Benjamin Colman papers, 1641–1806 (microfilm)

New York, Franklin D. Roosevelt Presidential Library
Livingston family papers, 1630–1901 (microfilm)

Printed primary sources

Archives of Maryland: proceedings and acts of the general assembly of Maryland, April 26, 1715–August 10, 1716, xxx, ed. William Hand Brown (Maryland Historical Society, 1910)

Archives of Maryland: proceedings of the council of Maryland, 1696/7–1698, xxiii, ed. William Hand Brown (Maryland Historical Society, 1903)

Archives of Maryland: proceedings of the council of Maryland, 1698–1731, xxv, ed. William Hand Brown (Maryland Historical Society, 1905)

Beardsley, Eben Edwards, *Life and correspondence of Samuel Johnson, D.D.*, New York 1874

Calendar of state papers colonial, America and West Indies, ed. W. Noel Sainsbury, J. W. Fortescue and Cecil Headlam, London 1860–1969

Correspondence of the Rev. Robert Wodrow, minister of Eastwood, and author of the History of the sufferings of the Church of Scotland, ed. Thomas McRie, Edinburgh 1842

Diary of Cotton Mather DD, FRS, 1712, ed. William Manierre, Charlottesville, VA 1964

Diary of Samuel Sewall (Collections of the Massachusetts Historical Society vii, 1882)

Documents relating to the colonial history of the State of New Jersey, xiv (New Jersey Historical Society, 1880)

Documents relative to the colonial history of the State of New-York procured in Holland, England, and France by John Romeyn Brodhead, v, ed. F. B. O'Callaghan, Albany, NY 1853

[George I], *His majesty's most gracious speech to both houses of parliament*, Boston 1716

– *His majesty's most gracious speech to both houses of parliament, on Thursday October 11, 1722*, London 1722

Historical collections relating to the American colonial Church, ed. William Stevens Perry, ii, New York 1969

[Hunter, Robert], *His excellency's speech to the General Assembly of his majesty's colony of New York*, New York 1716

Journal of the Board of Trade and Plantations (1704–1782), ed. K. H. Ledward, London 1920–8

Life and character of the Reverend Benjamin Colman, DD: late pastor of a church in Boston, New England, ed. Ebeneezer Turell, Boston 1749

Papers relating to the history of the Church in Virginia, 1650–1776, ed. William Perry, n.p. 1870

Papers of William Penn, III: 1685–1700, ed. Richard Dunn, Mary Maples Dunn and others, Philadelphia 1986

The report of the committee of the honble House of Commons: appointed to inspect the examinations given in by Dominick Langton, clerck, formerly a fryar in this kingdom, Cork Hill 1711

Selected letters of Cotton Mather, ed. Kenneth Silverman, Baton Rouge, LA 1974

'Some unpublished letters of Benjamin Colman, 1717–1725', ed. Neil Caplan, *Proceedings of the Massachusetts Historical Society* lxxvii (1965), 101–43

Newspapers

American Weekly Mercury
Boston News-letter
Daily Courant
Flying Post
New England Courant
Post Boy

Contemporary books and articles

Anon., *An abstract of the French king's will*, Boston 1715

— *An account of the fair and impartial proceedings of the Lords proprietors, governour and council of the colony of South Carolina, in answer to the untrue suggestions, contained in the petition of Jos. Boon and others, and of a paper intituled, The case of the Church of England in Carolina*, London 1706

— *The case of the Church of England in Carolina*, London 1706

— *Gloria Britannorum; or, The British worthies*, Boston 1723

— *Instructions by the citizens of London, to their representatives for the ensuing parliament*, Boston 1715

— *A letter to the clergy of the Church of England: on occasion of the commitment of the right reverend the Lord Bishop of Rochester to the Tower of London*, London; repr. Boston 1722

— *The madness of the Jacobite party, in attempting to set a popish pretender on the British throne*, Boston 1724

— *A modest proof of the order and government of the Church as settled by Christ and his Apostles*, Boston 1723

— *The whole tryal and examination of Dr. Welton, rector of White-Chapel and the church-wardens, on Monday last, in the bishop of London's court*, London 1714

Bird, Benjamin, *The Jacobites catechism*, Boston 1692

Boyer, Abel, *The reign of Queen Anne, digested into annals: year the fifth*, London 1707

[Checkley, John], *Choice dialogues between a godly minister and an honest countryman concerning election and predestination*, Boston 1720

[Checkley, John], *A modest proof of the order and government of the Church as settled by Christ and his Apostles*, Boston 1723

Checkley, John, *A defence of a book lately reprinted at Boston, entitled A modest proof of the order and government settled by Christ and his Apostles in the Church*, Boston 1724

Clough, Samuel, *The New-England almanack for the year of our Lord, MDCCII*, Boston 1702

— *The New-England almanack for the year of our Lord, MDCCIII*, Boston 1703

— *Clough's farewell, 1708: an almanack for the year of our Lord (according to the common account) 1708*, Boston 1708

Colman, Benjamin, *A brief enquiry into the reasons why the people of God have been wont to bring into their penitential confessions, the sins of their fathers and ancestors, in times long since past*, Boston 1716

— *A sermon preach'd at Boston in New-England on Thursday the 23d. of August. 1716: being the day of publick thanksgiving, for the suppression of the latevile and traiterous rebellion in Great Britain*, Boston 1716

— *A thanksgiving sermon for the suppression of the late vile and traiterous rebellion in Great Britain*, Boston 1716

Dalcho, Fredrick, *An historical account of the Protestant Episcopal Church in South Carolina, from the first settlement of the province to the War of the Revolution*, Charleston, SC 1820

Defoe, Daniel, *Party-tyranny; or, An occasional bill in miniature: as now practised in Carolina humbly offered to the consideration of both houses of parliament*, London 1705

— *The case of Protestant Dissenters in Carolina, shewing how a law to prevent occasional conformity there, has ended in the total subversion of the constitution in Church and*

State: recommended to the serious consideration of all that are true Friends to our present Establishment, London 1706

Dickinson, Jonathan, *Remarks upon the postscript to the defence*, Boston 1724

[Gordon, William], *A representation of the miserable state of Barbadoes*, London 1719

— *A sermon preached before the governor and council, & general assembly of the Island of Barbadoes*, London 1719

Holyoke, Edmund, *An almanack of the coelestial motions, aspects and eclipses, &c. for the year of the Christian aera, 1713*, Boston, 1713

— *An almanack of the coelestial motions, aspects and eclipses, for the year of the Christian aera, 1715*, Boston 1715

Hunter, Robert, *Androboros: a biographical [sic] farce in three acts, viz. The senate, The consistory, and The apotheosis*, New York 1716

— *His excellencys speech to the general assembly of New York*, New York 1715

Keith, George, *A journal of travels from New-Hampshire to Caratuck, on the continent of North-America*, London 1706

Leeds, Daniel, *The American almanack for the year of Christian account, 1705*, New York 1705

— *The great mistery of Fox-Craft discovered and the Quaker plainness & sincerity demonstrated*, New York, 1705

— *The second part of the mystry of Fox-Craft*, New York 1705

— *The American almanack for the year of Christian account, 1707*, New York 1707

— *The American almanack for the year of Christian account, 1710*, New York 1710

— *The American almanack for the year of Christian account, 1711*, New York 1711

Leslie, Charles, *The case of the regale and of the pontificat stated: in a conference concerning the independency of the Church, upon any power on earth, in the exercise of her purely spiritual power and authority*, London 1701

— *The new association: part II. &c: with farther improvements*, London [1702?]

— *The religion of Jesus Christ the only true religion; or, A short and easie method with the deists*, Boston 1719

— *A short and easie method with the deists*, 8th edn, London 1723

Mather, Cotton, *An history of seasonable interpositions: specifically relating to the twice memorable fifth of November*, Boston 1719

Mather, Increase, *Two discourses shewing, I: That the Lords ears are open to the prayers of the righteous; II: The dignity & duty of aged servants of the Lord*, Boston 1716

Mist, Nathaniel, *Collection of letters*, i, London 1722

Nichols, John, *Illustrations of the literary history of the eighteenth century consisting of authentic memoirs and original letters of eminent persons*, London 1818

Paine, Thomas, *An almanack of the coelestial motions, aspects and eclipses, &c. for the year of the Christian aera 1718*, Boston 1718

Palmer, John, *An impartial account of the state of New England; or, The late government there, vindicated in answer to the declaration which the faction set forth when they overturned that government*, London 1690

Parker, George, *Parker's ephemeris for the year of our Lord 1707*, London 1707

— *Parker's ephemeris for the year of our Lord 1711*, London 1711

— *Parker's ephemeris for the year of our Lord 1712*, London 1712

— *Parker's ephemeris for the year of our Lord 1713*, London 1713

Pemberton, Ebenezer, *A brief account of the state of the province of the Massachusetts-Bay in New-England, civil and ecclesiastical*, Boston 1717

Steele, Richard, *The crisis; or, A discourse representing from the most authentick records, the just causes of the late happy revolution*, Philadelphia 1725

To the king's most excellent majesty, the humble address of the lord mayor of London, and the rest of your majesty's commissioners of lieutenancy for your City of London, Boston 1715

Travis, Daniel, *An almanack of the coelestial motions for the year of the Christian epocha 1707*, Boston 1707

— *An almanack of the coelestial motions & aspects, for the year of the Christian aera, 1716*, Boston 1716

Trott, Nicholas, *The laws of the province of South Carolina*, Charleston, SC 1736

Turell, Ebeneezer, *The life and character of the Reverend Benjamin Colman, D.D.: late pastor of a church in Boston, New England*, Boston 1749

Walter, Thomas, *A choice dialogue between John Faustus a conjurer, and Jack Tory his friend*, Boston 1720

— *An essay upon that paradox, infallibility may sometimes mistake; or, A reply to a discourse concerning episcopacy, said in a late pamphlet to be beyond the possibility of a reply. to which is prefixed, some remarks upon said pamphlet, entitled A discourse shewing, who is a true pastor of the Church of Christ: as also remarks upon St Ignatius's Epistle to the Trallians*, Boston 1724

[Welton, Richard], *The whole tryal and examination of Dr. Welton, rector of White-Chapel and the church-wardens, on Monday last, in the bishop of London's court*, London 1714

— *The clergy's tears; or, A cry against persecution: humbly offered in a letter to the bishop of London, in our present great distress and danger*, London 1715

— *The certain comforts of God the Holy Ghost, &c, preached at the Episcopal Church in Philadelphia*, Philadelphia 1726

Whittemore, Nathaniel, *An almanack for the year of our Lord MDCCVI*, Boston 1706

Wigglesworth, Edward, *Sober remarks on a book lately re-printed at Boston, entituled, A modest proof of the order and government settled by Christ and his Apostles in the Church: in a letter to a friend*, 2nd edn, Boston 1724

Secondary works

Abbott, Susannah, 'Clerical responses to the Jacobite rebellion in 1715', *Historical Research* lxxvi (2003), 332–46

Alsop, J. D., 'Thomas Nairne and the "Boston Gazette no. 216" of 1707', *Southern Studies* xxii (1983), 209–11

Armitage, David and Michael Braddick (eds), *The British Atlantic world, 1500–1800*, Basingstoke 2002

Armory, Hugh and David D. Hall (eds), *The colonial book in the Atlantic world*, Cambridge 2000

Bailyn, Bernard, *Atlantic history: concepts and contours*, Cambridge, MA 2005

Barnard, Toby, 'Ireland 1689–91', in Harris and Taylor, *Final crisis of the Stuart monarchy*, 157–88

— 'The impact of print in Ireland, 1680–1800: problems and perils', in Eve Patten and Jason McElligott (eds), *The perils of print culture: books, print, and publishing in theory and practice*, Basingstoke 2014, 96–117

Bell, James, *The imperial origins of the king's Church in early America, 1607–1783*, Basingstoke 2004

— A war of religion: dissenters, Anglicans and the American Revolution, Basingstoke 2008

Beneke, Chris, Beyond toleration: the religious origins of American pluralism, Oxford 2006

— and Christopher Grenda (eds), The first prejudice: religious tolerance and intolerance in early America, Philadelphia 2011

Bennett, G. V., White Kennett: bishop of Peterborough: a study in the political and ecclesiastical history of the early eighteenth century, London 1957

— The Tory crisis in Church and State, 1688–1730: the career of Francis Atterbury, bishop of Rochester, Oxford 1975

Bennett, J. Harry, 'The SPG and Barbadian politics, 1710–1720', Historical Magazine of the Protestant Episcopal Church xx (1951), 190–206

Black, Jeremy, The English press, 1621–1861, London 2001

Bonomi, Patricia, A factious people: politics and society in colonial New York, New York 1971

— Under the cope of Heaven: religion, society, and politics in colonial America, Oxford 1986

— The Lord Cornbury scandal: the politics of reputation in British America, Chapel Hill 1998

Bowie, Karin, Scottish public opinion and the Anglo-Scottish union, 1699–1707, Woodbridge 2007

Breen, T. H., 'An empire of goods: the anglicization of colonial America', JBS xxv (1986), 467–99

Bridenbaugh, Carl, Cities in the wilderness: the first century of urban life in America, 1625–1742, New York 1955

— Mitre and sceptre: transatlantic faiths, ideas, personalities, and politics, 1689–1775, Oxford 1962

Brinsfield, John W., 'Daniel Defoe: writer, statesman, and advocate of religious liberty in South Carolina', South Carolina Historical Magazine lxxvi (1973), 107–11

— Religion and politics in colonial South Carolina, Easley, SC 1983

Broxap, Henry, The later nonjurors, Cambridge, 1924

Brydon, George McClaren, Virginia's mother Church and the political conditions under which it grew, Richmond, VA 1947

Buranelli, Vincent. The king and the Quaker: a study of William Penn and James II, Philadelphia 1962

Burnard, Trevor, 'The British Atlantic', in Jack P. Greene and Phillip D. Morgan, (eds), Atlantic history: a critical appraisal, Oxford 2009, 11–136

Burr, Nelson R., The Anglican Church in New Jersey, Philadelphia 1954

Bushman, R., King and people in provincial Massachusetts, Chapel Hill, NC 1985

Butler, Jon, Awash in a sea of faith: Christianising the American people, Cambridge, MA 1990

Canny, Nicholas (ed.), The Oxford history of the British Empire, I: The origins of empire: British overseas enterprise to the close of the seventeenth century, Oxford 1998

Capp, Bernard, Astrology and the popular press: English almanacs, 1500–1800, London 1979

Carney, Thomas E., 'A tradition to live by: New York religious history, 1624–1740', New York History lxxxv (2004), 301–30

Chaplin, Joyce, 'The British Atlantic', in Nicolas Canny and Phillip Morgan (eds), The Oxford handbook of the Atlantic world, c. 1450–1850, Oxford 2011, 219–34

Clark, Charles, *The public prints: the newspaper in Anglo-American culture, 1665–1740*, Oxford 1994

— 'Periodicals and politics: part one: early American journalism: news and opinion in the popular press', in Hugh Amory and David D. Hall (eds), *A history of the book in America, I: The colonial book in the Atlantic world*, Chapel Hill 2010, 347–65

Clark, G. N., 'War trade and trade war, 1701–1713', *Economic History Review* i (1928), 262–80

Clark, J. C. D., *English society, 1668–1832, religion, ideology, and politics during the ancien régime*, Cambridge 1985

— *The language of liberty, 1660–1832: political discourse and the social dynamics in the Anglo-American world*, Cambridge 1994

— 'The many restorations of King James: a short history of scholarship on Jacobitism, 1688–2006', in Paul Monod, Murray Pittock, and Daniel Szechi (eds), *Loyalty and identity: Jacobites at home and abroad*, Basingstoke 2010, 9–56

Clarke, Tristram, '"Nurseries of sedition?": the Episcopal congregations after the Revolution of 1689', in James Porter (ed.), *After Columba, after Calvin: religious communities in North-East Scotland*, Aberdeen, 1999, 61–9

Colley, Linda, *In defiance of oligarchy, 1714–1760*, Cambridge 1982

— *Britons: forging the nation, 1707–1837*, 2nd edn, New Haven 2005

Collis, Robert, 'To a fair meeting on the green: the Order of Toboso and Jacobite fraternalism, 1726–c. 1729', in McInnes, German and Graham, *Living with Jacobitism*, 125–38

Connolly, S. J., *Religion, law, and power: the making of Protestant Ireland, 1660–1760*, Oxford 1992

Conroy, David, *In public houses: drink and the revolution of authority in colonial Massachusetts*, Chapel Hill 1995

Corp, Edward (ed.), *The Stuart court in Rome: the legacy of exile*, Burlington, Vᴛ 2003

— *A court in exile: the Stuarts in France, 1689–1718*, Cambridge 2004

— *The Stuarts in Italy, 1719–1766: a royal court in permanent exile*, Cambridge 2011

Cowan, Brian, *The social life of coffee: the emergence of the British coffeehouse*, New Haven 2005

— 'Geoffrey Holmes and the public sphere: Augustan historiography from the post-Namierite to the post-Habermasian', *PH* xxviii (2009), 166–78

— 'The spin doctor: Sacheverell's trial speech and political performance in a divided society', *PH* xxxi (2012), 28–46.

Cranfield, G. A., *The development of the provincial newspaper, 1700–1760*, Oxford 1962

Crawford, M.J., *Seasons of grace: colonial New England's revival tradition in its British context*, Oxford 1991

Cruickshanks, Eveline, *Political untouchables: the Tories and the '45*, New York 1979

— 'Religion and royal succession: the rage of party', in Clyve Jones, (ed.), *Britain in the first age of party, 1680–1750: essays presented to Geoffrey Holmes*, London 1987, 19–44

— and Richard Harrison, 'Lowther, Robert (1681–1745), of Maulds Meaburn, Westmld', in D. Hayton, E. Cruickshanks and S. Handley (eds), *The history of parliament: the House of Commons, 1690–1715*, London 2002, iv. 703–4

— (ed.), *Ideology and conspiracy: aspects of Jacobitism, 1689–1759*, Edinburgh 1982

Dickinson, H. T., *Bolingbroke*, London 1970

Dobson, David, *Scots on the Chesapeake, 1607–1830*, Baltimore, MD 1992

— *Scottish emigration to colonial America*, Athens, GA 1994

— *Directory of Scots banished to the American plantations, 1650–1775*, 2nd edn, Baltimore 2010

Dunn, Richard, 'The Glorious Revolution and America', in Canny, *Oxford history of the British Empire* i. 445–66

Enright, Brian J., 'An account of Charles Town in 1725', *South Carolina Historical Magazine* lxi (1960), 13–18

Erskine-Hill, Howard, 'Twofold vision in eighteenth-century writing, *ELH* lxiv (1997), 903–24

Every, George, *The High Church party, 1688–1718*, London 1956

Farooq, Jennifer, *Preaching in eighteenth-century London*, Woodbridge 2014

Fischer, David Hackett, *Albion's seed: four British folkways in America*, Oxford 1989

Flaningan, John, 'The occasional conformity controversy: ideology and party politics, 1697–1711', *JBS* xvii (1977), 38–62

Foote, H. W., *Annals of Kings Chapel: from the Puritan age of New England to the present day*, Boston 1882

Foster, S., *The long argument: English Puritanism and the shaping of New England culture, 1570–1700*, Chapel Hill, NC 1991

Fox, E.T., 'Jacobitism and the "golden age" of piracy', *International Journal of Maritime History* xxii (2010), 277–303

Fritz, Paul, *The English ministers and Jacobitism between the rebellions of 1715 and 1745*, Toronto 1975

Gallup-Diaz, Ignacio, Andrew Shankman and Daniel J. Silverman (eds), *Anglicizing America: empire, revolution, republic*, Philadelphia 2015

Games, Alison, 'Migration', in Armitage and Braddick, *The British Atlantic world*, 31–50.

Geiter, Mary, 'William Penn and Jacobitism: a smoking gun?', *Historical Research* lxxiii (2000), 213–19

Genet-Rouffiac, Nathalie, *Le Grand Exil: les Jacobites en France, 1688–1715*, Paris 2007

Gibney, John, 'Ireland's restoration crisis', in Harris and Taylor, *The final crisis of the Stuart monarchy*, 133–56

Gibson, William, *The Church of England, 1688–1832: unity and accord*, London 2001

Glasson, Travis, *Mastering Christianity: missionary Anglicanism and slavery in the Atlantic world*, Oxford 2012

Glickman, Gabriel, *The English Catholic community, 1688–1745: politics, culture and ideology*, Woodbridge 2009

— 'Political conflict and the memory of the revolution in England, 1689–c. 1750', in Harris and Taylor, *The final crisis of the Stuart monarchy*, 243–71

Goldie, Mark, 'The nonjurors, episcopacy, and the origins of the Convocation Controversy', in Cruickshanks, *Ideology and conspiracy*, 15–35

— 'The damning of King Monmouth: pulpit Toryism in the reign of James II', in Harris and Taylor, *The final crisis of the Stuart monarchy*, 33–55

Goodfried, Joyce, *Before the melting pot: society and culture in colonial New York City, 1664–1730*, Princeton 1992

Graham, Aaron, *Corruption, party, and government in Britain, 1702–1713*, Oxford 2015

Grasso, Christopher, *A speaking aristocracy: transforming discourse in eighteenth century Connecticut*, Chapel Hill 1999

Greene, Jack P., *Peripheries and center: constitutional development in the extended polities of the British Empire and the United States*, Athens, GA 1986

— '"Empire and identity" from the Glorious Revolution to the American revolution', in Marshall, *Oxford history of the British Empire*, ii. 208–30

— and J. R. Pole, 'Reconstructing British-American colonial history', in Jack P. Greene and J. R. Pole (eds), *Colonial British America: essays in the new history of the early modern era*, Baltimore 1984, 1–17

Gregory, J., 'Refashioning Puritan New England: the Church of England in British North America, c. 1680–1770', *Transactions of the Royal Historical Society* xx (2010), 85–112

— 'Transatlantic Anglican networks, c. 1680–c.1770: transplanting, translating and transforming the Church of England', in Jeremy Gregory and Hugh McLeod (eds), *International religious networks*, Woodbridge 2012, 127–42

— 'The later Stuart Church in North America', in Grant Tapsell (ed.), *The later Stuart Church, 1660–1714*, Manchester 2013, 150–72

Guthrie, Neil, *The material culture of the Jacobites*, Cambridge 2013

Habermas, Jurgen, *The structural transformation of the public sphere: an inquiry into a category of bourgeois society*, trans. Thomas Burger, Boston 1989

Hanham, Andrew, '"So few facts": Jacobites, Tories and the Pretender', *PH* xix (2000), 233–57

Hardy, Beatriz Betancourt, 'A papist in a Protestant age: the case of Richard Bennett, 1667–1749', *Journal of Southern History* lx (1994), 203–28

Harris, Bob, *Politics and the rise of the press: Britain and France, 1620–1800*, London 1997

Harris, Michael, *London newspapers in the age of Walpole*, London 1987

Harris, Tim, *Politics under the later Stuarts: party conflict in a divided society, 1660–1715*, London 1993

— and Stephen Taylor (eds), *The final crisis of the Stuart monarchy: the revolutions of 1688–91 in their British, Atlantic and European contexts*, Woodbridge 2013

Hawkins, Jonathan, 'Imperial '45: the Jacobite rebellion in transatlantic context', *Journal of Imperial and Commonwealth History* xxiv (1996), 24–47

Hayton, David, 'Traces of party politics in early eighteenth-century Scottish elections', *PH* xvi (1996), 74–99

— *Ruling Ireland, 1685–1742: politics, politicians, and parties*, London 2004

— 'Irish Tories and victims of Whig persecution: Sacheverell fever by proxy', *PH* xxxi (2012), 80–98

— E. Cruickshanks and S. Handley (eds), *The history of parliament: the House of Commons, 1690–1715*, London 2002

Heyd, Uriel, *Reading newspapers: press and public in eighteenth-century Britain and America*, Oxford 2012

Hills, George Morgan, *A history of the church in Burlington, New Jersey: comprising the facts and incidents of nearly two-hundred years, from original, contemporaneous sources*, Trenton, NJ 1885

Hoffman, Ronald, *Princes of Ireland, planters of Maryland: a Carroll saga, 1500–1782*, Chapel Hill 2000

Holmes, Geoffrey, *The trial of Dr. Sacheverell*, London 1973

— *British politics in the age of Anne*, 2nd edn, London 1987

Hunter, Phyllis Whitman, 'Transatlantic news: American interpretations of the scandalous and heroic', in Leslie Howsam and James Raven (eds), *Books between Europe and the Americas: connections and communities, 1620–1860*, Basingstoke 2011, 63–82

Ihalainen, Pasi, 'Preaching in an age of party strife, 1700–1720: contributions to the conflict', in Peter McCullough, Hugh Adlington and Emma Rhatigan (eds), *The Oxford handbook of the early modern sermon*, Oxford 2011, 495–513

Jannuzzi, L. R., '"And let all the people say amen": priests, presbyters, and the Arminian uprising in Massachusetts, 1717–1724,' *Historical Journal of Massachusetts* xxvii (1999), 1–27

Johnson, Richard, *Adjustment to empire: the New England colonies, 1675–1715*, New Brunswick, NJ 1981

Juster, Susan, 'Heretics, blasphemers, and sabbath breakers: the prosecution of religious crime in early America', in Beneke and Grenda, *The first prejudice*, 123–42

Keith, Charles P., 'Sir William Keith', *Pennsylvania Magazine of History and Biography* xii (1888), 1–33

Kidd, Colin, 'Religious realignment between the restoration and the union', in John Robertson (ed.), *A union for empire: political thought and the union of 1707*, Cambridge 1995, 145–68

Kidd, Thomas S., *The Protestant interest: New England after Puritanism*, New Haven, CT 2004

Knights, Mark, *Representation and misrepresentation in later-Stuart Britain: partisanship and political culture*, Oxford 2005

– 'The Tory interpretation of history in the rage of parties', *Huntington Library Quarterly* lxviii (2005), 353–73

– 'How rational was the later Stuart public sphere', in Lake and Pincus, *The politics of the public sphere*, 252–67

– 'Introduction: the view from 1710', *PH* xxxi (2012), 1–15

Lake, Peter and Steven Pincus, (eds), *The politics of the public sphere in early modern England*, Manchester 2007

Landsman, Ned, *From colonials to provincials: American thought and culture, 1680–1760*, New York 1997

– 'Roots, routes, and rootedness: diversity, migration and toleration in mid-Atlantic pluralism', *Early American Studies: An Interdisciplinary Journal* ii (2004), 267–309

– *Crossroads of empire: the middle colonies in British North America*, Baltimore 2010

Lemay, J. A. Leo, 'Francis Knapp: a red herring in colonial poetry', *New England Quarterly* xxxix (1966), 233–7

Lenman, Bruce, 'The Scottish Episcopal clergy', in Cruickshanks, *Ideology and conspiracy*, 36–48

Little, Thomas J., 'The origins of southern Evangelicalism: revivalism in South Carolina, 1700–1740', *Church History* lxxv (2006), 768–808

Lovejoy, David, *The Glorious Revolution in America*, New York 1972

Lustig, Mary Lou, *Robert Hunter, 1666–1734: a New York Augustan statesman*, Syracuse 1983

McConville, Brendan, *These daring disturbers of the public peace: the struggle for property and power in early New Jersey*, Ithaca, NY 1999

– *The king's three faces: the rise and fall of royal America, 1688–1776*, Chapel Hill 2006

MacInnes, Allan I., Kieran German and Lesley Graham (eds), *Living with Jacobitism, 1690-1788: the three kingdoms and beyond*, London 2014

Marshall, P. J. (ed.), *Oxford history of the British Empire, II: The eighteenth century*, Oxford 1998

Miller, P., *The New England mind: from colony to province*, Cambridge, MA 1953

Minardi, M., 'The Boston inoculation controversy of 1721-1722: an incident in the history of race', *WMQ* lxi (2004), 47-76

Monod, Paul, *Jacobitism and the English people, 1688-1788*, Cambridge 1989

— 'Pierre's white hat: theatre, Jacobitism and popular protest in London, 1689-1760', in Eveline Cruickshanks (ed.), *By force or default? The revolution of 1688-89*, Edinburgh 1989, 159-89

— 'The Jacobite press and English censorship, 1689-1695', in Corp, *The Stuart court in exile*, 125-42

— 'A restoration? 25 years of Jacobite studies', *Literature Compass* x (2013), 311-30

— Murray Pittock and Daniel Szechi, (eds), *Loyalty and identity: Jacobites at home and abroad*, Basingstoke 2010

Murdoch, Steve, *Network north: Scottish kin, commercial and covert associations in Northern Europe, 1603-1746*, Leiden 2006

— 'Tilting at windmills: the Order del Toboso as a Jacobite social network', in Monod, Pittock and Szechi, *Loyalty and identity*, 243-64

Nelson, John, *A blessed company: parishes, parsons, and parishioners in Anglican Virginia, 1690-1776*, Chapel Hill 2002

Nicholson, Eirwen, '"Revirescit": the exilic origins of the Stuart oak motif', in Corp, *The Stuart court in Rome*, 25-48

Ó Buachalla, Breandán, 'Irish Jacobite poetry', *Irish Review* xii (1992), 40-9

O'Ciardha, Eaomon, *Ireland and the Jacobite cause, 1685-1766: a fatal attachment*, Dublin 2002

O'Connor, Thomas, (ed.), *The Irish in Europe, 1580-1815*, Dublin 2001

Olson, Alison Gilbert, *Anglo-American politics, 1660-1775: the relationship between parties in England and colonial America*, Oxford 1973

— 'Governor Robert Hunter and the Anglican Church in New York', in Anne Whiteman, J. S. Bromley, and P. G. M. Dickson (eds), *Statesmen, scholars, and merchants: essays in eighteenth century history presented to Dame Lucy Sutherland*, Oxford 1973, 44-64

— *Making the empire work: London and American interest groups, 1690-1790*, Cambridge, MA 1992

Parker, Anthony, *Scottish highlanders in colonial Georgia: the recruitment, emigration, and settlement at Darien, 1735-1748*, Athens, GA 1997

Parrish, David, 'A party contagion: party politics and the inoculation controversy in the British Atlantic World, c.1721-1723', *Journal for Eighteenth-Century Studies* xxxix (2016), 41-58

Pennington, Edgar, *Apostle of New Jersey: John Talbot, 1645-1727* (Church Historical Society, 1938)

Pestana, Carla, *Protestant empire: religion and the making of the British Atlantic world*, Philadelphia 2009

Petrie, Charles, *The Jacobite movement: the first phase, 1688-1715*, New York, 1948

Pincus, Steve, '"Coffee politicians does create": coffeehouses and Restoration political culture', *Journal of Modern History* lxvii (1995), 807-34

– 'Addison's empire: Whig conceptions of empire in the early 18th century', *PH* xxxi (2012), 99–117
– 'Rethinking mercantilism: political economy, the British Empire, and the Atlantic world in the seventeenth and eighteenth centuries', *WMQ* lxix (2012), 3–34
Pittock, Murray, *The invention of Scotland: the Stuart myth and the Jacobite identity, 1638 to the present*, London, 1991
– *Poetry and Jacobite politics*, Cambridge 1995
– *Jacobitism*, Basingstoke 1998
– *The myth of the Jacobite clans: the Jacobite army in 1745*, 2nd edn, Edinburgh 2009
– 'Treacherous objects: towards a theory of Jacobite material culture', *Journal for Eighteenth-Century Studies* xxxiv (2011), 39–63
– *Material culture and sedition, 1688–1760: treacherous objects, secret places*, Basingstoke 2013
Plank, Geoffrey, *An unsettled conquest: the British campaign against Acadia*, Philadelphia, 2001
– *Rebellion and savagery: the Jacobite rising of 1745 and the British Empire*, Philadelphia 2006
Pomfret, John E., *Colonial New Jersey: a history*, New York 1973
Purcell, Richard J., 'Irish colonists in colonial Maryland', *Studies: An Irish Quarterly Review* xxiii (1934), 279–94
Raffe, Alisdair, 'Presbyterians and Episcopalians: the formation of confessional cultures in Scotland, 1660–1715', *English Historical Review* cxxv (2010), 570–98
Raymond, Joad, *News, newspapers, and society in early modern Britain*, London 1999
– 'The newspaper, public opinion, and the public sphere', in Raymond, *News, newspapers, and society*, 109–40
Reeves, T. C., 'John Checkley and the emergence of the Episcopal Church in New England', *Historical Magazine of the Protestant Episcopal Church* xxxiv (1965), 349–60
Rhoden, Nancy, *Revolutionary Anglicanism: the colonial Church of England clergy during the American Revolution*, Basingstoke 1999
Richards, James, *Party propaganda under Queen Anne: the general elections of 1702–1713*, Athens, Ga 1972
Rogers, Nicholas, *Crowds, culture, and politics in Georgian Britain*, Oxford 1998
Roper, L. H., *Conceiving Carolina: proprietors, planters, and plots, 1662–1729*, New York 2004
– 'Conceiving an Anglo-American proprietorship: early South Carolina history in perspective', in L. H. Roper and B. Van Ruymbeke (eds), *Constructing early modern empires: proprietary ventures in the Atlantic world, 1500–1750*, Leiden 2007, 389–410
Rowlands, Guy, *Dangerous and dishonest men: the international bankers of Louis XIV's France*, Basingstoke 2014
Runcie, John D., 'The problem of Anglo American politics in Bellomont's New York', *WMQ* xxvi (1969), 191–217
Salinger, Sharon, *Taverns and drinking in early America*, Baltimore 2002
Sankey, Margaret, *Jacobite prisoners of the 1715 rebellion: preventing and punishing insurrection in early Hanoverian Britain*, Burlington, Vt 2005
Sedgwick, Romney (ed.), *The history of parliament: the House of Commons, 1715–1754*, London 1970

Shields, David, *Oracles of empire: poetry, politics, and commerce in British America, 1690–1750*, Chicago 1990

— *Civil tongues and polite letters in British America*, Chapel Hill 1997

Sirmans, Eugene, *Colonial South Carolina: a political history, 1663–1763*, Chapel Hill 1966

Sirota, Brent, *The Christian monitors: the Church of England and the age of benevolence, 1680–1760*, New Haven, 2014

Slafter, Edmund, *John Checkley; or The evolution of religious tolerance in Massachusetts Bay*, Boston 1897

Sloan, David, 'The *New England Courant*: voice of Anglicanism: the role of religion in colonial journalism', *American Journalism* viii (1991), 108–14

Smith, Hannah, *Georgian monarchy: politics and culture, 1714–1760*, Cambridge 2006

Smith, S. D., *Slavery, family, and gentry capitalism in the British Atlantic: the world of the Lascelles, 1648–1834*, Cambridge 2006

Sowerby, Scott, 'Opposition to anti-popery in restoration England', *JBS* li (2012), 26–49

— *Making toleration: the repealers and the Glorious Revolution*, Cambridge, MA 2013

Spaeth, Donald, *The Church in an age of danger: parsons and parishioners, 1660–1740*, Cambridge 2000

Speck, W. A., *Tory and Whig: the struggle in the constituencies, 1701–15*, London 1970

— *The birth of Britain: a new nation, 1700–1710*, Oxford 1994

— 'The current state of Sacheverell scholarship', *PH* xxxi (2012), 16–27

Stanwood, Owen, 'The Protestant moment: antipopery, the Revolution of 1688–1689, and the making of an Anglo-American Empire', *JBS* xliv (2007), 481–508

— 'Catholics, Protestants, and the clash of civilizations in early America', in Beneke and Grenda, *The first prejudice*, 218–40

— *The Empire reformed: English America in the age of the Glorious Revolution*, Philadelphia 2011

Starkie, Andrew, *The Church of England and the Bangorian controversy, 1716–1721*, Woodbridge 2007

Stasavage, David, *Public debt and the birth of the democratic state: France and Great Britain, 1688–1789*, Cambridge 2003

Steele, Ian K., *Politics of colonial policy: the Board of Trade in colonial administration, 1696–1720*, Oxford 1968

— *The English Atlantic, 1675–1740: an exploration of communication and community*, Oxford 1986

— 'The anointed, the appointed, and the elected: governance of the British Empire, 1689–1784, in Marshall, *Oxford history of the British Empire*, ii. 105–27

Stephen, Jeffrey, *Defending the revolution: the Church of Scotland, 1689–1716*, Burlington, VT 2013

Stowell, Marion Barber, *Early American almanacs: the colonial weekday Bible*, New York 1977

Swingen, Abigail, *Competing visions of empire: labor, slavery, and the origins of the British Atlantic empire*, New Haven 2015

Szechi, Daniel, *Jacobitism and Tory politics, 1710–1714*, Edinburgh 1984

— *The Jacobites: Britain and Europe, 1688–1788*, Manchester 1994

— *George Lockhart of Carnwath, 1689–1727: a study in Jacobitism*, East Linton 2002

— *1715: the great Jacobite rebellion*, New Haven 2006

Talbott, Siobhan, 'Commerce and the Jacobite court: Scottish migrants in France, 1688–1718', in McInnes, German and Graham, *Living with Jacobitism*, 99–110

Thompson, Peter, *Rum punch and revolution: taverngoing & public life in eighteenth century Philadelphia*, Philadelphia 1999

Thorpe, F. J., 'George Vane', in *Dictionary of Canadian biography online*, ‹http://www.biographi.ca/EN/009004-119.01-e.php?id_nbr=1139›

Tucker, B., 'The reinvention of New England, 1691–1770', *New England Quarterly* lix (1986), 315–40

Voorhees, David William, 'The "fervent zeale" of Jacob Leisler', *WMQ* li (1994), 447–72

— '"To assert our right before it be quite lost": the Leisler rebellion in the Delaware River Valley', *Pennsylvania History* lxiv (1997), 5–27

Waller, George, *Samuel Vetch, colonial enterpriser*, Chapel Hill 1960

Walsh, John and Stephen Taylor, 'Introduction: the Church and Anglicanism in the "long" eighteenth century', in John Walsh, David Hayton and Stephen Taylor (eds), *The Church of England c. 1689–1833*, Cambridge 1993, 1–66

Warner, Michael, *The letters of the republic: publication and the public sphere in eighteenth century America*, Cambridge, MA 1990

Webb, Stephen Saunders, *Marlborough's America*, New Haven 2013

Weir, Robert, *Colonial South Carolina: a history*, Millwood, NY 1983

— '"Shaftsbury's darling": British settlement in the Carolinas at the close of the seventeenth century', in Canny, *Oxford history of the British Empire*, i. 375–97

Wendal, Thomas, 'Jacobitism crushed: an episode concerning loyalty and justice in colonial Pennsylvania', *Pennsylvania History* xl (1973), 58–65

Whatley, Chris, 'Reformed religion, regime change, Scottish Whigs and the struggle for the "soul" of Scotland, c. 1688 – c. 1788', *Scottish Historical Review* xcii (2013), 66–99

Wills, Rebecca, *The Jacobites and Russia, 1715–1750*, East Linton 2002

Woolverton, John, *Colonial Anglicanism in North America*, Detroit 1976

Wright, David McCord, 'Mr. Ash: a footnote in constitutional history', *South Carolina Historical Magazine* lxiii (1962), 227–31

Unpublished dissertations

Chapman, Paul, 'Jacobite political argument in England, 1714–1766', PhD, Cambridge 1983

Murrin, John M., 'Anglicizing an American colony: the transformation of provincial Massachusetts', PhD, Yale 1966

Online resources

Bell, James, *Colonial American Clergy of the Church of England Database*, ‹www.Jamesbbell.com›

Index